THE PROMISE OF
TRINITARIAN THEOLOGY

THE PROMISE OF TRINITARIAN THEOLOGY

Colin E. Gunton

Second Edition

T&T CLARK
EDINBURGH

T&T CLARK LTD
59 GEORGE STREET
EDINBURGH EH2 2LQ
SCOTLAND

First edition copyright © T&T Clark Ltd, 1991
Second edition copyright © T&T Clark Ltd, 1997

First edition 1991
Second edition 1997

ISBN 0 567 08574 0

Typeset by Fakenham Photosetting Ltd, Fakenham
Printed and bound in Great Britain by Bell & Bain Ltd, Glasgow

For
Daniel W. Hardy
Robert W. Jenson
Thomas F. Torrance
John D. Zizioulas

CONTENTS

PREFACE TO THE FIRST EDITION

The Promise of Trinitarian Theology is neither a set of essays thinly disguised as a unified book nor a fully unified book, but a set of essays for which is claimed a unity of theme, direction and development. The unity is provided not only by a concentration on the doctrine of the Trinity, but also by a specific orientation within the immense range of possibilities opened up by trinitarian thought. The centre is to be found in a quest for ontology, in something like a traditional sense, for I believe that it is only through an understanding of the kind of being that God is that we can come to learn what kind of beings we are and what kind of world we inhabit.

The danger of such an approach is well indicated by the use of that word 'understanding': of a rationalism that claims too much for the intellect. Some of those who have discussed the papers have pointed out that they riskily, if not mistakenly, set on one side the soteriological dimension. I hope that careful readers will realise that the concerns of *The Actuality of Atonement*, far from being abandoned, have in fact been advanced by these explorations, one of whose concerns is to hold creation and redemption together. I recognise the danger that discussions of ontology apart from the reconstitution of our being and that of the world through the cross and resurrection of Jesus are perilously near abstraction. But what is theology apart from intellectual risk? And the doctrine of the Trinity *is* crucial to ontology – to any ontology that would hold together creation and redemption – although its implications in this field are rarely explored.

The fact is that the loss of a trinitarian dimension has gravely impoverished the Christian tradition over recent decades, and one of the hopeful signs of recent years has been a renewal of interest. Indeed, as will be argued, particularly in chapter three,

xi

the reasons for the modern belief in the irrelevance of trinitarian theology lie in large part in the shape the Western tradition took after Augustine, so that in many respects the Enlightenment can be seen less as a rejection of traditional Western thought than as the reinforcement and radicalisation of some of its leading features. However, although I believe that we should look to the Cappadocians among the ancient writers for some of the resources we need, I am less tempted than I was to run the risk of romanticising the Eastern tradition. That tradition, too, has a history of abstraction, and particularly of developing a breach between the being of God and his action in the economy of creation and redemption. But to the Cappadocians are owed crucial steps in a process of conceptual development which, despite some parallels in the West, has for the most part been neglected. Many of the papers in this volume are intended to carry forward a programme of ontological exploration in the light of concepts which owe much of their shape to the Cappadocians.

Some of the papers have been used elsewhere, and I wish to acknowledge permission to reuse them. The first three set the scene: in the possibilities for trinitarian theology and the problems of the present, both cultural and theological. An ancestor of the first was given in two places, Chichester Theological College and the seminar on the theology of the Trinity at the meeting of the Society for the Study of Theology in Oxford, 1989. The second is an adaptation of 'The Christian Doctrine of God: Opposition and Convergence', *Heaven and Earth: Essex Essays in Theology and Ethics*, edited by Andrew Linzey and Peter Wexler, Churchman Publishing Ltd., 1986, pp. 11–22. The third, first given at the weekly research seminar in systematic theology at King's College, London in 1987, was subsequently published in the *Scottish Journal of Theology*, vol. 43 (1990), pp. 33–58. I am grateful for the permission of the Scottish Academic Press to reprint the article.

The following five papers are intended to be substantive contributions to ontology in a number of important areas of human life and thought. Chapter four has already been published in a separate collection by T. & T. Clark: *On Being the Church*, edited by C. E. Gunton and D. W. Hardy (1989). Chapter five is a slightly revised version of my inaugural lecture in the Chair of

Christian Doctrine at King's College, London, published by the College in 1985. Chapter seven was a lecture given at a conference in honour of Robert W. Jenson at Gettysburg, Pennsylvania, in December 1988. It belongs in the book because it is a treatment of one area of trinitarian theology not otherwise present: the relation between God and human freedom. It thus supplements the two other chapters, five and six, devoted to the relation between trinitarian thought and the human condition. It was published in *Dialog*, Winter 1991.

It will be apparent that whereas there are three papers on matters anthropological, there is only one on the doctrine of the non-human creation. Chapter eight was written to fill the gap and complete the collection. It was prepared also for the first international conference of the Research Institute in Systematic Theology at King's College in September 1990, and is less comprehensive than the papers on anthropology, being designed to fill out some of the hints thrown out in them, and especially those towards the end of chapter six. It requires supplementation, and is, I hope, a pointer to the direction work will take after the completion of the collection here published. It remains to be said that chapter nine [chapter eleven in the second edition of this book], like chapter one, was written for this book, after the completion of the other papers, and is designed to round off the collection by bringing together some of the main discoveries and developments, and in particular to summarise the conceptual explorations.

I am, as ever, immensely grateful to many who have helped along the way. The stimulus of my colleagues and students in the Research Institute in Systematic Theology at King's College, London, has been central to the process, and not only because a number of the chapters first took shape as papers for research seminars. As always in recent years I have received more than I can say from the learning and critical judgement of my colleague and friend Christoph Schwöbel, who has had a hand in the shaping and reshaping of almost every paper. I am also grateful to Marcelle Letacq who has typed on to disk a number of papers which were not originally written by word processor, and so saved me much time; to Geoffrey Green for continuing encouragement; and to Sarah Gunton for her careful reading of the proofs.

The dedication of the book is a small attempt to signal my debt to a number of my seniors who have shaped my development in this rewarding craft, and in particular have impressed on me in different – some of them may think very different – ways the importance of thinking in a trinitarian way.

King's College, London
Advent 1990

PREFACE TO THE SECOND EDITION

I *Six years later*

Suddenly we are all trinitarians, or so it would seem. As the result of a number of influences, both churchly and secular, the doctrine of the Trinity is now discussed in places where even a short time ago it would have been regarded as an irrelevance. Among the former influences are the increasing bearing of the thought of Eastern Orthodox theology on Western theology, as well as the continuing growth of Pentecostalism and the consequent attention given to the doctrine of the Spirit. So far as the latter are concerned, the continuing anxiety about the decline of civility in the Western world and its increasing depersonalisation have called attention to the importance of personal being, apparently in some way related to the concepts of social and communal relations which are encouraged by trinitarian thinking. But the net can be thrown still more widely. There is also to be discerned in some recent theology the less easily quantifiable presence of Hegelian influences, whether in what is effectively the purely rationalised form in books like Peter Hodgson's recent one volume systematic theology,[1] or the far more concretely Christian theology of Daniel Hardy,[2] where there is at least a trace of Hegelian influences in his subtle characterisations of the dynamic interactions of the triune God with the world of space and time.

---

[1] Peter C. Hodgson, *Winds of the Spirit. A Constructive Christian Theology*, London: SCM Press, 1994, pp. 44–50, 151–172.

[2] Daniel W. Hardy, *God's Ways with the World. Thinking and Practising Christian Faith*, Edinburgh: T. & T. Clark, 1996.

We shall return to the dangers of the Hegelian tendency, which itself has deep roots in neoplatonic emanationism. But first, some brief account should be given of what has happened, brief because much that needs to be said of the detail is to be found in Christoph Schwöbel's introduction to the collection he edited, *Trinitarian Theology Today*. I simply cite two statements:

> Trinitarian theology therefore appears to be a summary label for doing theology that affects all aspects of the enterprise of doing theology in its various disciplines ... This concerns not only major doctrinal topics such as the doctrine of creation, the destiny of humankind, the person and work of Christ, the church, its ministries and sacraments, and eschatology, but also those areas where doctrinal reflection and non-theological modes of enquiry overlap, such as the conversation with the natural sciences, anthropological inquiries, historical investigation and social theory.

> ... the doctrine of the Trinity matters. It is not a topic reserved for austere theological speculation or the language and practice of worship. The conceptual form in which the doctrine of the Trinity is expressed will affect not only the content and emphases of the doctrinal scheme of theology but also the forms of community organization in the church and its life of worship.[3]

As Professor Schwöbel remarks, other matters such as the relation of the Christian doctrine of God to the tradition of philosophical theism are also being rethought in the light of the revival,[4] and the list could be extended. We might add that he has himself contributed to consideration of the relation of trinitarian thinking to inter-religious dialogue,[5] while the matter of feminism has come within the purview of trinitarian

---

[3] Christoph Schwöbel, editor, *Trinitarian Theology Today. Essays in Divine Being and Act*, Edinburgh: T. & T. Clark, 1995, pp. 1–30 (pp. 1f, 4).

[4] Schwöbel, *Trinitarian Theology Today*, p. 8.

[5] Christoph Schwöbel, 'Particularity, Universality and the Religions. Towards a Christian Theology of Religions' in *Christian Uniqueness Reconsidered. The Myth of a Pluralistic Theology of Religions*, ed. Gavin D'Costa, New York: Orbis Books, 1990, pp. 30–46.

theologians,[6] as has an argument that neglect of the Trinity has been instrumental in generating modern atheism.[7]

However, with revival come also the dangers of over-simplification and the superficiality so often attendant on being fashionable. They lie to the right and to the left of the narrow path which all theology must tread, though it is important to remember that that metaphor is not intended to be a political one. The first set of dangers derives from a mistaken attempt to remain concretely relevant by casting doubt on the necessity of an immanent, or, better, ontological Trinity – of any doctrine of who and what kind of being God is in himself, in the eternal *taxis* or order of persons in relation. Two recent and influential books on the doctrine of the Trinity have in different ways advocated the limitation of enquiry to the historical or economic Trinity, thus reinforcing tendencies revealed in the work of Robert W. Jenson discussed in chapter seven of this book. As Professor Jenson has himself said in response to this point, confessional differences continue to reappear in discussions of these matters. In this respect Lutheran theology's tendency to restrict what we may say of the being of God to his being for and in relation to us contrasts with a concern, more characteristic of the Reformed tradition, for ontology. Thus it is with Ted Peters' *God as Trinity*, in which the author takes to task even Jenson's justification of a doctrine of the immanent Trinity in the interest of the freedom of God. Against this, Peters concludes that all we need to affirm is that 'God is in the process of self-relating through relating to the world he loves and redeems. God is in the process of constituting himself as a God who is in relationship with what is other than God.'[8] No more than that, it seems, is needed.

A second book is by a Roman Catholic, Catherine Mowry LaCugna, who contends, in a thesis similar to Harnack's judgement about the development of early theology, that the move into ontology in the early centuries – an account of God's

---

[6] Alvin Kimel, editor, *Speaking the Christian God. The Holy Trinity and the Challenge of Feminism*, Leominster: Gracewing, 1992.

[7] Michael Buckley, *At the Origins of Modern Atheism*, New Haven and London: Yale University Press, 1987.

[8] Ted Peters, *God as Trinity. Relationality and Temporality in Divine Life*, Louisville, Kentucky: Westminster/John Knox Press, 1993, p. 145.

being rather than simply his action – was mistaken.[9] It follows that any doctrine of an immanent Trinity, even one derived from an understanding of the economy, is to be rejected. For her, even Rahner, in retaining vestiges of *theologia*, does not go far enough. From the outset it is made clear that we must not 'reify the idea of communion by positing an intradivine "community" or society of persons that exists alongside, or above, the human community'.[10] All talk of the Trinity must therefore be in some way a function of the economy of salvation, so that *perichoresis* is not an analogy between divine and worldly being, but a kind of univocal principle. 'The starting point ... locates *perichoresis* not in God's inner life, but in the mystery of the one communion of all persons, divine as well as human'. 'There are not two sets of communion – one among the divine persons, the other among human persons, with the latter supposed to replicate the former.'[11]

In face of both of these polemics against the doctrine of the ontological Trinity, and against any suggestion that it is *only* the freedom of God that is at stake here, it can be argued that on the contrary that doctrine serves as a foundation for the relative independence and so integrity of worldly reality also, and thus for human freedom. It is because God is a communion of love prior to and in independence of the creation that he can enable the creation to be itself. The question that must be asked therefore is whether Peters' and LaCugna's approaches finally escape the pantheism which results from any attempt to bring God and the world too close. The danger is particularly manifest in the latter. In one crucial passage, the author sounds as though she owes more to John Scotus Erigena, one of the fountainheads of modern pantheism, than the Cappadocian Fathers:

> This chiastic model of emanation and return, *exitus* and *reditus*, expresses the one ecstatic movement of God outward by which all things originate from God through Christ in the power of the Holy Spirit, and all things are brought into union with God and returned to God. There is neither an

[9] Catherine Mowry LaCugna, *God for Us. The Trinity and Christian Life*, New York: HarperCollins and Edinburgh: T. & T. Clark, 1991.
[10] LaCugna, *God for Us*, p. 15.
[11] LaCugna, *God for Us*, p. 274.

economic nor an immanent Trinity; there is only the *oikono-mia* that is the concrete realization of the mystery of *theologia* in time, space, history and personality.[12]

The source of the malaise that such a doctrine reveals can be found in the principle of self-communication, with its emana-tionist and neoplatonic – and thus ultimately pantheist – overtones.[13] There is ultimately only one reality, the divine-worldly emanation, which constitutes the world and then swallows it up. Against this it must be contended that far from ensuring the relevance of trinitarian categories, the outcome of such a process is to destroy it. God's personal otherness from the world is needed if there is to be a true establishing of the world in its own right.

The second set of perils derives from the opposite tendency, to use the doctrine to validate, on the basis of a doctrine of the immanent or ontological Trinity, causes the theologian believes, for whatever reasons, to be worthy ones. That is to say, the doctrine of the Trinity is used as a kind of principle of explanation and ethics. Because God is like this, it is argued, then the world is, or ought to be, like that. Like almost all arguments it is one from analogy, and none the worse for that. Much has rightly been made, for example, of the way in which the relational being of the immanent Trinity can provide a model for personal relations in human social order. There are chapters in this book which argue precisely that. But the corresponding danger of analogical arguments is to be seen in premature appeals to something called the social analogy, as if

---

[12] LaCugna, *God for Us*, p. 223.

[13] Much of the above is repeated from a review of LaCugna in *Scottish Journal of Theology* 47 (1994), pp. 135–137 (p. 137). The following passage might also be repeated, for, like the argument about pantheism, it raises the matter of the personal: 'It must be said that the current fashion for political correctness in theological language, like so many other well-meaning modern enterprises, has the effect of making the cure worse than the disease. Robert Jenson has already commented on the polytheistic overtones of "Godself", and indeed it implies the presence of something other than the subject in a way that the true reflexive pronoun does not. ("The Father gives the Father's self to the creature ...", p. 157. Really? But, we are still bound to ask, does he truly give *himself*, or are we being presented with a *thing* that is not the personal God in personal relation to his creatures?) The outcome is thus both modalistic and impersonal, so that "The Son is named Son according to *its* procession from the Father ..." (p. 156, my emphasis). Does even the Son lose his personal pronoun? What, then, finally, of yours and mine?'

it is easily distinguishable from what is opposed to it as the psychological analogy to support a vision of society without first passing through a difficult and complex process of inter-mediate argumentation. The assumption often seems to be that these are both fixed and intelligible quantities, when they are neither.[14] It may be true that the Trinity encourages neither an individualist nor a collectivist form of social order, as I can scarcely deny in view of my use of them in various papers in this book, and in a successor.[15] Yet it remains true that moves from the immanent Trinity to the created world are not obvious, and are fraught with dangers of idealising and projection. This is especially the case with those books in the Hegelian tradition which use trinitarian categories to discern the work of the divine Spirit largely or chiefly from immanent patterns of modern history and social development. Their chief defect is that they turn Christ into a world principle at the expense of Jesus of Nazareth, and treat his cross as a focus for the suffering of God rather than as the centre of that history in which God overcomes sin and evil. That is to say, if the doctrine of the Trinity is abstracted from the doctrine of the atonement, according to which history does not develop but is disrupted and has to be redirected by the unique incarnation, ministry, death, resurrection and ascension of Jesus of Nazareth, it is no longer the Christian Trinity but, as Kierkegaard rightly claimed to be the case with Hegel, simply an uncritical validation of modern culture – or whatever – and so effectively Christianity's opposite.

This is the chief fault of Peter Hodgson's book, however much at times it seeks to overcome this tendency and remain Christian by careful ambiguity. As in the case of LaCugna, the danger here too is of pantheism, and for similar reasons, because although her economy begins as being the economy realised in Jesus of Nazareth, it too comes near – at least – to turning him into a historical principle. Hodgson takes this step far earlier, losing at the outset the definitive place given to Jesus of Nazareth: 'Christ is not contained in a single historical

---

[14] Something further is said of this in chapter eleven, below, p. 195.

[15] Colin E. Gunton, *The One, the Three and the Many. God, Creation and the Culture of Modernity. The 1992 Bampton Lectures*, Cambridge University Press, 1993.

individual.'[16] The result is a deep ambiguity about the significance of the cross, which is neither the unique act of God reconciling the world to himself nor simply one focus in a market of religious possibilities, but tries to be both. 'The significance of the crucifixion of Jesus for God' is that it 'means the death of God, and that in turn means that suffering and tragedy are incorporated into the divine life'.[17] The objection to this is clear. To incorporate something into the divine life is to affirm it, and so to deny the central character of Christianity as a religion of redemption, in which evil is not affirmed but conquered, eschatologically and by anticipation, in the cross and resurrection of Jesus of Nazareth.[18]

II *Further specifications*

Both dangers – of limiting expression to the economic Trinity and of using an ontological trinitarianism as an immanent principle of reality – are finally the same in leading to a pantheism which nullifies the proper being and autonomy of the created world. To avoid this, it is necessary to maintain a careful systematic consideration of what is said on the basis of which theological warrant. I continue to believe that Irenaeus provides an essential biblically-based starting point for discussion. He is biblical in the sense that he maintains that the economy of creation, recapitulation and redemption is constituted by the achievement of the Father's work by the Son and the Spirit. They, as the two hands of God, mediate the will and work of the Father in perfecting what can be called the project

[16] Hodgson, *Winds of the Spirit*, p. 49. The dominating concepts are pluralism, postmodernism, liberation and feminism – in fact everything that is modish according to the modernist canon.

[17] Hodgson, *Winds of the Spirit*, p. 263.

[18] Another ambiguity to be found in this book is between pantheism and a Christian doctrine of creation according to which God creates a world truly other than himself, though in continuing relation to him. What are we to make of this: 'God goes out from godself, creates a world seemingly infinite in extension but strictly nondivine in its perishability and contingency, yet enters into relationship with the world, makes it God's own "body" ...'? Hodgson, *Winds of the Spirit*, pp. 163f. The ambiguity is revealed by the quotation marks, but a choice cannot be evaded. If the world is God's body, it is not finite and contingent, for it participates in divinity rather than being truly the creation. The alternatives are mutually exclusive.

of creation: the final perfecting through redemption of what was created perfect in the beginning. It is often said that when the New Testament speaks of God, *simpliciter* its writers are referring to God the Father, and in that respect Irenaeus maintains a balance that later writers often lose in their over-anxiety to maintain the unity of the Trinity and the absolute co-equality of the three persons.

Irenaeus' trinitarianism is often referred to as relatively undeveloped, and although he may not have a formed doctrine of the immanent Trinity it is false to say that his is only an economic trinitarianism, though that is often suggested or assumed.[19] There is a doctrine of the eternal being of the Son in relation to God the Father in Irenaeus, a doctrine which is, in any case, implied by his anti-gnostic doctrine of the media-tion of creation through the Son.[20] It is also clear that this early theologian held to the eternity of the Spirit.[21] In fact, the case in Irenaeus' favour could be strengthened if it is pointed out that later speculations about the being of the immanent Trinity moved far beyond his careful self-limitation to Scripture, and generated doctrines of the immanent Trinity which tended both to move beyond the limits of the biblical narration of the economy and, worse, to divorce the immanent from the econ-omic Trinity. As is suggested elsewhere in this volume, that happened both in Augustine's psychological speculations and in the Eastern tendency to place the divine energies in the place where the activities of Son and Spirit in mediating the work of the Father are so firmly established in Irenaeus.

The proper reason for seeking to move beyond Irenaeus' supposedly primitive conception is not to be found in a need to avoid subordinationism; that is, any doctrine that supposes that the Son and the Spirit are in some way less truly God than God

---

[19] Maurice Wiles cites both G. L. Prestige and Leonard Hodgson as attribut-ing to Origen the development of the doctrine of the eternal generation of the Son. 'Dr. Hodgson speaks of the "doctrine of eternal generation by which Origen freed trinitarianism from one element of subordinationism, i.e. temporal secondariness." ', 'Eternal Generation', *Working Papers in Doctrine*, London: SCM Press, 1976, pp. 18–27 (p. 21).

[20] Irenaeus, *Haer* III. 16 is particularly significant: 'that he was the only begotten, and that he became incarnate for our salvation ...'

[21] Irenaeus, *Haer* V. xii. 2: 'The breath, then, is temporal but the Spirit eternal.'

the Father. Irenaeus is not an ontological subordinationist, though that is sometimes suggested. There is a sense in which the work of the Son and the Spirit are subordinate in the respect that they perform the will and work of God the Father, but, as we shall argue below, that is not subordinationism proper. We shall, however, approach the questions this topic raises not yet through a discussion of Irenaeus but through an examination of one aspect of recent controversy over the significance of the trinitarianism of the Cappadocian Fathers. In the first edition of this book it was suggested that there are difficulties with John Zizioulas' development of one Cappadocian theme.[22] In it, a move is made beyond Irenaeus' teaching that the Father is the one whose work is done by the Son and Spirit, to a claim that the Father must be understood as the eternal cause of the being and divinity of the other two persons.[23] The problems with this view have recently been discussed at length by Alan Torrance. Of the questions he raises, the chief for our purposes concerns whether Zizioulas' description of the Father as the cause of the Trinity endangers his own identification of being and communion. 'The thrust of these arguments suggests a failure to interpret the Oneness of God in the Light of the free communion and mutuality of God. An *a posteriori* ontology of the free communion and mutuality of God risks being subsumed by a cosmological category of causality.'[24] Torrance asks whether communion should not rather be construed as ontologically primordial, and quotes T. F. Torrance's appeal to Cyril of Alexandria. Should we not prefer to the doctrine that the Father is the cause of the Trinity 'Cyril's conception of the interrelation of the three, perfect, coequal, coeternal, enhypostatic Persons ...'[25] and again, Athanasius' view 'of their coinherent and undivided wholeness, in which each person is "whole of the whole".'?[26]

[22] See below, chapter eleven, pp. 196f.

[23] See, for example, John D. Zizioulas, 'On Being a Person. The Ontology of Personhood', *Persons, Divine and Human. King's College Essays in Theological Anthropology*, edd. Colin E. Gunton and Christoph Schwöbel, Edinburgh: T. & T. Clark, 1991, pp. 33–46 (p. 40).

[24] Alan J. Torrance, *Persons in Communion. Trinitarian Description and Human Participation*, Edinburgh: T. & T. Clark, 1996, p. 291.

[25] Torrance, *Persons in Communion*, p. 294, citing Thomas F. Torrance, *The Trinitarian Faith*, Edinburgh: T. & T. Clark, 1988, p. 340.

[26] T. F. Torrance, *The Trinitarian Faith*, p. 238.

The chief issue in contention between Torrance and Zizioulas concerns the manner in which we are to characterise the distinctive ways of being of the three persons. It might be suggested, particularly in the light of the citations from Cyril and Athanasius, that there is in the tradition of trinitarian theology an opposition of extremes both of which might well be avoided. On the one side is the tendency so to stress the primacy of the Father that there is a danger of an ontological subordinationism, with the Son and the Spirit at least appearing to be less truly God than the Father. On the other side, the tendency of the two Alexandrians is to over-stress the equality of the persons, something that might be present also in Athanasius' much cited teaching that we must affirm of the Son everything that we affirm of the Father except that he is the Son and not the Father. The weakness of the Augustinian tradition is similar, and, as is argued in chapter three below especially, is manifested in a tendency, if not to obliterate, then at least to obscure the particularity of the persons. Against any such tendency to homogenise the persons, much of the argument of this book is devoted to suggesting the necessity of identifying the concrete particularly, individuality even, of each person, though that is not to imply that the persons can be called *individuals*.[27] If there is to be a point in speaking of Father, Son and Spirit, rather than simply of God, then it is incumbent upon the theologian to say something of that in which their differences consist, whether by means of an identification of the (eternal) being of the persons, or a characterisation of their historic forms of action – or, best of all, by a relating of the two.

Wolfhart Pannenberg has here contributed major insights to the discussion, especially in his insistence that the Patristic treatments concentrated too exclusively on relations of origin: on characterising the distinctions between the three persons of the Trinity in terms of who causes whom or who derives from whom. 'The mistaken formulation of Augustine points ... to a defect which plagues the trinitarian theological language of both East and West, namely, that of seeing the relations among Father, Son and Spirit exclusively as relations of origin.'[28]

---

[27] See here especially *The One, the Three and the Many*, chapter seven.
[28] Wolfhart Pannenberg, *Systematic Theology Volume 1*, E.T. by Geoffrey W. Bromiley, Edinburgh: T. & T. Clark, 1991, p. 319.

Against this, he argues that the relations of the persons of the Trinity must also be understood in ways more closely tied to the historical relations of, for example, the Son and his Father. 'In the handing over of lordship from the Father to the Son, and its handing back from the Son to the Father, we see a mutuality in their relationship that we do not see in the begetting.' Similar things, he continues, should also be the case in the relation of the Spirit to the Father and the Son.[29]

That, it seems to me, takes us some of the way. In general, however, I believe that if we are to conceive the inalienable marks of the distinctive personhood of the three, we should also attempt to identify their characteristic modes or forms of action as they are made known in the economy of creation, salvation and redemption. And it is here that we must return to Irenaeus and explore why things had to be said which went beyond his theology. What he was developing was a theology of mediation: an account of the way in which the eternal counsel of God the Father, that all things in heaven and on earth should be reconciled to him through Jesus Christ, is achieved in course of time. Much of the point of Irenaeus' polemic against the Gnostics was directed against their subordination-ism. According to them, it was beneath the dignity of their high deity to involve himself in the inferior realms of matter. That was the work of inferior, lower – subordinate, though, it appears, often insubordinate – deities or godlets. Against this mythological nonsense, Irenaeus affirmed that, because of the incarnation, we can be sure that *God himself* takes thought for the ordering of the whole world, material and spiritual alike. He does this through his Son and Spirit, who, it might be said, are subordinate in doing his behest, but not subordinate in being, for Irenaeus' point against the Gnostics is that the Son and the Spirit are the ways by which God himself is *personally* involved in the created order; hence the apparently anthro-pomorphic, but actually highly sophisticated metaphor of the

---

[29] Pannenberg, *Systematic Theology Volume 1*, p. 313, cf. pp. 313–327. The logic of the link between economic and ontological Trinity is nowhere better expounded than by Karl Barth. For an exploration of the logic of Barth's move from revelation to eternal God, see my *Becoming and Being. The Doctrine of God in Charles Hartshorne and Karl Barth*, Oxford and New York: Oxford University Press, 1978, pp. 127–130. I now believe that he failed to give adequate account of the distinction of persons.

two hands of God (material analogies for God's material involvement in the world). The point could be strengthened and illustrated by saying that a subordinate activity does not imply something less than God, but the reverse. We must not forget that, as Barth repeatedly reminds us on trinitarian grounds, it is as Godlike to be humble as to be exalted. In the words of the British Council of Churches' report:

> It does not follow that a 'subordination', an 'ordering below' entails an inferiority of personhood, dignity or being. It often appears so to us because – for example – obedience is often a merely external relation rather than a hearing stemming from love. As Christians, however, we would want to argue to the contrary, that Jesus' humiliation, whether we see that demonstrated in his birth, his washing of the disciples' feet or his sacrificial death, is a mark of his divinity and glory, not his inferiority.[30]

Something else that should not be forgotten is that Irenaeus' insistence on the freedom of God's creation of the world is implicitly a doctrine of the immanent Trinity, in that it distinguishes the being of God from that of the world he creates. If, then, there is a deficiency in Irenaeus' account it is to be found more in his failure to specify the distinctive features of the work of the two hands of God the Father – to distinguish, that is to say, the characteristic ways of working of the Son and the Spirit respectively – than to go further into the way of being of the immanent Trinity.[31] The fact remains that though there are hints of a distinction, and particularly in Irenaeus a strong eschatological orientation that can only be achieved through attention to the work of the Spirit, the characteristic identities of the two are rarely expressed in anything more than a linking of them in common work.

Perhaps the most important attempt to go beyond this is to be found in Basil of Caesarea's characterisation of the distinctive work of the three persons in relation to the created world.

---

[30] British Council of Churches, *The Forgotten Trinity. 1. Report of the BCC Study Commission on Trinitarian Doctrine Today*, London: British Council of Churches, 1989, p. 33.
[31] I owe the point to my student, Mark Butchers.

In a much quoted saying from his treatise on the Holy Spirit he elaborates the distinctive functions of the Spirit, and, while affirming that the Holy Spirit is 'inseparable and wholly incapable of being parted from the Father and the Son', he distinguishes: 'the original cause of all things that are made, the Father; ... the creative cause, the Son; ... the perfecting cause, the Spirit'.[32] Here, as in Scripture, the Father calls the tune, so to speak, and it is played in different modes by his two hands. Calvin's characterisation is similar: 'to the Father is attributed the beginning of activity, and the fountain and well-spring of all things; to the Son, wisdom, counsel and the ordered disposition of all things; but to the Spirit is assigned the power and efficacy of that activity'.[33]

Generalising and extending this, we can say that because the Son is the mode of God's free involvement in the world which is other than he, as is realised above all in the incarnation, it follows that 'The Person of the Son is the principle of otherness, of difference in the Trinity ... as the personal other of his love'. Whether, with Pannenberg, we should go on to speak of the Son's self-distinction from the Father is doubtful, because it appears to give the Son almost an autonomy over against the Father which makes him something more than the mediator of the Father's action. Better to say with Christoph Schwöbel that, 'Because of his origin in the freedom of the Father, the Son can freely respond to the Father by doing his will, by making the will of the Father his own'.[34] Similarly, because the Holy Spirit is the agent of the Father's perfecting and transforming work as it is realised by relating the creation to God through Jesus Christ, it follows that we can cautiously draw conclusions from the Spirit's perfecting work to a speculation that he may, similarly, perfect the being of God, in a way parallel to, but distinctly different from, Augustine's teaching that the Spirit is the bond of love between Father and Son.[35]

[32] Basil of Caesarea, *On the Holy Spirit*, XV.36 and 38.

[33] John Calvin, *Institutes* I. xiii. 18.

[34] Christoph Schwöbel, 'God, Creation and the Christian Community. The Dogmatic Basis of a Christian Ethic of Createdness', *The Doctrine of Creation*, ed. Colin E. Gunton, Edinburgh: T. & T. Clark, forthcoming.

[35] I have attempted this in 'God the Holy Spirit. Augustine and his Successors', *Theology through the Theologians. Selected Essays, 1972–1995*, Edinburgh: T. & T. Clark, 1996, pp. 105–128.

It does not follow, however, that because there are *distinctive* forms of action and ways of being of the three persons of the triune God that they can be conceived to be or to act *separately*. There is therefore no room for what sometimes appears to happen in modern theology, a severing of the Spirit from Jesus Christ, as if a work of God the Spirit, in creation and human culture, can somehow be generally discerned apart from him. It may be the case that modern emancipationist movements, whether feminist or other forms of liberationism, are in part the work of the Spirit. It may be the case that the Spirit brings about the rule of God in all kinds of pagan religions and secular cultures. But if those phenomena are to be affirmed or assimilated into theology, it must surely be an empirical question, in which of each particular instance it is asked whether or not it is of the God of Jesus Christ and the Spirit who makes holy. If the Spirit relates created beings to God – thus making them holy, in the sense of finally acceptable to God – he achieves this through the Son, the mediator of creation, for there is no other way. Both, together, do the work of the Father, and in that sense the works of God the Trinity are undivided. We might say here that on an Irenaean conception of the two hands we can expect in this case the left hand to know what the right is doing! Whatever is achieved in perfecting and redeeming the created order, is the work of the Father, mediated by the Son and Spirit. Yet may we not – *must* we not – distinguish their forms of mediation, despite all this, and does this not bring in its train some implications for the being of the ontological Trinity?

The point of moving beyond this to a cautious character-isation of the eternal being of Father, Son and Spirit in their mutual constituting is to show that the distinctive particularity and otherness of each of the three – their very differences within relation – enable us to articulate something of an understanding of who – rather than what – is the God who creates and redeems through the Son and Spirit. The much maligned doctrine of the relations of origin at least establish the point that there is personal otherness within the being of God. As many of the existing chapters, and particularly those which open and close the collection indicate, there is much to be said for the articulation not so much of some inner view, but of a mapping, strictly derived from the economy of creation, reconciliation and redemption, so far as it is made known in Scripture, of the kind of God with whom we have to deal. As is often said, much of the point of this, in turn, is doxological: to enable true worship and praise. But how much more needs to be said? As we have seen, there are lessons to be drawn about the implications of the being of God for our personal being and the being of the rest of the created order. The movement into ontology – into a theology of God's eternal being – enables something of a move back into the world, in order to throw light on the being of that world. From God's personal otherness in relation there can be argued to derive that otherness in relation that is so important for our personal being, but also a doctrine of creation which enables us to respect the diversity in relation of the whole world in which we are set.[36] Beyond that, however, there must be limits on speculation, certainly about the inner being of the deity, if the doctrine of the ontological Trinity is not to fly free from its basis in revelation.

There is therefore much to be said for the view, mentioned in the citations from Christoph Schwöbel in the remarks which opened this preface, that the value of the theology of the Trinity lies more in enabling a rethinking of the topics of theology and culture than in offering a privileged view of the being of God. The two new major chapters which precede the theological postscript are included in order to strengthen the points made in this preface about the importance of a concrete rather than theoretical trinitarianism, and thus to reinforce the concern already present in the shape of chapters four and seven to think the church and the world trinitarianly through Christ and the Holy Spirit.[37] The two new chapters are both studies of major theological topics – the relation between church and culture and the atonement – which demonstrate the impact of not so much arguing from the Trinity to the world by analogy as thinking trinitarianly through the focus

[36] This is the burden of the second half of Gunton, *The One, the Three and the Many*.

[37] The intention is, therefore, to shift the balance of the book rather than to offer a wide-ranging recantation. That is not to suggest that nothing of the other chapters would be changed were the book to be rewritten *de novo*; it is that the series of studies with introduction and postscript which constitute the book has been enlarged to provide two studies which take account of considerations arising from more recent discussion.

provided by the action of God in the world mediated by his 'two hands'. Conventional treatment of both the topics suffers from a failure to integrate the pneumatological dimension into their development, with distortions particularly of the christological dimensions. This is because christology which is abstracted from a discussion of the relation to it of pneumatology is not christology rooted in the actual human career of the incarnate Lord. That is the motive for a stress on the importance of both of the hands of God in their distinctive forms of action, the Son being revealed as the agent of God's immanent involvement with the created order, the Spirit of his eschatological perfecting activity through the Son.

Part of the point of chapter nine on the church and contemporary culture is to focus the question of the distinction between the way in which the triune God acts in and towards the church and in and towards what is called the world. Jürgen Moltmann has recently characterised the false forms of eschatology, particularly those taking the form of misplaced millennialism, which scarred the church's relation with the societies in which it has been set.[38] The chapter focuses on one aspect of this broad question, and suggests a better co-ordination of the functions played by christology and pneumatology, and the triune God they mediate, in our thinking on these matters. By this means, we may urge on our era the necessity of its institutions being undergirded by belief in God, while disavowing the – no doubt exaggerated – repression of past Christian institutional forms.[39]

As has already been suggested, the treatment of the atonement operates in some way as a criterion for a trinitarian theology. Because the atonement has its centre in the particularity of Jesus' life, death and resurrection, a doctrine intrinsically related to it is unlikely to slide into idealism or ideology of the kind we have met in some recent treatments of the Trinity. We might say that the doctrine of the atonement in this respect functions to prevent trinitarian theology from becoming a kind of problem solving device rather than theology bound up with repentance and worship. But, as chapter ten serves also to

---

[38] Jürgen Moltmann, *The Coming of God*, London: SCM Press, 1996.
[39] Exaggerated, because to a certain kind of modernist mind, any form of authority is to be repudiated, except, of course, its own.

suggest, that atonement is itself likely to be better expounded if both its unity as the act of the one God and its many-sidedness as a work of God achieved by both Son and Spirit are both held in view. Doctrines of the Trinity have sometimes appeared to suggest a dualism of will and action between God the Father and God the Son, particularly in those doctrines known by the usually misleading label of 'penal substitution'. But if the incarnate Son achieves what he does through obedience to the (Father's) Spirit who enables him freely to be what he is, distorted versions of the relationship between the Son and the Father are less likely to eventuate.

Finally, it remains to express my thanks to Geoffrey Green for his encouragement to prepare a second edition of a book whose reception has surprised me, at least to the extent that it seems to have been more enthusiastically received than some I thought – and am inclined still to think – rather better written. My colleagues and students at King's, Christoph Schwöbel, who has always maintained his connection with the Research Institute in Systematic Theology, as well as those named on the dedication page, continue to provide inspiration, encouragement and the friendship – indeed, the koinonia which is the gift of the triune God – without which theology can never be done.

Colin Gunton
King's College, London
November 1996

CHAPTER 1

TRINITARIAN THEOLOGY TODAY

I   *Where we stand: the situation of trinitarian theology*

There are, in recent theology, two opposite reactions to the possibilities of trinitarian theology. On the one hand, there is renewed interest and debate. Signalling this, the British Council of Churches has recently received a report of its working party, *The Forgotten Trinity*. Further into the past, there have been in this century at least three major treatises on the Trinity, which have each in a different way renewed the theology of their confessions. Outstanding is without doubt that of Barth (1932), whose central concern can perhaps be said to be the question of the identity of the Christian God over against what Barth held to be the too easy accommodation of the gospel to the main currents of modern thought. From the Roman Catholic tradition has come Rahner's influential attempt (1967) to redirect the dogmatic labours of his church, which, he argued, in its tendency to separate the dogmatic treatises 'On the one God' and 'On the triune God' introduced an intolerable rent in the fabric of theology. From the East, there came (1944) Lossky's attempt to identify in trinitarian terms the basis of the rift between East and West.

More recently, there have been treatises representing many of the main traditions of Christendom: Roman Catholic (Kasper, Hill), Orthodox (Zizioulas), Lutheran (Jenson), Reformed (Moltmann) and Anglican (Brown).[1] If there can be

---

[1] Karl Barth, *Church Dogmatics* Vol. I. Part 1, Edinburgh: T. & T. Clark, 1975 (first German ed. 1932), Chapter II. Karl Rahner, *The Trinity*, London: Burns and Oates, 1970; Vladimir Lossky, *The Mystical Theology of the Eastern Church*,

1

found common threads of interest in so diverse a range of approaches, they are perhaps seen in two general areas of problematic. The first is the problem of Western 'theism', manifested in the widespread feeling that many of the constituents of the crisis that Christianity is facing in the West derive from weaknesses in the way that the doctrine of God has taken shape in the tradition. Lossky, of course, is sure that this is so, and tends to attribute much, if not all, the blame to the doctrine of the *Filioque*. One of the theses to be argued in this set of essays is that there is much to be said for the claim that the way in which Augustine formulated the doctrine of the Trinity did bequeath problems to the West, and that in solving them some help is to be sought from the Cappadocian Fathers. The second general area of problematic is to be found in what can generally be identified as the problem of Christianity and culture, or church and society. What is the relation of Christian faith and its embodiment in institutions to the world about it, particularly in a time when the common Christian culture of our civilisation can no longer be taken for granted?

The other widespread reaction to the doctrine of the Trinity is one of hostility, dismissal or indifference. It is, in the recent public words of a colleague, a 'distortion', and that is all there is to be said. Why should this be so? It is sometimes claimed that modern critical studies of the Bible have ruled out that kind of interpretation of the Bible's God, though A. W. Wainwright suggests that the case is otherwise.[2] However, the view is more likely to be that we have here an inherited dogma that is of no interest or relevance to the modern world. Most famously, this dismissal was voiced in J. A. T. Robinson's expression of dislike in having to preach on Trinity Sunday. Overall, there is a

London: James Clarke, 1957; Walter Kasper, *The God of Jesus Christ*, London: SCM Press, 1984; W. J. Hill, *The Three-Personed God. The Trinity as the Mystery of Salvation*, Washington: Catholic University of America Press, 1982; John D. Zizioulas, *Being as Communion. Studies in Personhood and the Church*, London: Darton, Longman and Todd, 1985; R. W. Jenson, *The Triune Identity*. Philadelphia: Fortress Press, 1982; Jürgen Moltmann, *The Trinity and the Kingdom of God*, London: SCM Press, 1981; David Brown, *The Divine Trinity*, London: Duckworth, 1985. See also *The Forgotten Trinity, The Report of the BCC Study Commission on Trinitarian Doctrine Today*, London: British Council of Churches, 1989.

[2] Arthur W. Wainwright, *The Trinity in the New Testament*, London: SPCK, 1969.

suspicion that the whole thing is a bore, a matter of mathematical conundrums and illogical attempts to square the circle.

Such complaints should not be dismissed out of hand. There is no smoke without fire: in this case there are at least two sets of reasons why things have come to the pass that they have. The first is the assault on christology that has been made by the logicians of the Enlightenment. If the classical dogmatic formulations of the divinity and humanity of Christ, and particularly the former, are irrational and impossible, the Trinity becomes automatically problematic. The Jesus who was believed to be God incarnate becomes interesting not as the presence or revelation of God in person, but as a man pointing to God, providing an instance of religious experience or in some way symbolising a God who is essentially *other* than he. God becomes a more or less shadowy figure *behind* Jesus rather than the one known through him. The Trinity on this account is an improper attempt to provide an ontology of God that is, after Kant, impossible. In chapter two, some kind of conversation will be held with a proponent of a radically post-Kantian view of the impropriety of all 'objective' talk of God.

But the problem is not simply the product of recent history, as will be argued in chapter three. The unfortunate fact is – and it underlies Bishop Robinson's lament – that the shape of the Western tradition has not always enabled believers to rejoice in the triune being of God. The Trinity has more often been presented as a dogma to be believed rather than as the living focus of life and thought. That, I think, is in large measure what underlies Rahner's complaint about the tearing apart of the one and the three: if the real God is known as one, the tacking on of his threeness simply appears as an unnecessary complicating of the simple belief in God. Hence there developed the apparent mathematical dimensions: the hopeless quest for analogies that will somehow make sense of the otherwise illogical. As we shall see, this has much to do with Augustine's famous quest in the latter part of his *De Trinitate* for threefold patterns in experience, and particularly mental experience, which might be seen in some way to mirror the being of God as three. Three chief features of Augustine's and later Western trinitarian thinking can be seen to derive from his approach.

The first is that by seeking for patterns of threeness apart from the economy of salvation – what actually happens in Christ and with the Spirit – Augustine introduces a tendency to draw apart the being of God – what he is eternally – and his act – what he does in time. The second feature is the development of the principle, *opera trinitatis ad extra sunt indivisa* (the actions of the Trinity outwards are undivided). No objection can be taken to this principle if it means that everything that God does, he does in the unity of his being. But if it is taken to mean, as it sometimes appears to be, that no characteristic and distinctive forms of action can be ascribed to Father, Son and Spirit, there appears to be no point in distinguishing between them. All we really need is the action of the one God, so that once again the Trinity appears an irrelevance to our actual understanding of the ways of God towards us.[3] The third problematic feature of Augustine's formulation is the inadequacy of his concept of the person. Here again – as will be argued in detail – the distinctive *personae* of Father, Son and Spirit in the being of the one God fall short of adequate identification, so that the drive is to treat God *unipersonally*, with his personhood located in his oneness, not his threeness. Once again, the actual economy, the way God meets us in time as Father, Son and Spirit is at best secondary to the way we are to understand that he really is, in himself.

Over against this, the collection of papers is designed both to argue for and to illustrate in different ways the importance of a trinitarian account of God's being. It is not meant to be a merely pragmatic justification of the doctrine of the Trinity, because I believe, and will give reasons for the belief in the course of the papers, that God is triune, one being in three persons. But the two, truth and relevance, being and life, are meshed inextricably. Because God is triune, we must respond to him in a particular way, or rather set of ways, corresponding to the richness of his being. (That is one of the implications of the fact that he is in this way and not another.) In turn that means that everything looks – and, indeed, is – different in the

[3] Interestingly, the same kind of development has been discerned by Dorothea Wendebourg in Palamite Orthodox theology, whose doctrine of the energies goes against important dimensions of the theology of the Cappadocians. Her title says it all: 'From the Cappadocian Fathers to Gregory Palamas. The Defeat of Trinitarian Theology', *Studia Patristica* 17.1 (1982), pp. 194–198.

light of the Trinity. But before we come to such matters, there is further introductory work to be done.

II *Where we stand: the basis of trinitarian theology*

Systematic Theology is a programme of thought based in the life of the Christian community of worship. It is important to be aware of the fact that there is no thought or culture without a context, and that theology's context is essentially, in however derivative a sense, churchly. That is not to say, as we shall see in later chapters, that a theology based in a particular community has no bearing on the world outside that community. Quite the reverse. It is rather that any process of thinking has to begin somewhere: where the thinker is. But where are those of us who wish to think in an essentially trinitarian way? Karl Barth saw himself primarily as standing before the God made known – revealed – in Scripture, and as is well known, his preoccupation with revelation gave to his theology a strongly epistemic drive, which at the same time showed him to be working in some way in the context of, although also against, the Enlightenment. Barth's achievement should not be under-rated. His insight is surely correct, that theology cannot rely on the world for a place in which to begin: after Kant, it is bound to stand on its own intellectual feet.[4] But the relative abstractness of his position drives us, it seems to me, to seek a place that is somewhat more concrete, more expressive of Christianity as not merely a religion of revelation – which it is, and must continue to be – but as a faith that takes shape as the faith of a community of worship.

As a number of recent theologies have claimed,[5] theology has its basis in worship. And as soon as we begin to look at worship in the Christian church, the importance of the trinitarian dimension immediately becomes apparent. Worship is not

---

[4] Colin Gunton, 'Barth on the Western Intellectual Tradition. Towards a Theology After Christendom', *Theology Beyond Christendom. Essays on the Centenary of the Birth of Karl Barth May 10, 1886*, ed. John Thompson, Pennsylvania: Pickwick Press, 1986, pp. 285–301.

[5] See especially Edmund Schlink, *The Coming Christ and the Coming Church*, Edinburgh: Oliver and Boyd, 1967.

activity in which we contemplate or observe a being who is over against us – though in a sense God is that also – but it is relational, something that happens between persons. And the happening between persons is worship in the Son and through the Spirit. The sense in which worship is in the Son has been spelled out in various writings by Professor T. F. Torrance.[6] His conception depends on a theology of the mediatorship of Christ. Through his humanity the risen Christ is present in and with the church in order that as God he may lift the community into the presence of the Father. The matter can, and must, also be understood pneumatologically. The church is the true church at worship insofar as – only, but really insofar as – the Spirit ever and again constitutes the community of believers as the church by bringing them into the life of God through the Son. Theology does not therefore begin in abstract observation, but in the work of those who stand in a particular relation to God.

The basis and starting point of theology, however, should not be limited to the relation that is worship, but rather is to be taken as the paradigm case of what takes place also in other dimensions of life. To be a human being is to be related to the Father through the Son and in the Spirit, and it is the character of Christian experience to realise that relationship. Calvin's definition of faith is a splendid and classic expression. 'Now we shall possess a right definition of faith if we call it a firm and certain knowledge of God's benevolence toward us, founded upon the truth of the freely given promise in Christ, both revealed to our minds and sealed upon our hearts through the Holy Spirit.'[7] That is not to deny that as things are human sin brings about a distortion and so failure of that relationship, just as the atonement relocates – again through the Son and in the Spirit – the creature in its destined relationship to God. The point is that because we are established in our being in the Trinity, we are enabled to think *from*, and, with careful qualification, *about* the triune being of God. (The qualification consists in the fact that we may only speak about God while remaining within the relationship: any purely 'objectivising' approach

[6] See especially T. F. Torrance, *Theology in Reconciliation*, London: Geoffrey Chapman, 1975.

[7] John Calvin, *Institutes of the Christian Religion*, III.ii.7.

would be false abstraction.) Theology, on this account, is a trinitarian process, from the being of God through whom we are, to the articulation of the manifold relationships in which we have our created and redeemed being.

Theology, that is to say, is the enterprise of thought which seeks to express conceptually and as well as possible both the being of God and the implications of that being for human existence on earth. Because it is God to whom we are related by Son and Spirit, theology is required in order to come to terms with the universal implications of the relationship in which we have our being. The God met and made known in Christ and the Spirit is the God of all, whether or not they acknowledge it. The theological task is therefore the conceptual exploration of the rationality of the God so experienced and made known. As such, the task can be seen to have two main focuses.

The first is the articulation of the faith for its own sake as the faith of the worshipping community. That is part of theology's responsibility to the claims of truth that Christianity makes. But even that is not a concern for truth in the abstract, for Christian truth, because it is centred on Jesus who is the truth, is truth that edifies, builds up. What might be called the internal orientation of theology is its calling to enable the believing community better to understand and so live the truth by which it is what it is. The second focus of theological activity is the elucidation of the content of the faith for those outside the community of belief: the apologetic or missionary function. It is part of the pathos of Western theology that it has often believed that while trinitarian theology might well be of edificatory value to those who already believe, for the outsider it is an unfortunate barrier to belief, which must therefore be facilitated by some non-trinitarian apologetic, some essentially monotheistic 'natural theology'. My belief is the reverse: that because the theology of the Trinity has so much to teach about the nature of our world and life within it, it is or could be the centre of Christianity's appeal to the unbeliever, as the good news of a God who enters into free relations of creation and redemption with his world. In the light of the theology of the Trinity, everything looks different. To show something of that, by means of an exploration of what might be called the inner rationality of the God who relates himself to us as Father, Son and Holy Spirit, is the chief aim of this book. But before we come to the body of the book, there are further introductory matters to be outlined.

III   *Where we stand: the contribution of history*

The historical claim I wish to make is that the history of trinitarian thought has enabled us to think about God and the world – about reality – in a way otherwise impossible. Inevitably simplifying what is a very complex story, it can be claimed that a number of conceptual advances were made as the result of thought about the God who is indwelt and known in worship. The first conceptual development happened in the centuries up to and after the council of Nicaea in AD 325. The process began with the impact upon the Christian community of the historic act of God in Christ. There is widespread New Testament testimony, albeit expressed in different ways, that Jesus is the one through whom God created the world now come in person to restore it. In the earlier writings of the New Testament, the confession of the mediatorship of Christ in creation begins early and culminates in the 'cosmic christologies' of Hebrews, the Johannine writings and the so-called deutero-pauline epistles to Colossae and Ephesus.[8] An expression of the same theme in the different key provided by their different perspectives is to be found also in the synoptic gospels, where Jesus is presented in the narratives as expressing the lordship of God over the creation, particularly in healing it from its bondage to decay manifested in sickness and death.

It was inevitable and right, certainly in the context in which these things happened, that the historical – 'economic' – sharing of Jesus in the work of the Father should lead to ontology, to questions about the being of the God whose work is done both by Christ and by the Spirit who was understood to be in such close relation to him. If Jesus – to leave on one side for the moment the Spirit – is understood, in the monotheistic context which was both Judaism and the Christian movement that sprang from it, to do the work of God, he cannot finally be

[8] J. G. Gibbs, *Creation and Redemption: A Study in Pauline Theology*, Supplement to *Novum Testamentum* xvi, Leiden, 1971.

separated in thought and being from God. It was the function of the *homoousion*, the teaching that the Son is 'of one being' with the Father, to express the ontological relation between the Son and God the Father. While the precise meaning of this word in its historical context is the subject of much debate, the kind of function that it performs can be pointed quite simply. It is to establish a new ontological principle: that there can be a sharing in being. According to Greek ontology, to be is either to be universal or to be individual: to be defined by virtue of participation in universal form or by virtue of material separation from other beings. The Arian objection to classical christology is that it violates sacred and traditional ontology and divides up the being of God: God cannot be one God if he is Son as well as Father. Arius' definition of God, with its repeated 'alone', is essentially non-relational: 'one God, alone unbegotten, alone everlasting, alone unbegun, etc.'. By insisting, to the contrary, that God is eternally Son as well as Father, the Nicene theologians introduced a note of relationality into the being of God: God's being is defined as being in relation. Such is the impact of the doctrine of the incarnation on conceptions of what it is to be.

To the Cappadocian theologians can be credited a further stage in the process. As a result of their attention to the character of the Holy Spirit, the intellectual revolution – a much misused word, but here surely appropriate – was consolidated. God is being in communion. 'The substance of God, "God", has no ontological content, no true being, apart from communion.'[9] There is, and will continue to be, much argument about how far this is the achievement of the Cappadocians, how much the building upon their work by later theologians, East and West, up to and including John Zizioulas, who has made this theme peculiarly his own. But the points to be made here can be made without the establishing of one or other particular historical theory about origins. The first is that the Cappadocians were in large measure aware of the kind of ontological innovation in which they were sharing. According to the letter variously attributed to Basil of Caesarea and Gregory of Nyssa, we have 'a new unity'. Of course it was

[9] John D. Zizioulas, *Being as Communion*, op. cit., p. 17.

paradoxical, for it stood in opposition to all Greek ontology against whose background it had been thought. It was a major conceptual and theological innovation: God is 'a sort of continuous and indivisible community'.[10]

The crucial move in the process was to distinguish between two words whose meaning had until then been virtually synonymous, *ousia* and *hypostasis*, both meaning 'being'. It is worth mentioning here, after Coleridge but with the help of Stephen Prickett,[11] that the capacity of a language increases by a process of de-synonymy: that is, the process whereby two words which are in the beginning synonymous take on different shades of meaning, and are so able to perform different functions. The desynonymising of *ousia* and *hypostasis*, which previously had meant the same – being or substance – made possible the distinction and yet holding together of the unity and plurality of God. God is indeed one in being: there is only one God. But this very oneness is not a mathematical oneness, as Arius and Greek theology had taught, but a oneness consisting in the inseparable relation of Father, Son and Spirit, the three *hypostases.*

The doctrine of the Trinity has, it can now be seen, nothing to do with attempting a mathematical innovation, apparently contradictory. And this brings us to the second point, that this was a theological revolution, in the primary sense of the word: a revolution in the way in which the word *God* was to be understood. God *is* no more than what Father, Son and Spirit give to and receive from each other in the inseparable communion that is the outcome of their love. Communion is the *meaning* of the word: there is no 'being' of God other than this dynamic of persons in relation. The charge against Augustine and many of his Western successors is that because he failed to appropriate the ontological achievement of his Eastern colleagues he allowed the insidious return of a Hellenism in which being is not communion, but something underlying it. That is the matrix out of which the objectionable features of Western

[10] Basil of Caesarea, Letter 38 4, MPG 32 332a14f and 333d5–333el, E.T. in Maurice Wiles and Mark Santer (edd.), *Documents in Early Christian Thought*, Cambridge University Press, 1975, pp. 34 and 35.

[11] Stephen Prickett, *Words and the Word. Language, Poetics and Biblical Interpretation*, Cambridge University Press, 1986.

'theism' have arisen: the breach between East and West and the dualisms of which Barth and Rahner have made us aware, between God's 'being' and his 'becoming', and between the one God and the triune.

The third point concerns the conceptual possibilities that the theological revolution makes possible. It is not just a matter of the being of God, but of what can be said also about other things. We might say that the developments are of philosophical as much as theological significance, in introducing new conceptual possibilities, new possibilities for speech, into the language. This book is devoted to exploring and developing some of them. At the heart of the doctrine that being is communion are four central concepts: person, relation, otherness and freedom. Let me say a little about each of them here as an introduction to some of the main themes of the papers that follow. The concept of the person is the chief, as well as the most difficult, of the four. I believe that it is impossible to find a definition of it in other words, because it is both ontologically and logically primitive: the personal is both that from which other realities take their meaning and that which is irreducible to other (less than personal) entities. But we can, only by a combination of ostensive and reflective definition, say something of what is meant by the term. Central will be the point that a person is different from an individual, in the sense that the latter is defined in terms of *separation from* other individuals, the person in terms of *relations with* other persons.

To think of persons is to think in terms of relations: Father, Son and Spirit are the particular persons they are by virtue of their relations with each other. That, too, enables us to understand what is meant by *relation*. A relation is first of all to be conceived as the way by which persons are mutually constituted, made what they are. (That does not mean, as will be argued in chapter eight, that the concept is limited to the relations we call personal. On the contrary, it is also fruitful for an understanding of the character of the whole of reality.) But we cannot understand relation satisfactorily unless we also realise that to be a person is to be related as an *other*. One person is not the tool or extension of another, or if he is his personhood is violated. Personal relations are those which constitute the other person as other, as truly particular. And, finally, persons are those whose relations with others are – or should be, for it is the nature of fallenness to distort our being – free relations. By 'free' is not meant what is understood by the reigning conception of the term, a freedom from others. It has to do with a free and mutually constitutive relationship with other persons, as well as with a way of being in the world. The question of freedom will particularly concern the argument of chapter seven.

IV   *Where we stand: the possibilities for trinitarian theology*

⎮As we have seen, the conceptual and philosophical revolution with which we are concerned centres on the doctrine of God, who now comes to be understood as a communion of three persons – not individuals – in mutually constitutive relations with one another.⎮Each is only what he is by virtue of what the three give to and receive from each other; and yet, by virtue of their mutually constitutive relations each is distinctive and particular.⎮But, as has already been suggested, the doctrine of God has important implications for other, indeed all, aspects of human life and the being of the world. The purpose of this final introductory section is to sketch some of them, and to serve as a summary of some of the arguments that will be developed at greater length in the chapters that follow.

We begin with the doctrine of the church, whose character is immediately illuminated if seen in the light of the Trinity. It is remarkable how often Paul, for example, uses the word *koinonia*, communion or community, when speaking of the church and its way of being in the world. The church is the human institution which is called in Christ and the Spirit to reflect or echo (to use a favourite word of chapter four which treats this topic) on earth the communion that God is eternally. The church is therefore called to be a being of persons-in-relation which receives its character as communion by virtue of its relation to God, and so is enabled to reflect something of that being in the world.

But the doctrine of the Trinity is not restricted to the religious sphere, for if what is said about God is true the same kind of implications must be spelled out for other spheres of life also. We can illustrate this by reference to two major questions which face the world at present: the nature of human being in society and human responsibility for the world. The problem of human society becomes immediately apparent when we recall the two forms of political order which have rivalled each other since the Enlightenment, and which in effect present a kind of coincidence of opposites: individualism and collectivism. Individualism is represented by the remark Mrs Thatcher is supposed to have made, that there is no society, only individuals and their families. On such a conception, we do not exist in mutually constitutive relations with each other. We do not need our neighbour in order to be human. In a collective form of society, the opposite is true, for the many exist only for the one. Although we can see the elements of truth in collectivism's reaction against the excesses of individualism, it is on the whole, as history is beginning to teach us, even worse, for it leads to the suppression of the *particular person* in the name of the collective, and, indeed, to some of the worst iniquities of history.

The fact is, however, that neither system is adequate, for each alike derives from a failure to give priority to the person as free, other and yet constituted by relations to other persons. In chapter five is to be found a treatment of some of the problems of the concept of the person as it has been understood in recent Western philosophical tradition and, more important, of the contributions which a theological concept of the person can make to the discussion. The person is neither an individual, defined in terms of separateness from others, nor one who is swallowed up into the collective. Just as Father, Son and Spirit are what they are by virtue of their otherness-in-relation, so that each *particular* is unique and absolutely necessary to the being of the whole, so it is, in its own way, for our being in society.

The problem of human responsibility to the world is twofold, because the crisis we are experiencing derives, on the one hand, from a false conception of the human relation to the world, and, indeed, a false anthropology and ethic; and on the other from a false assessment of the nature of the world. We have overstressed the role of the human race as dominating lords – made ourselves in a false image of God – and treated the world as a machine, empty of meaning except as we choose to confer it. The anthropological question is raised in chapter six, where it is argued that to be in the image of God is to exercise particular forms of relatedness to other human beings and to the world.

But perhaps the most central question of all is the relation between trinitarian theology and our understanding of the kind of world in which we live. The question arises very early in the book, in the discussion in chapter two between the two approaches to the doctrine of the Trinity in recent theology, where Coleridge's concern to develop a theology of a world supportive of human and personal values is discussed. But a direct approach to the question is to be found in chapter eight, where it is argued that the doctrine of Trinity enables us to think both the otherness, and so relative autonomy of the world, from God, and the relatedness of the world to God. The world is created through the Son and in the Spirit, that is to say by persons in relation who freely relate themselves to that which is not themselves. As the creation of the love of God the world is not impersonal process, a machine or a self-developing organism – a cosmic collective into which the particular simply disappears – but that which itself has a destiny along with the human: it is that whose destiny is to be realised along with and by the agency of the human creation, so that that which is not personal may come to be itself in being offered back perfected to its creator through Christ and in the Spirit.

CHAPTER 2

THE QUESTION OF GOD IN THE MODERN WORLD

Trinitarian possibilities

I One recent debate

Readers of Christian theology during recent years have witnessed two debates, apparently quite separate, about the Christian doctrine of God. The first concerns whether we can believe at all in God conceived as a being other than the world, and it comes into sharpest focus in the directly opposed writings of Don Cupitt and Keith Ward.[1] On the face of the matter, it may seem absurd to suggest that there can be Christianity without belief in a God to whom prayer and worship are offered, and who is conceived to make a difference to both worshippers and world. But Cupitt's view that there not only can but should be a rejection of an 'objective' God has to be understood against the background of a tradition which has developed momentum during the past few centuries and asserts that the whole idea of a transcendent 'other' God is alienating and dehumanising. The fundamental dogma of this tradition, and it is a dogma Cupitt accepts almost without question, is that the existence of an objectively 'metaphysical' God and human freedom are incompatible.

This dogma is, in turn, supported by another: that the proper condition of the human agent is autonomy, being a law unto oneself, the implication being that to take one's direction for life from another, whether that other be God or man, is to be less than fully human. The autonomous individual – and this is

---

[1] Don Cupitt, *Taking Leave of God*, London: SCM Press, 1980. Keith Ward, *Holding Fast to God*, London: SPCK, 1982.

mostly an individualistic creed, because systems of thought which are collectivist tend to take an authoritarian or heteronomous form – is the one who legislates for him- or herself. Cupitt belongs to this tradition, increasingly, it seems, turning to the thought of Nietzsche, and holds both that belief in God of a traditional kind is to be rejected on moral grounds and that as a matter of fact philosophical criticism has made it untenable. In his response to Cupitt, Keith Ward rejects both the factual claim and the dogma that God and freedom are incompatible. The former case is made by an appeal to something like a traditional metaphysical theology, but Ward argues also that this does not entail an alienating heteronomy. God and freedom are not incompatible, because 'I assert, in total opposition to Cupitt, ... that it is God's love which arouses the religious response of loving commitment' (p. 74). Piece by piece, Ward demolishes Cupitt's arguments. As Professor John McIntyre said of a similar piece of destruction, Ward has no compunction in shooting a sitting duck; not a feather remains. And yet the verdict of a relatively disinterested observer of the debate, Stewart Sutherland, is that while the demolition is successful, Ward's alternative construction is not entirely convincing.[2] Could it be that there is more to Cupitt's position than can be met by argument of this kind? We shall return to this question.

II   *A second discussion*

The second debate about the doctrine of God appears to be altogether different. It is not about whether there is a God, but rather about his nature: the kind of being God is. To put the matter in specifically Christian terms, it is to ask the question of the relationship of God to ourselves and the implications of such a relationship for our understanding of what it is for God to be God. To take the matter a step further, it is to begin with somewhat different assumptions, not so much in a different context as with a different conception of the context of theology. Cupitt's assumption is a general cultural one, that

---

[2] Stewart R. Sutherland, 'A Theological Fable', *King's Theological Review* 6 (1983), pp. 17–19.

certain developments have taken place in the modern world which make anything like traditional theology impossible. The developments cannot be denied. What can be questioned is their significance, and, indeed, the shape of chapter one was in part developed to show that there is another context to be taken into account than the cultural. On such alternative assumptions, theology cannot simply react to culture, but must approach it from a particular context of worship and life.

If that is done, a different question is asked: Who is the God who enters into saving relationship with us in Jesus of Nazareth? The earliest full scale Christian answer to the question was to develop a doctrine of the Trinity. One feature of recent theology has been a widespread tendency to doubt the propriety of the process. But the centrality of the doctrine to a Christian understanding of God has always had its advocates, and was strongly reasserted in the 1930s by Karl Barth. More recently there have been published a number of books more or less directly devoted to the Trinity, and the flow shows no signs of abating.[3] They are very different from each other, but a glance at some of them will indicate the concerns underlying this side of the debate about the Christian doctrine of God.

Robert W. Jenson's *The Triune Identity* is significant in diagnosing entirely differently from Don Cupitt the Western culture they share, albeit from different sides of the Atlantic. Cupitt's world is modern secular culture, self-confident in its technological progress. He even makes one revealing allusion to the offence caused by Western secularism, particularly in what he calls 'more backward countries of the Third World and the socialistic block' (pp. 16f). By contrast, Jenson believes the modern world to be like the declining Mediterranean world in which Christianity first took form, 'presenting a different divine offering on every street corner' (p. ix). It is not secularism but modern religiosity which presents the chief challenge to Christianity, and so the theological task is not to defend religion – or,

---

[3] See footnote 1, chapter one, for a list of representative twentieth century studies of the Trinity. Also among recent books are Eberhard Jüngel, *The Doctrine of the Trinity*, Edinburgh: Scottish Academic Press, 1976 and *God as the Mystery of the World*, Edinburgh: T. & T. Clark, 1983; Jürgen Moltmann, *The Crucified God*, London: SCM Press, 1974; James P. Mackey, *The Christian Experience of God as Trinity*, London: SCM Press, 1983.

with Cupitt, to develop an atheist or subjectivist form of it – but to identify the Christian God in a world of competing religious systems. 'The Western Church must either renew its trinitarian consciousness or experience increasing impotence and confusion' (ibid.). The question for us is, Why should the Trinity be supposed to be so important?

A number of possible answers centre on the matter of the nature of Christianity. The first appeals to tradition, and argues from origins. From the very beginning the church had a trinitarian faith, even though it took some time to work out its intellectual implications and expression. Many New Testament texts have an apparently threefold structure (for example, Mt. 28.10 and Rom. 8.11), while it can also be argued that the roots, even part of the plant, are to be found already in the overall teaching of the Canon.[4] Similarly, the worship and creeds of the early church quickly developed a trinitarian shape. The argument to tradition is a strong one, because a church that changes its conception of God as radically as the abandonment of trinitarianism would entail could scarcely find it possible to claim to be the same church. In the New Testament and the earliest traditions of theology and worship, we have documents dating from the time Christianity took shape. Such considerations, however, are not completely compelling, because traditions go dead, and because we can still ask, Was the early church right to develop in the way it did? It is now widely contended that early theology made a mistake in attempting to derive an ontology from the Bible. The biblical documents are best understood as a record of experience, not a quarry for trinitarian construction. We should therefore, it is argued, be free to develop a doctrine of God that conforms to our experience, even if that involves taking the apparently atheist path of Don Cupitt.

A second type of argument is similar to the first, but links the appeal to what is taken to be the definitive tradition with a systematic attempt to discern a continuity of theology: what God did then is argued to provide the pattern, so to speak, for what he does now. It is held that what we find witnessed or

---

[4] Arthur W. Wainwright, *The Trinity in the New Testament*, London: SPCK, 1969.

described in the Bible is the presence of God in certain specific ways to time, and that this involvement of God in the world provides a way of understanding the kind of being that God (always, and therefore now) is. Such an approach is rooted in the Jewish apprehension of God, according to which – in some contrast to the typical Greek approach, as Jenson points out – time was the place where God made himself known.[5] For Christian theology, the temporal history of Jesus and the life of the church in the Spirit provided a focus, and inevitably drew theology in a trinitarian direction.

Recent Western theology has tended to concentrate on the latter of those two focuses, and move to trinitarianism on the basis of various understandings of the significance of Jesus. The most influential treatise on the Trinity this century has been that of Karl Barth, who centred his development on a conception of Jesus Christ as revelation.[6] His Trinity of revelation, revealer and revealedness has received much criticism, particularly for its apparent tendency to make all depend on the noetic rather than – say – on the saving significance of Jesus, but has fathered a number of similar offspring. Thus Jüngel, in a paraphrase of Barth, concentrates on the notion of the doctrine of the Trinity as theology's interpretation of God's self-interpretation;[7] while Jenson, drawing on discussions of identity in Anglo-Saxon philosophy, speaks of God's self-identification. '"Father, Son and Holy Spirit" became the Church's name for its God because it packs into one phrase the content and logic of this God's identifying descriptions. These in turn embody the Church's primal experience of God.'[8] On understandings such as these, the trinitarian pattern of Christian worship, life and thought once was and now continues to be the appropriate human response to the way God relates himself to us in time: 'through Christ we ... have access in one Spirit to the Father' (Eph. 2.18). The theology of the Trinity, even in its sometimes convoluted abstractions, is the intellectual articulation

[5] Jenson, *The Triune Identity*, op. cit., ch. 1, n. 1, pp. 57ff. See also R. S. Anderson, *Historical Transcendence and the Reality of God*, London: Geoffrey Chapman, 1975.
[6] Karl Barth, *Church Dogmatics* Vol. I. Part 1, Edinburgh: T. & T. Clark, 1975 (first German ed. 1932), Chapter II.
[7] Jüngel, *The Doctrine of the Trinity*, op. cit., pp. 15ff.
[8] Jenson, op. cit., p. 21.

of this simple insight. In worship, Christians are brought into relationship with the Father through Jesus Christ in the Holy Spirit. To be true to the logic of such experience, we are bound to say that if God is truly God, he must be eternally what he shows himself to be in time. The threeness of the trinitarian understanding of the Godhead is the outworking of the implications of the threeness of his movement into time.

Before we move to the next stage of the argument, one observation should be made. None of the three treatments of the Trinity just mentioned is particularly concerned with apologetic. The preoccupation of Cupitt and his less radical colleagues with the defence or reconstitution of Christianity in modern cultural conditions is not a primary concern. Theirs is rather an attempt to articulate what they take to be the centre of a Christian conception of God as it is presented in Bible, tradition and experience. Indeed, one of them, Jenson, is positively aggressive, measuring modern culture in the balance of the Christian gospel, and finding it wanting. As is well known, that is the strategy associated with the name of Barth, and would appear to place the preoccupations of these authors in an entirely different world from that of the Cupitt-Ward debate. We appear to be faced with an opposition between culture's mission to Christianity and Christianity's mission to culture. But, as will be argued in the next section, such an opposition is a distinct oversimplification. We shall rather discover one central preoccupation that the two sides have in common.

III   *A community of interest*

A way into the topic is provided by a glance at two recent approaches to the Trinity, both originating in Tübingen, which make direct links to the concerns of Cupitt. The first is that of Jürgen Moltmann, adumbrated in *The Crucified God* and developed at length in *The Trinity and the Kingdom of God*. Moltmann's direction is at once apologetic and systematic. It is apologetic in the sense that he wishes to develop a theology of the Trinity which will help to overcome the antagonism of the cultured modern mind to Christianity. Two features dominate the cultural landscape as Moltmann paints it. The first is the apparent responsibility of God for evil, particularly as that is crucially instantiated in the evil of Auschwitz. Against the notion of a God conceived as overwhelmingly active, as *doing* everything and therefore as, apparently, the cause of evil, Moltmann in the earlier work introduced a counter-balancing stress on the suffering of God on the cross, developing a theology of the Trinity from the conception of Jesus as the crucified Son, in dialogue with the Father who was – in contradiction of the traditional teaching of the impassibility of God – also understood to suffer in and with the Son.

The second feature is to be found in a critique of the Christian tradition developed at greater length in the later work. The weakness of theology in the West is, on Moltmann's account, its theism or monotheism. Theism elevates beyond measure the unity of God, and produces a theology with socially destructive consequences. 'The monotheistic God is "the Lord of the world". He is defined simply through his power of disposal over his property, not through personality and personal relationships' (*The Trinity*, p. 198). The tendency to depersonalise God, to turn him into the ideological support of authoritarianism, is not adequately countered by the mainstream trinitarian theologies of the West. They too easily lose hold of the interpersonal reality of God, and have been at the root of political and ecclesiastical tyranny. A change in the way God is conceived, opposing monotheism with a more truly trinitarian doctrine, will not only be more faithful to the nature of God as Christianity understands him, but will obviate the more scandalous aspects of the tradition. Thus for Moltmann the doctrine of the Trinity is the source at once of the renewal of Christianity from within and its defence against often justified criticisms from without.

A parallel concern is at the heart of the work of the Tübingen Roman Catholic theologian, Walter Kasper. *The God of Jesus Christ* has as its dominating background the contemporary debate about God: 'The denial of God in modern atheism', and 'The predicament of theology in the face of atheism' are the titles of two early chapters. Kasper's account of the predicament is very much that to be found in countless other books by modern theologians. The distinctive feature of his treatment is like that of Moltmann, and although he distinguishes his own position from the latter's (pp. 60f), his response to the problems raised by modern atheism is centred on a treatment of the Trinity. Unfortunately, the bulk of the book consists in a fairly straightforward discussion with the Christian tradition, and the question dominating the opening chapters is returned to only briefly towards the end. At stake in all theology is what can broadly be termed the question of salvation, of what, if any, the overall meaning of things is. Thus, says Kasper (p. 290), the question of unity is the question of salvation; but, he adds, quoting Pascal and echoing Moltmann, unity without multiplicity is the route to tyranny. The question of God's unity in Trinity is therefore one of the clues to the problem about the nature of human life on earth (pp. 290ff).

The value of the work of the two Tübingen theologians for our purpose is that they link the two matters which are the subject of this paper, the equation of God with pernicious heteronomy by Don Cupitt and Christianity's traditional conception of God as triune. Moltmann and Kasper conceive the challenge in terms similar to those of Cupitt: the traditional concept of God is an enemy of human freedom. Their trinitarian theology is in part an attempt to provide a reasoned answer to the same problem. But therein lies also the weakness of their proposals. By allowing their theology to be dominated by one dimension they are prevented from penetrating below the surface of the underlying questions. Moltmann's much criticised tendency to identify God too closely with his historical manifestations may well derive from too great a preoccupation with apologetic questions. And it is only summarily that Kasper comes to face the central ontological question of the one and the many. What is the world and how is it structured both in relation to ourselves and to such meaning as might be conceived to inform it?

Underlying the concerns of all the authors we have reviewed, although very different distances from the surface of their discussion, is the matter of ontology, without which none of the questions will receive satisfactory treatment. The reason for the importance of ontology is not only that if it is ignored it will be assumed, and therefore will shape theology in an unacknowledged way. It is also for the more positive reason that only if we root a proper concern with apologetics, culture and the renewal of Christianity in a wider and deeper theology of being will we be able to relate the different concerns that we have met without reducing one to the other. To find out more about the matters in common to both Cupitt and the trinitarian theologians, the question will be pursued with the help of one who long ago saw both sides of the question with prophetic clarity.

IV *One dialogue with modern culture*

The link between the two debates we have outlined was perceived more than a hundred and fifty years ago by Samuel Taylor Coleridge. Coleridge was as aware as Don Cupitt of the pressures making for atheism in the modern Western world. The difference is that he was prepared to enter into a critical dialogue with movements of thought deriving from the Enlightenment. What Cupitt has swallowed whole Coleridge tasted, spitting out some of the less palatable bits. For unpalatable they are, and for the following reasons. At the centre for Coleridge was the question of human life on this earth, and in particular the search for its meaning and redemption. He examined the two fashionable doctrines of his day, mechanist unitarianism and romantic pantheism. Both the mechanical philosophy, deriving from the deist doctrines of the Enlightenment, and the pantheism of Spinoza had the same outcome; the human 'I' was turned into an 'it', human freedom was abolished, the human moral agent turned into a cog in an impersonal machine or organism. Where for Cupitt any objectively existing God is an enslaving tyrant, for Coleridge slavery was the outcome of a world foreign to personal values. The whole issue was centred on the matter of the Trinity. Why? The central puzzle was found in the relation between the 'I' and the 'world'.

On the one hand, the 'it' philosophy of deism, mechanism and pantheism swallowed up the personal 'I', and so deprived it of personhood. We meet here considerations that will receive treatment in further papers of the collection. At the heart of the question is the distinction between personal and logical relations, in this case between God and what is not God, a distinction reaching back to the very beginnings of theology.

The tendency of much early Greek theology, with its quest to show the inherence of the 'many' in the 'one', is to make the many in some way or other a logical implication of the one, whether as emanation or as a more strictly logical outworking, as characteristically exemplified in the geometrical philosophy of Spinoza. What 'I' am is in some way a logical implication of what 'reality' is, so that I am deprived of particularity, otherness and freedom. Some of the anthropological implications of this tendency will be considered in chapter six.

On the other hand – and this is the outcome of some aspects of Cupitt's philosophy – the 'I' philosophy of idealism endangered, according to Coleridge, the objective reality of the world, turning it into the unreal play of the fancy. The need rather was for a conception of the reciprocity of the human mind and its objects, something only possible on an understanding of God as a structure of reciprocities, in which the 'I' and the other are related through a third.[9] Coleridge's proposals, with their tendency to be fragmentary and schematic, are in some ways more important for what they suggest and make conceptually possible than for what they actually deliver. What is significant for our purpose is the different way in which he and Cupitt conceived the intellectual possibilities. For Cupitt, as for many contemporary theologians, certain questions about the relation of God to the world have been decided by the course of Western culture in the past few centuries. The world is mechanistic in character, closed to any meaning deriving from outside it, and so able to be understood only in the categories of immanence. Cupitt's is an extreme version of this 'immanentism', in that he holds the world to be lacking any meaning in itself, such value as it has being granted it by the human mind, the sole source of truth and value. In effect he is saying that there is only one possibility open to the theologian: picking up the pieces remaining after the modern destruction of options other than his.

[9] See especially Thomas McFarland, *Coleridge and the Pantheist Tradition*, Oxford: Clarendon Press, 1969. Part One of my *Enlightenment and Alienation. An Essay Towards a Trinitarian Theology*, Basingstoke: Marshall, Morgan and Scott, 1985, makes use of Coleridge's insights in a similar context to that of this paper. For the development of the rest of this section I am indebted to Daniel W. Hardy, 'Coleridge on the Trinity', *Anglican Theological Review* LXIX (1988), pp. 145–155.

It was the genius of Coleridge to see that there are, and have always been in some form or other, at least two distinct ways of conceiving the world and God. Other modern thinkers have made the point that the matter is more open than is sometimes made to appear, for example Kierkegaard: 'the only consistent position outside Christianity is that of pantheism ...'.[10] In his discussion of the origins of different cosmologies, Coleridge saw three possibilities, the Phoenician, the Hebrew and the Greek, and he sets them out in his important paper, 'On the Prometheus of Aeschylus'. 'The Phoenician confounded the indistinguishable with the absolute', with the result that 'their cosmogony was their theogony, and vice versa'.[11] By contrast, the Hebrew wisdom imperatively asserts 'an unbeginning creative One ... who willed and it was' (p. 354). The Greek view stands somewhere between, containing three terms in contrast to the Phoenician two ('a self-organizing chaos, and the omniform nature as the result', p. 354), and the Hebrew four (p. 355).

The lesson to be learned from such an analysis is that there are a limited number of ways – perhaps finally only two – in which the fundamental nature of the universe can be conceived, and that they are distinct conceptual frameworks within which other enterprises such as the sciences can be comprehended. Such a typology of world-views is more illuminating than the more fashionable opposition of the scientific and pre-scientific, because such possibilities are to be found in both ancient and modern views of things. Accordingly, a main difference is to be found between conceptions of the world as owing its origin to personal agency and as in some way self-organised – Coleridge's distinction between the Hebrew and the Phoenician. In the name of modern enlightenment and science, Cupitt has opted for a version of the latter of these, in a characteristically mechanistic version. The most naive questions can cast doubt upon Cupitt's position. It may not be easy to co-ordinate the Bible's openness to miracles and the world of

---

[10] Soren Kierkegaard, *Concluding Unscientific Postscript*, E.T. by David F. Swenson and Walter Lowrie, Princeton University Press, 1941, p. 203.

[11] Samuel Taylor Coleridge, 'On the Prometheus of Aeschylus', *The Complete Works of Samuel Taylor Coleridge*, ed. W. G. T. Shedd, New York: Harper and Brothers, 1853, Vol. 4, pp. 344–365.

modern science, but is not modern science more various than uniformly to conform to the mechanist picture so implicitly believed by certain theologians? And is there not at least a strong current in the philosophy of science which by its realism presupposes that the world is intrinsically meaningful and open to the human mind? That question leads to another: if scientific, factual, meaning imposes itself on us from outside, so that the scientist is, at least in part, the humble listener to truth, is it any more alienating to seek and hope to find *ethical* meaning also inhering in the world? All these questions suggest that the matter is much more open than Cupitt supposes. Once it is established that there is more than one way in which the world and its relation to us may be conceived, Cupitt's naive dogmatism is exposed and the way made clear for taking seriously the questions with which trinitarian theology confronts us.

V   *The debate again*

We have seen that the subject of the debate between Ward and Cupitt and the concerns animating those theologians who have in recent years turned their attention to the doctrine of the Trinity come together in two related questions: What is the world and what is the nature of human life within it? They were linked from the very beginnings of Christian theology in the conception of the eternal Word of God. 'In the beginning was the Word, and the Word was God ... All things were made through him' (John 1.1f). With the help of such texts, the great patristic theologians developed a theology in which creation and redemption were linked. The Word is the agent through whom God the Father creates, and is therefore the way by which God's eternal nearness to his creation is conceived. The world is a place in which evil has been let loose by human wickedness. Christianity grew and flourished because it taught that in the Word made flesh God has himself engaged with that evil in order to deprive it of its power.

There is no doubt that the Christian church has at times in its history turned that gospel of human liberation by the self-giving of God into its authoritarian opposite. But the response of those like Cupitt who wish in effect to transfer from God to humankind the centre of value is at once unrealistic and enslaving. It is at once to ignore the depths of human evil and to impose on the finite the impossible and alienating burdens of divinity. Against this recent books on the Trinity have asserted two features of the Christian doctrine of God which repeat something of the teaching of the Fathers. The first feature is found in the subtitle of one of the recent books, that of W. J. Hill: *The Three-Personed God. The Trinity as the Mystery of Salvation.* His title is taken from John Donne: 'Batter my heart, three person'd God'. Human wholeness, lost through sin, must be restored through the action of God, not heteronomously but by his 'battering' on hardened hearts, from within our human condition. Hill sees the doctrine of the Trinity as the articulation of the doctrine of God under the impact of the Christian scheme of salvation.

The second feature we have already met in Coleridge, and is found in Jüngel's title: *God as the Mystery of the World.* Christianity is not just a matter of personal salvation, out of a lost or empty world. Christian teaching has sometimes suggested this, and thus far has anticipated Cupitt's position. The latter's dualism of human value and impersonal world can in large measure be understood as an atheist version of an earlier dualism of human salvation out of a lost and perishing creation. By contrast, to understand God as the mystery of the world is to go back beyond manichaean distortions of Christianity to a more biblical understanding of salvation in the context of and along with a restored creation. According to Jüngel, 'God is ... grasped as the mystery of the world as he comes to the world',[12] and that means as he identifies himself on the cross of Jesus.

Both of these recent studies, however, disappoint in one central respect. Jüngel in particular, by his concentration on justification as the place where God is present, fails to show in in what sense God is the mystery of *the world*, while Hill's emphasis continues to appear rather limitedly dogmatic and ecclesiastical. It is not that these two dimensions are unimportant. Far from it; but, as I hope to show in the progression of topics in this book, an adequate theology of the Trinity will take us far further, into matter of more universal concern. Part of

[12] Jüngel, *God as the Mystery of the World*, op. cit., p. 378.

the point of doing theology from the Trinity is, to repeat a phrase from chapter one, that 'everything looks different in the light of the Trinity'.

This brings us back to Messrs Coleridge and Cupitt. The latter's overriding desire is for a theology that will do justice to modern culture. So is that of the former, whose programme is like Cupitt's even to the extent of seeking the clue to the being of things in the structure of human rationality. The difference, and it is all the difference in the world, lies in what he finds there. The idea of the triune God is what it is because it is a given – not a construct – which contains the clue to everything else: 'that *Idea Idearum*, the one substrative truth which is the form, manner, and involvement of all truths'.[13] The underlying claim is that the notion of the Trinity takes us to the heart of our being and of our being in the world. What is at stake, therefore, in this discussion is not only, as Jenson rightly sees, the future of the church, but also the being and flourishing of all humankind. Is the world, or is it not, a place in which human beings may live, love, flourish and find redemption? Indeed, is it a realm *along with which* we may seek the perfection of our being? Daniel Hardy sees that this is at the heart of what Coleridge was doing with his doctrine of the Trinity. 'For not only personal salvation but also full understanding of the created order relies always on a freely willed personal activity, one which follows the rich pattern of the "unitrine" God and thereby participates in the rich energies he affords.'[14]

To end with another of Cupitt's concerns, the matter of heteronomy and autonomy, we must ask what it is that truly establishes us according to the law of our being. Is it unstructured freedom, or our relation to God? That will be the burden of chapter seven. What must be said here is that the conviction, derived from the doctrine of the Trinity, that God is personal and loving in himself and in his relationship with the world requires us to think in other terms than that of simple opposition. There is, of course, a relationship of authority, for God is creator and Lord. But the authority is exercised personally, and from within our human plight. God is the mystery of the world,

---

[13] Coleridge, 'Notes on Waterland', op. cit., Vol. 5, p. 407.
[14] Hardy, op. cit., p. 155.

the salvation of the person and the redeemer of the cosmos. That is the heart of the Christian doctrine of God, and the doctrine of the Trinity is at the centre of that faith as the means by which its understanding of God takes conceptual shape. That is why the debate outlined in the second section of this paper is of far greater significance than that with which the discussion began: it takes us wider and deeper into the mystery of what it is to be a human being in the world.

CHAPTER 3

AUGUSTINE, THE TRINITY AND THE THEOLOGICAL CRISIS OF THE WEST

I *The problem of the unknowability of God*[1]

We live in a culture marked, as few others have been, by persistent and deep-seated scepticism about the existence and knowability of God. Not only is the intellectual leadership of our times for the most part atheist or agnostic, but theology itself, certainly since the time of Kant, has been in fundamental disarray about the question – as witness, for example, the recent preoccupation with the question of revelation. In this paper I want to argue two theses. The first is that the problem does not begin with Kant, because at least one of the causes of Western atheism is a theological tradition which encourages thought in the essential unknowability of God. Here, a distinction must be drawn. In one sense, of course, the doctrine of the unknowability of God is essential to theology. But to hold it in such a way as to suggest or teach that the unknowable God can in no way make himself known – so that there can be no theological ontology at all – is to offer the kind of hostages to fortune which so much Western theology has done. Can it really be a historical accident that it is here rather than anywhere else that atheism has found so fertile a soil?

Second, I want to argue that the problem has much to do

[1] This paper was first presented to a seminar on the doctrine of the Trinity at King's College, London, on 26 January 1988. I am grateful to members of the seminar, particularly John Zizioulas and Christoph Schwöbel, the latter of whom read the paper in draft and made some characteristically helpful suggestions.

with the way in which the doctrine of the Trinity has been treated in our tradition. It is worth notice that while the theology and worship of Eastern Orthodoxy continue to be saturated with trinitarian categories, the doctrine of the Trinity has in the West come into increasing question. Where there has been no explicit move to call the doctrine in question – as it has most obviously been questioned by those such as Robinson, Lampe and Wiles who have in recent years been among the most quoted of English theologians – there has for long been a tendency to treat the doctrine as a problem rather than as encapsulating the heart of the Christian Gospel. It is as if one had to establish one's Christian orthodoxy by facing a series of mathematical and logical difficulties rather than by glorying in the being of a God whose reality as a communion of persons is the basis of a rational universe in which personal life may take shape.

The aim of this chapter is to bring together the two questions – of the problem about the knowledge of God and of the relegation to secondary status of the doctrine of the Trinity – by enquiring how far responsibility for the state of affairs is to be laid at the door of St Augustine. His formulation of the doctrine of the Trinity has been much discussed in recent times, and some attempt to examine the main issues is overdue. On the face of it, to accuse of undermining the doctrine of the Trinity one whose treatment of the topic is among the glories of Western theology may appear to be perverse; to accuse of undermining the knowledge of God one for whom the knowledge of God was a prominent concern may appear odd at the very least. Yet much hangs on what or who is supposed to be known, and how.

Here, one of the first recent Western theologians to voice suspicions of the Augustinian tradition was Karl Rahner. As is well known, his polemic was against the separation of the dogmatic treatises, *On the One God* and *On the Triune God,* a development he attributes to the time when 'the *Sentences* of Peter Lombard were superseded by the Summa of St Thomas'.[2] Nonetheless, the intellectual origin of the tendency he inclines

---

[2] Karl Rahner, *The Trinity*, E.T. by Joseph Donceel, London: Burns and Oates, 1970, p. 17.

to attribute to Augustinian theology in general (p. 17). Rahner's analysis is confirmed by that of the translator of Augustine in his introduction to the CUA edition:

> [T]he very plan that he [Augustine] follows differs from that of the Greeks. They begin by affirming their belief in the Father, Son and the Holy Spirit according to the Scriptures ... But to Augustine it seemed better to begin with the unity of the divine nature, since this is a truth which is demonstrated by reason. ... The logic of this arrangement is today commonly recognized, and in the textbooks of dogma the treatise *De Deo Uno* precedes that of *De Deo Trino*.[3]

According to Rahner, the weakness of that development is that 'It looks as if everything which matters for us in God has already been said in the treatise *On the One God*' (p. 17). The result is that salvation history comes to appear irrelevant to the doctrine of God. The implication for conceptions of the knowledge of God we can then suppose to be something as follows. Because the one God is the real God, and known in a different way from the God who is three, God as he is in himself would appear to be, or at least conceivably is, other than the God made known in salvation history. The outcome is either a modalistic conception of God, or two competing sources of knowledge which tend to discredit each other.

Can Augustine's doctrine of the Trinity justly be accused of fathering such a development? The claim has been made by Harnack that 'Augustine only gets beyond Modalism by the mere assertion that he does not wish to be a Modalist, and by the aid of ingenious distinctions between different ideas.'[4] The fact is, however, that Augustine is a many-sided figure so that, as Wolfson has shown, the matter cannot be so easily decided.[5] Therefore what has to be examined is not simply his statement of doctrine *but the underlying presuppositions which give the doctrine the shape that it has.* Christian theologising about the knowledge of God in the early centuries was always carried out, as it is now,

---

[3] Stephen McKenna, 'Introduction' to *Saint Augustine. The Trinity*, Washington, D.C.: Catholic University of America Press, 1963.

[4] Adolf Harnack, *History of Dogma*, E.T. by E. B. Speirs and James Millar, London: Williams and Norgate, 1898, Vol. IV, p. 131.

[5] H. A. Wolfson, *The Philosophy of the Church Fathers*, Cambridge: Harvard University Press, 1956, p. 358.

in the context of the philosophical teaching and assumptions of the day. In Arianism, for example, one important aspect of the debate concerned whether or not God had truly given himself to be known in Christ, or whether philosophical axioms of his unknowability should come to rule the day. The question to Augustine concerns similarly the impact of platonising doctrines upon his thought. Are they such as to take away with the left hand what had already been given with the right, to undermine the doctrine of the God known as triune even while it is being stated?

II The problem of materiality

It is well known that Augustine was suspicious of the material world. With the platonists, he found it difficult to believe that the material and sensible realm could either be truly real or the object or the vehicle of knowledge. The kind of assumptions that he held have since come to cast doubt upon the doctrine of the incarnation. For Augustine, that doctrine was central (e.g. IV.27f);[6] and yet when we come to examine what he made of it, we shall be able to understand why his doctrine of the Trinity took the shape that it did. Our enquiry will be concerned with two related aspects: with the use Augustine makes of christology in his development of the doctrine of the Trinity, and with what in general he makes of the humanity of Christ.

There are moments of truth in the frequent complaints of modern theologians that theology has in the past tended to be 'docetic' about the humanity of Christ. In that respect, the ill-fated quest of the historical Jesus can be understood as a proper concern to do justice to Chalcedon's insistence that in respect of his humanity, Jesus Christ was of one substance with

---

[6] References to the *De Trinitate* will appear in the text in parentheses, the book number being followed by the section reference in Arabic numerals, as in CCL vols. L and L A. Where translations are taken directly from either the Catholic University Press edition (note 3 above) or from *Augustine: Later Works*, E.T. by John Burnaby, Library of Christian Classics, Vol. VIII, London: SCM Press, 1955, the reference will be followed by either 'CUA' or 'LCC'. In some places I have made my own translations, erring on the literal side, because the translations often obscure Augustine's language or smooth out difficulties.

ourselves. With few exceptions, the English Puritan John Owen and the nineteenth century Scot Edward Irving among them, Western theology has for the most part failed to develop adequate conceptual equipment to ensure due prominence to Christ's full humanity. Part of the cause of this may be found in Augustine's reluctance to give due weight to the full materiality of the incarnation.

In considering the relation of christology to trinitarian theology, two distinct considerations must be held in mind. The first is that some account of the divinity of the historical Christ is a necessary condition of a Christian Trinity, as distinct from some merely rational triad. The second is that a firm hold on the material humanity of the incarnate Son is a prerequisite for a doctrine of the Trinity that does not float off into abstraction from the concrete history of salvation. In that connection, it must be said that the doctrine of the divinity of Christ is more important for Augustine than that of the humanity. The refutation of Arianism is central for him, as it was for his predecessor Hilary of Poitiers, and it means that much of his effort is directed to assaults on those who would in any way compromise the divinity of the saviour. Indeed, anti-Arian zeal may be thought to be among the causes of any inadequacies that may be found in Augustine's treatment of Chalcedon's second *homoousion*. And yet the problems are so pervasive, that there must be at least a suspicion that other influences are also at work, specifically, of course, neoplatonic assumptions of the material order's incapacity to be really and truly the bearer of divinity.

The first suspicion of anti-incarnational platonism is to be found in Augustine's treatment of the Old Testament theophanies. The use of these, it seems to me, is one indication of whether a theology is genuinely incarnational. If it is, it should be able to look back at the Old Testament with eyes given by the person of Christ and see there further evidences of that interrelationship of God with his creation which comes to its perfection in Jesus. (Conversely, if we are doubtful whether the theophanies are instances of God's interrelationship with the world, we are less likely to be able to develop adequate conceptual equipment to cope with the incarnation.) Here it must be said that although what Augustine says is not absolutely

clear, there are signs that he is rather embarrassed by too close
an involvement of God in matter. The prefiguring of the Son in
the Old Testament is not by means of the Word, but by angels;
God is not *substantially* involved:

> even though appearing in visible and sensible forms, it is
> however through his creature, not in his own substance (per
> suam substantiam) . . . (III.27)
>
> If, then, I am asked how either the voices or the sensible
> forms and figures (species) were produced before the incar-
> nation of the Word . . . I answer that God made them through
> the angels (IV.31).

The angels tend in Augustine to take the place of the Word as
the mediators of God's relation with the world. This has two
effects, both of them bad. The first is noted by TeSelle who,
in alluding to 'Augustine's principle that God . . . relates himself to the realm of matter only through soul – angels, the
human mind of Christ, men with their arts and sciences. . .'[7]
points us to a spiritualising tendency in Augustine's thought.
The second is that Augustine, by losing the mediatorship of
the Word at once distances God from the creation and flattens
out the distinctions between the persons of the Trinity, a
process which can only encourage belief in the irrelevance of
conceiving distinct persons and therefore of a doctrine of the
Trinity:

> . . . in which angels there were undoubtedly the Father and
> the Son and the Holy Spirit; and sometimes the Father,
> sometimes the Son, sometimes the Holy Spirit, sometimes
> God without any distinction of person, was figured by
> them . . . (III.26).

In place of the tradition, going back to Irenaeus, of the Father
relating himself to the world by means of the Son and Spirit, we
are in danger of supposing an unknown God working through
angels. Augustine's shying away from the involvement of God
with the material order should be contrasted with the more
concrete modes of speech of both Irenaeus and Tertullian.
A fragment, once attributed to Irenaeus and certainly not

---

[7] Eugene TeSelle, *Augustine the Theologian*, London: Burns and Oates, 1970,
pp. 229f.

inconsistent with his theology, sees a continual involvement of
the Word in creation in saying that: 'it is He who sailed along
with Noah, and who guided Abraham; who was bound along
with Isaac, and was a wanderer with Jacob ...'.[8]

Tertullian is equally concrete:

> For it was he who always came down to converse with men ...
> always from the beginning preparing beforehand in dream
> and in a mirror and in an enigma the course that he was
> going to follow out to the end. Thus he was always learning
> (ediscebat) how as God to company with men, being none
> other than the Word who was to be flesh.[9]

It would be a mistake to conclude from the more fanciful
examples of this genre that the contrast between the earlier
writers and Augustine is between the primitive and the more
sophisticated. 'Irenaeus' and Tertullian write as those who
believe that because the Word was incarnate in Jesus it is right
to attempt identifications of the divine action through him
elsewhere in salvation history. They have a conception of
trinitarian divine action in which the incarnation and its Old
Testament anticipations mutually reinforce each other. Augustine backs off this trinitarian conception of action, and in effect
replaces it with a conception of angelic mediation to which the
Trinity is later fitted.

A similar story can be told of the way in which Augustine
treats the human story of Jesus. As has already been suggested,
it is one thing to treat the person of Christ merely dogmatically,
another to do it in such a way that the fullness of the humanity
is given due weight. That Augustine does not do the latter is
suggested by his treatment of that event which is so central for
an account of Jesus' humanity, the baptism by John in the
Jordan. Augustine cannot handle the story:

> It would be utterly absurd for us to believe that he received
> the Holy Spirit when he was already thirty years old ... but

---

[8] 'Irenaeus', Fragment LIII, *The Apostolic Fathers, with Justin Martyr and
Irenaeus*, Library of the Fathers, Vol. I, Grand Rapids: W. B. Eerdmans, 1977, p.
577.

[9] Tertullian, *Against Praxeas* 16, *Tertullian's Treatise Against Praxeas*, edited
and E.T. by Ernest Evans, London: SPCK, 1948, p. 153.

[we should] believe that he came to that baptism both
entirely sinless and not without the Holy Spirit (XV.46).

The least that we must take from the New Testament here is
that at his baptism Jesus entered a new form of relationship
with the Spirit, a relationship which then took shape in his
enduring and conquest of temptation. That, at any rate, was
what Basil made of it:

> After this every operation was wrought with the co-operation
> of the Spirit. He was present while the Lord was being
> tempted by the devil. ... He was inseparably with Him while
> working His wonderful works. ... And He did not leave Him
> when He had risen from the dead ...[10]

Augustine appears to treat the Spirit, in anticipation of a long
tradition of Western thought, substantially rather than personally and relationally: as if the Spirit was a substantial presence,
given in the womb and, so to speak, preprogramming Jesus'
life, rather than the means by which his humanity was realised
in relationship to the Father. The point may appear to be a
small one, making much of a minor detail. Yet in the light of
what happens elsewhere, it can be seen to fit the pattern.

The third instance of Augustine's suspicion of the material is
a more general than strictly incarnational one, but it is related.
One of the implications of the doctrine of the incarnation for
ontology is that it gives us reason to understand the material
world as the place where meaning, including theological meaning, can be found. If the human reality of Jesus is the presence
of God to the world, it would appear to follow that the world is
the kind of place that is patient of that kind of meaning.
Augustine, however, does not really believe it. When he seeks
his analogies of the Trinity, he judges the material world to be
the least adequate source of assistance. Book XI is an argument
for the inferiority of the outer, as distinct from the inner,
rational, nature to serve as an analogy of the Trinity. The point
is scarcely worth arguing, for such considerations are to be

---

[10] Basil, *On the Holy Spirit* XVI.38, *The Treatise de Spiritu Sancto, etc., of Saint
Basil the Great*, E.T. by B. Jackson, A Select Library of Nicene and Post-Nicene
Fathers, Vol. VIII, New York: Christian Literature Company, 1895, pp. 23f.

found in many places.[11] It does, however, serve to introduce the next major section.

III   *Substance and persons*

What is the real source of Augustine's understanding of the Trinity? The textbooks assure us that it is Scripture and the dogmatic tradition of the church.[12] Augustine takes the Trinity as given, and proceeds on its basis to seek such understanding as is possible for the finite mind. To remain on that level, however, is not to begin to understand what is going on. The fact is that during the process of reflection – an extremely appropriate word to use here[13] – the tradition is changed, unsubtly and radically. It is in the changes that Augustine introduces that is to be found the real tendency of his thought. And there is a major question to be asked. Are the changes that

[11] See, for example, VIII.3: '... we reject everything that is material. Even in the world of spirit, nothing that is changeable must be taken for God' (LCC p. 40). As Christoph Schwöbel pointed out, we here reach matters of great significance for an understanding of the relation between the doctrines of creation and incarnation. Despite the important part that Augustine played in the development of the doctrine of creation, there can be no doubt that because the mutual support that the two doctrines should give to each other is lacking, it is difficult for him to treat the world *as creation*, and so to hold together more adequately the realms of creation and salvation. That he does find it difficult, by virtue of his platonising assumptions, to treat the material order as the vehicle of intrinsic meaning emerges in a number of areas. I have tried to isolate aspects in relation to christology and the nature of time in *Yesterday and Today. A Study of Continuities in Christology*, London: Darton, Longman and Todd, 1983, pp. 108–110; and in aesthetics, 'Creation and Recreation. An Exploration of Some Themes in Aesthetics and Theology', *Modern Theology* 2 (1985), pp. 1–19 (p. 2).

[12] For example, W. J. Hill, *The Three-Personed God. The Trinity as the Mystery of Salvation*, Washington, D.C.: Catholic University of America Press, 1982, pp. 55f.

[13] Reflection is a problematic activity for at least two reasons. The first is that it can suggest an objectivising process, whereby the thinker reflects upon the subject matter as something external, and therefore to an extent freely disposable. While it would be unfair to ascribe this to Augustine, there is no doubt that his method of beginning with dogma as something given which is then the object of rational analysis sails very close to the wind. The second is that it can encourage the notion that theology is essentially an inner process, consisting in large measure in the bringing to expression of the contents of the mind. Here again, Augustine has something to answer for. The overall difficulty is a rather static conception of dogmatics, along with a loss of the communal and participatory elements of theology.

he introduces the price of dogmatic advance, as textbooks tend to proclaim, or a failure to appropriate many of the developments that had taken place since the time of Origen? I believe the latter, and wish to show that Augustine either did not understand the trinitarian theology of his predecessors, both East and West, or looked at their work with spectacles so strongly tinted with neoplatonic assumptions that they have distorted his work. The tragedy is that Augustine's work is so brilliant that it blinded generations of theologians to its damaging weaknesses. Our problem is, where to begin?

An introduction is made possible by examining what Augustine made of the work of his predecessors, and in particular of their central concepts. We begin with the concepts *person* and *relation*. By the time of the Cappadocians, the Greek *hypostasis* had come to be used in distinction from *ousia* to refer to the concrete particularity of Father, Son and Spirit. Whatever the origins of the term, it is now no longer adequate, as some commentators do, to translate it as *individual*, simply because the three are not individuals but persons, beings whose reality can only be understood in terms of their relations to each other, relations by virtue of which they together constitute the being (*ousia*) of the one God. The persons are therefore not relations, but concrete particulars in relation to one another.

By this conceptual development, two things are achieved. The first is that a distinction is made between the threeness and the oneness of God; concepts are developed, that is to say, by means of which the Christian God can be thought as triune without loss to his unity. The second is that, as this is done, a new ontology is developed: for God to be is to be in communion.[14] *Hypostases* and *ousia* are conceptually distinct, but inseparable in thought, because they mutually involve one another. To use Rahner's terms, there can be no distinction between the dogmatic loci *De Deo Uno* and *De Deo Trino* if we are to be true to the being of God. Similarly, thought about the Trinity cannot proceed in abstraction from the history of salvation because the being of God is thought by means of the concrete and revealed threeness of hypostasis.

[14] John Zizioulas, *Being As Communion. Studies in Personhood and the Church*, London: Darton, Longman and Todd, 1985.

When we look at Augustine's treatment of the topic, it becomes evident that he has scarcely if at all understood the central point. It is difficult for him to understand the meaning of the Greek *hypostasis*. One reason is that he can make nothing of the distinction so central to Cappadocian ontology between *ousia* and *hypostasis*: 'I do not know what distinction they wish to make'(V.10). Certainly, it is unfair to say that he gets nothing of the point at all, for he goes on to say that, in view of the difficulty of translating the Greek terms into Latin, he prefers to say, with his Latin tradition, *unam essentiam* or *substantiam* and *tres personas*. Augustine at least realises that different concepts are required if we are to express the distinction between the way in which God is one and the way in which he is three. It becomes clear, however, that the adoption of the correct Latin equivalents does not enable him to get the point, for, in a famous statement, he admits that he does not really see why the term should be used. 'Dictum est tamen *tres personae* non ut illud diceretur sed ne taceretur'(V.10, cf. VII.7: 'this formula was decided upon, in order that we might be able to give some kind of answer when we were asked, what are the three').

One translator, in rendering *diceretur* 'to give a complete explanation' (CUA p. 188), is perhaps putting into Augustine's mouth what he ought to have said rather than what he actually did say. To say that a term is used merely in order not to be silent seems to be too agnostic, and to fall short of what the Cappadocians had done, far more constructively, with the concept. Moreover, Augustine reveals that he is unaware of what is going on when he makes it appear to be merely a matter of linguistic usage (forte secundum linguae suae consuetudinem, VII.11). However, a decision about that matter will be bound up with an examination of the second reason why Augustine appears not to understand the Cappadocian conceptual revolution. For, despite his avowed reason for the use of the term, he had prepared the way for the later, and fateful, *definition* of the person as a *relation*. His relatively brief and sketchy discussion of the ontological status of the three persons in God shows him asking a different kind of question from that asked by the Cappadocians: not, What kind of being is this, that God is to be found in the relations of Father, Son and Spirit? but, What kind of sense can be made of the apparent logical oddity of the threeness of the one God in terms of Aristotelian subject-predicate logic? The one God is the substance, being single and unchanging. There is no problem there in terms of the philosophical tradition:

> ... there can be no accidents ... in God. Therefore, only the substance of God, or the essence which God is, is unchangeable (V.3).

Augustine is here operating with a distinction between the one God of whom no accidents are predicated, and all other things of which they are. But where do the three persons fit? Uncomfortably, it must be confessed. Augustine uses the concept of *relation* to designate that which can be predicated of God in the plural but which is yet not accidental:

> For something can be said of God with respect to relation (ad aliquid), for example of the Father to the Son and the Son to the Father. This is not an accident because the one is always Father and the other always Son ... (V.6).

What, it will be asked, is wrong with that? The chief problem seems to be that his method of treating the concepts has left Augustine unable to break out of the stranglehold of the dualistic ontology which underlies the logic. The unfortunate implications emerge in a very revealing passage a few pages further on:

> The particulars in the same Trinity that are properly predicated of each person are by no means predicated of them as they are in themselves (ad se ipsa), but in their relations either to one another or to the creature, and it is therefore manifest that they are predicated relatively, not substantially. (V.12, compare VII.3, where Augustine says that with predicates like 'begotten' 'the essence is not revealed, since they are spoken of relatively').

In all this, Augustine is taking a clear step back from the teaching of the Cappadocian Fathers. For them, the three persons are what they are in their relations, and therefore the relations qualify them ontologically, in terms of what they are. Because Augustine continues to use relation as a logical rather than an ontological predicate, he is precluded from being able to make claims about the being of the *particular* persons, who, because they lack distinguishable identity tend to disappear into the all-embracing oneness of God.

It is for reasons such as this that there is in Augustine, and in most Western theology after him, a tendency towards modalism, and it is not surprising that we find him denying what for Basil was the truth about the being of God, that 'three somethings subsist from one matter (materia) which, whatever it is, is unfolded in these three' (VII.11). But if the being of God does not derive from the 'unfolding' of the three persons, in what does it consist? Does Augustine believe that the true being of God *underlies* the threeness of the persons? That is certainly the view of Wolfson: 'Unlike Tertullian and like Aristotle ... he identifies the substratum not with the Father but with something underlying both the Father and the Son.'[15] In that case, the danger is that the being of God will either be unknown in all respects – because it modalistically underlies the being of the persons – or will be made known other than through the persons, that is to say, the economy of salvation. That is the suspicion which must be examined as we approach what for many commentators is the heart of Augustine's contribution to trinitarian theology.

Whatever is the case with the doctrine of substance, the outcome of the discussion so far is that by the time that Augustine reaches the famous discussion of the analogies for the Trinity, a conceptual and ontological framework has already been developed. It is, moreover, a gross oversimplification to say that analogies are merely illustrative of the church's dogma, a penetration into its inner logic. What we find in Augustine is one distinctive reading of the church's dogma, an outworking indeed, but one which, as we have already seen, is distinctly different from that developed by the Cappadocians.

IV   *The trinitarian analogies*

In this section I want to suggest that the problem with the trinitarian analogies as Augustine presents them is that they impose upon the doctrine of the Trinity a conception of the divine threeness which owes more to neoplatonic philosophy

---

[15] Wolfson, *Philosophy*, pp. 326f.

than to the triune economy, and that the outcome is, again, a view of an unknown substance *supporting* the three persons rather than *being constituted* by their relatedness. The true ontological foundations of the doctrine of the Trinity, that is to say, are to be found in the conception of a threefold mind and not in the economy of salvation. If that appears to be a sweeping claim, it should be remembered that Augustine's treatise reveals some very odd features from the outset. One of them is that remarkably little space is expended on an exposition of what the doctrine of the Trinity actually is, only summary statements of the dogma being given (see, for example, IX.1). Augustine's concern appears to be not so much to penetrate more deeply into the topic, but to illustrate, from outside, so to speak, a given form of words. (That is an exaggeration, but none the less indicates the baneful legacy Augustine left for later generations.)

The main evidence for the contention, however, must come from what Augustine actually says. I begin with two general features of his approach, what can be called his individualism and intellectualism. By the former I mean the tendency to illustrate the nature of the Trinity by comparing it not to persons in relation, as, for example, does Richard of St Victor later, but to the individual human mind. Book XIV in particular will provide plentiful illustration of this tendency, which ineluctibly brings with it a stress on the oneness of God, and can, unless very carefully qualified, encourage the suggestion that God is primarily a kind of eternal mind. So we reach the parallel tendency, the intellectualism. Now, in introducing this I do not wish to deny that Augustine has a view of intellect very different from the typical post-Enlightenment concept of the calculating machine. His notion of mind is strongly religious in character, so that of him it could be said as it has also been said of Hegel, that his motto was, 'I think, therefore I am religious.'[16] Nonetheless, it is in categories taken from the inner mental world that he seeks to unpack his analogies for the threefold being of God.

Three features of the work will serve to illustrate the tendency to intellectualism, the third of them taking us into the next main topic for discussion. The first is Augustine's

---

[16] James Yerkes, *The Christology of Hegel*, Albany: State University of New York Press, 1983, pp. 53f.

outlining of a hierarchy of adequacy in images of the Trinity, for example in the recapitulation of his argument in the opening pages of Book XV. Least suitable are those containing any element of materiality, and the argument is summarised as moving to a point when it emerged that 'the Trinity became apparent in the image of God which is man with respect to his mind (secundum mentem)' (XV.5). Second is Augustine's tendency to think of God as a kind of supermind as, for example, in the dominance of the category of knowledge in the discussion of the divine inner being in XV.23. Third is an odd feature of Augustine's thought, which builds upon the suspicion of materiality already expounded in section II above, in which he expounds his concept of the eternal Word. Here, once again, there is a movement away from any concrete, 'material' conceptions of the topic: 'the word which sounds outwardly is sign of the word that shines inwardly, and to this latter the name of "word" is more appropriate' (XV.20). This means – and here Augustine perpetuates the breach we have already met between the incarnation and the Old Testament theophanies – that 'We speak here not of that word which came to one or another of the prophets ...' Rather, the Word has to be understood mentally as: 'the word that precedes all the tokens by which it is signified, and is begotten of the knowledge which remains in the mind ...' (ibid., LCC p. 147). The eternal Word is the word as *abstract*, rather than the concrete person of the Son in relation to the Father and Spirit. So much, then, for general points about intellectualism and individualism.[17]

[17] I owe to Christoph Schwöbel the suggestion that there can be developed in this context another link between substance ontology and individualism and intellectualism. A starting point in substance, as distinct from one in the threefold economy, give the whole development a radically different shape. He points out that individualism is engendered by the fact that for a substance it is of no concern whether it is exemplified by one, three or a hundred individuals. To demonstrate exemplification in one individual is quite sufficient, and on neoplatonic presuppositions necessary in the case of God. Similarly, intellectualism is encouraged by a starting place in a hierarchical ontology where the mental always has priority over the material, which in turn encourages Augustine to take his analogies from the mental acts of one individual. These observations reinforce the impression, already reported, that Augustine is doing far more than defend the given dogma of the Trinity. His is a systematic theology of massive consistency all of whose parts provide mutual support for each other, and, indeed, to a large extent mutually imply each other.

We come now to the most difficult part of the evidence to handle, the use by Augustine of the celebrated triad, memory, understanding and will. We must not be deceived by two facts that are often brought to bear on the discussion, Augustine's avowal of the limited nature of these and all analogies, and the fact, claimed as important in the secondary literature, that it is not Augustine's primary analogy, because he goes on to say that a superior analogy is that taken from the mind's memory, understanding and love of God (XIV.11ff). I believe, against all this, that the triad of memory, understanding and will is determinative for Augustine's conception of the Trinity. It is noteworthy that he has already appealed to it before the discussion of analogies begins (IV.30), and, more decisively, returns to it again after he has moved to other, supposedly more important, analogies to establish a point. Addressing his soul, Augustine affirms that 'the light itself shows you in yourself those three elements in which ... you may recognise the image of the Trinity' (XV.50). That, it must be realised, is Augustine's final solution for the problem of distinguishing between Son and Spirit. In the absence of any other more adequate argument, he makes a final appeal to the triad of memory, understanding and will. The conclusion is inescapable: *The crucial analogy for Augustine is between the inner structure of the human mind and the inner being of God, because it is in the former that the latter is made known, this side of eternity at any rate, more really than in the 'outer' economy of grace.*

What is the justification for such an outrageous claim? It is to be found on many pages of the *De Trinitate*, and particularly in those latter books which the editors of the Library of Christian Classics appear to regard as the important ones. But let us attempt to itemise the evidence. The crucial and illuminating hermeneutic is provided when we analyse the triad in the terms of a platonising doctrine of knowledge as recollection. According to such a doctrine, the human mind is constituted in a threefold way because it contains, first, as its hidden storehouse the memory of the forms which, according to classic platonist theory, it brings into the world from eternity but forgets by virtue of its embodied state; second, the so to speak mental screen on which the contents of its store can be actualised; and third, the power by means of which the content is brought to actuality. Some such conception provides the framework for Augustine's unfolding of the being of God:

> To memory we assigned all that we know even though we are not thinking of it, and to understanding the impartation of a certain definite form to thought (quandam cogitationis informationem). . . .
>
> Love (dilectio) is that which takes the vision which has its seat in memory (in memoria constitutam), and the vision of thought which thence receives form, and joins them together as parent and offspring (XV.40 and 41, LCC pp. 168f).

We have already seen something of how the platonising drive affects Augustine's discussion of the Word, who is intellectualised as part of the contents of the divine mind. A similar fate befalls the Father, whose function in the Godhead is parallel to that of memory in the human mind: he is the storehouse of being and, as such, the fount of the Trinity. Augustine will not, of course, attribute memory to the Father alone, because his discussion of the persons, as we have seen, tends not to distribute particular functions or attributes between them. But the very fact that in XV.12 he argues that memory belongs to all three and not just to the Father indicates the powerful effect upon him of the platonic categories. More illuminating is Augustine's discussion of the distinction between the Son and the Spirit in the Trinity, a problem whose solution gives him much difficulty. He sets the scene by an attribution to the Spirit of the third function of the human mind: 'If indeed any Person in the Trinity is to be termed especially the will of God, the name is applicable rather. . . to the Holy Spirit. For what else is love (caritas) than willing?' (XV.38, first sentence from LCC p. 167). Why, we may ask, except under the constraints of Augustine's procrustean bed? If we were to think from the economy, would not the Father be a better candidate, as the one whose will is realised in the economy by the Son and the Spirit? The dominance of the platonic triad is demonstrated by the fact that after many contortions, Augustine establishes the difference between Son and Spirit, as we have already seen, by appeal to the distinction between understanding and will. 'And thus there is a suggestion in the mental reality of the difference between begetting and proceeding, inasmuch as to view in thought is not the same as to pursue or enjoy with the will' (XV.50, LCC p. 179). What is virtually the final argument of the *De Trinitate* makes its appeal to the triad of memory, understanding and will.

Once the dominance of the platonising conceptuality is understood, other pieces of the argument find their places in the jigsaw. For example, there is the major part played by the doctrine of recollection in building a conception of knowledge in Book X. Whatever he says, Augustine is not merely producing analogies by this analysis; he is in fact developing a doctrine of God, with the stress on the unity:

> [T]his triad of memory, understanding and will are not three lives, but one; nor three minds, but one. It follows that they are not three substances, but one substance. ... But they are three inasmuch as they are related to one another (ad se invicem referuntur). ... And these three constitute one thing, one life, one mind, one essence.
>
> We might now attempt to raise our thoughts ... (literally: Is an ascent now to be made ...?) towards that supreme and most exalted essence of which the human mind is an image – inadequate indeed, but still an image (X.18f, LCC pp. 88f).

Similarly, it becomes possible to understand how the doctrine of the Spirit comes in to complete the trinitarian circle rather than on the basis of aspects of the economy. The conception of the Spirit, the Achilles' heel, as if it needed one, of Augustine's Trinity, will require a section to itself. For the moment, I will bring this part of the argument to its end by an extended citation which illustrates many of the points which have been made in it. Augustine is, in Book XIV, summarising an earlier argument:

> [W]e developed an account of the mental trinity, in which memory supplied the source from which the thinker's view received its form, the conformation itself being a kind of image imprinted by the memory, and the agency by which the two are conjoined being love or will. Thus when the mind regards itself in the act of thought, it understands and takes knowledge of itself: we may say that it begets this understanding and self-knowledge. ... But this begetting by the mind of self-knowledge ... does not imply that it was

previously unknown to itself. ... And to these two, the begetter and the begotten, we have to add the love which joins them together, and is simply the will, pursuing or embracing an object of enjoyment (XIV.8, LCC pp.105f).

One further implication of Augustine's development of the doctrine of God should be mentioned, if only because it has had such fateful consequences for the history of Western theology. So strong a stress on the mind encourages the suggestion that knowledge of God is to be found primarily in the mind. We have already seen that, because of his suspicion of materiality, Augustine tends to call attention away from the concrete historical events in which God is present to the world in the economy of creation and salvation. The correlative effect is to overstress the knowledge of God found within the mind. Augustine is almost, if not quite explicitly, to be found at times saying that when we know ourselves correctly, we know God in the same act. It may be taking Augustine out of context to cite his saying that 'the man who knows how to love himself, loves God' (XIV.18), but there is no doubt that he is not far from that particular danger. In that respect, those modern theologies like Hegel's and Schleiermacher's which seek the knowledge of God in either the affective or the rational states of the consciousness are not very far from the kingdom of Augustine.[18]

V   *The third person of the Trinity*

We have seen already that Augustine's doctrine of the Spirit is, if not actually determined by, at least strongly affected by his need to have a third person corresponding to the will in the threefold mind. Augustine's concept of the Spirit as the love which unites Father and Son is among the most contested of his theologoumena, not only for its apparent derivation, but for the way it appears to sit ill with particular features of the

[18] Nicholas Bradbury, in a review in *Scottish Journal of Theology* 40 (1987), p. 159, cites the following summary of Jesuit spirituality: 'In brief: I want, above all else, the will of God; for I AM the will of God. I seek the grace to know myself.' We cannot blame Augustine for all of the decadent mysticism which has developed in the West, but neither can he be held to be without influence upon it.

economy. At the outset, it must be allowed that it has a superficial appeal. In a number of biblical passages, the Spirit does function as the giver of community (for example, in the Acts of the Apostles). What more appropriate, then, than that this function should be seen to be grounded in an inner-trinitarian function as the maker of the divine communion? What, then, are the problems?

We begin with Augustine's appeal to Scripture. There is now a considerable literature on the inadequacy of the attempt to justify from Scripture that particular way of identifying the person of the Spirit. As James Mackey comments: 'Undaunted ... and by dint of what John Burleigh ... called "rather desperate exegesis", Augustine fits out the Holy Spirit with the distinguishing and relative "name" of Gift ...'.[19] There is, as always, something in what Augustine says. Despite what Mackey suggests, it does seem reasonable to argue from the fact that the Spirit is God's gift bringing us to him to a corresponding reality in the inner divine being: 'the Holy Spirit, of whom (de quo) he has given us, makes us dwell in God and God in us' (XV.31, LCC p. 160). But what is more difficult is to distinguish on such grounds between the Spirit and the Son, in view of the fact that, particularly through the use it makes of the language of sacrifice (see, for example, Rom. 8.32) the New Testament describes the Son as God's gift to us.

As with gift so it is also with love. Augustine realises that he has no direct scriptural warrant for making the attribution: 'The Scripture has not said: "The Holy Spirit is charity"' (XV.27, LCC p. 157). Moreover, there is a sense in which Father, Son and Spirit together are love (XV.28f). 'Yet', he continues, 'there is good reason (non frustra) why in this Trinity we call none Word of God but the Son, none Gift of God but the Holy Spirit ...' (XV.29, LCC p. 158). What is the 'good reason'? It is not entirely clear, but would seem to have two main aspects. The first derives from the fact that the Spirit is, in some sense – and what that is we shall have further to consider – the 'common gift' of Father and Son. 'For hence it comes that the Word of God is by a special fitness called also the

---

[19] James Mackey, *The Christian Experience of God as Trinity*, London: SCM Press, 1983, p. 155.

Wisdom of God. ... If then one of the three is by a special fitness to be called charity, the name falls most appropriately to the Holy Spirit' (XV.29, LCC p. 159). The appeal is to a general appropriateness, on the grounds, it almost appears, that there are no real distinctions in the inner being of the deity: 'And this means that in the incomposite and supreme being of God, substance is not to be distinguished from charity; but substance is itself charity, and charity is itself substance, whether in the Father or in the Son or in the Holy Spirit, and yet by a special fitness the Holy Spirit is named charity' (ibid.). But what is this 'special fitness' (proprie)? We come to the second aspect of the 'good reason'. 'Thus the Holy Spirit ... makes us dwell in God, and God in us. But that is the effect of love. The Holy Spirit therefore is the God who is love' (XV.31, LCC p. 160). One can only conclude that the whole justification is very thin, and the result is that Augustine's conclusion in XV.37 has all the air of special pleading:

> Holy Scripture proclaims that God is charity. Charity is of God, and its effect in us is that we dwell in God and he in us. This we know because he has given us of his Spirit. It follows that the Spirit himself is the God who is charity. If among God's gifts there is none greater than charity, and there is no greater gift of God than the Holy Spirit, we naturally conclude that he who is said to be both God and of God is himself charity (LCC p. 165).

What is wrong with this? It is not that there is nothing in it, but that Augustine's singleminded desire to fit the Spirit into his scheme has meant that essential features of the economy scarcely feature. The first missing feature is the eschatological dimension to the work of the Spirit that is so prominent in the New Testament, and whose virtual absence from Augustine must be said to have been one of his worst legacies to the Western tradition. In the economy it is the action of the Spirit not simply to relate the individual to God, but to realise in time the conditions of the age to come. Augustine's discussion of eschatology tends to lack this dimension, because it is essentially dualistic, tending to require a choice between this world and the next, rather than seeking a realisation of the next in the materiality of the present. One dimension of Augustine's shortcoming here is that although he affirms the doctrine, the resurrection of the body plays no constitutive part in his theology. The second missing feature is a conception of the Spirit as realising the conditions of the age to come particularly through the creation of community. In Augustine we are near the beginning of the era in which the church is conceived essentially as an institution mediating grace to the individual rather than of the community formed on the analogy of the Trinity's *interpersonal* relationships.

And there is also a third missing feature, which is to be found in connection with the concept of love which is operative in the discussion. Because the notion of love centres on the unitive function of love in relating Father to Son and believer to God – a function that does not need to be denied – there seems to be little weight given in Augustine's treatment of the Trinity to a notion of love derived from the economy of the incarnation. There, the essence of the love of God is its outgoingness: its dynamic seeking of the other. One does not have to accept in its entirety the schematism of love adopted by Nygren to believe that a concept of love centred on its unitive rather than its agapeistic functions is likely to owe more to the platonic love of the *Symposium* than to the concrete economy of incarnation, cross and resurrection. By attributing to the Spirit the kind of love that he does, Augustine thus attracts attention away from the economy of salvation in two major ways: he minimises the part played in the development of the doctrine of the Trinity by the incarnation – for an incarnational conception of love is scarcely to be found – and he obscures the specific hypostatic uniqueness of the Holy Spirit. Because, we might also say, he has an inadequate conception of love as love for the other as other, he is unable to conceive true otherness in the Trinity, another feature which can be seen to be a function of too strong an emphasis on the unity of God.

The overall result is that because the doctrine of the Spirit has inadequate economic hypostatic weight in Augustine, the father of Western theology also lacks the means to give personal distinctiveness to the being of the Spirit in the inner Trinity. We have already seen some of the reasons for this unsatisfactory state of affairs. What others are there? We met above, in the discussion of the Spirit's characterisation as love, the passage in

Augustine which provides the crux for the discussion of his part in the development of the doctrine of the *Filioque*. His words are worth examining with care:

> Yet there is good reason why in this Trinity we call none Word of God but the Son, none gift of God but the Holy Spirit, none of whom the Word is begotten and from whom the Spirit originally proceeds, but God the Father. I add the word 'originally' (principaliter) because we learn that the Holy Spirit proceeds also from the Son.[20]

The editor of the Library of Christian Classics edition of the *De Trinitate* comments in a footnote (n. 60, p. 158) both that Augustine always maintained the double procession of the Spirit and that 'there is no real difference between his position and the Eastern doctrine of the Spirit's procession from the Father through the Son'. We have already seen, however, that there are major differences all along the line between Augustine and the Cappadocian Fathers. There are bound to be differences here also.

But what is at stake in the matter? In the first place, there is the question of loyalty to Scripture, not in the sense of proving the doctrine one way or another from proof texts, but in being able to give due weight in the doctrine of God to the part played by the Spirit in the economy. We have already seen that Augustine has difficulty with the narrative of the descent upon Jesus of the Spirit after his baptism by John. He is, to be sure, aware, both that Jesus must as man be in receipt of the Spirit and of aspects of the position taken by the Cappadocians:

> The Father alone is underived, and therefore alone called unbegotten ... The Son is begotten from the Father; and the Holy Spirit proceeds, ultimately,[21] from the Father, and by the Father's gift at no temporal interval from both in common. He could be called Son of Father and of Son, only if both had begotten him – a notion intolerable to all sound

---

[20] XV.29, LCC p. 158. There is some case for saying that the word 'originally' is in this context a systematically misleading translation, because if the Spirit's *origin* is from the Father, then it cannot be also from the Son. By contrast, 'principally' allows Augustine to make his point.
[21] Oddly, having used 'originally' as a translation for 'principaliter', this crucial term is now here translated 'ultimately'.

feeling. Thus he is not begotten of both, but proceeds from the one and the other as the Spirit of both (XV.47, LCC p. 176).

It is clear, then, that Augustine realises the first of the two requirements for a doctrine of the Trinity, a conceptual distinction between Son and Spirit. But if the doctrine of the Trinity is to be seen to be more than an exercise in conceptual mathematics, a second desideratum is an engagement with ontology. The fact that, as we have seen, his final argument for the nature of the distinction owes more to the structure of memory, understanding and will than to appeal to the economy of salvation must give us pause as to whether he is able to handle the ontological revolution that is required by a theology of the Trinity. We cannot escape the history of the matter, and that is that although Augustine was aware of the need to qualify the *Filioque* with a *principaliter*, the tradition which built upon his work eventually developed a doctrine of God which was materially different from that of its Eastern colleagues.

We have seen that the achievement of the Cappadocians, an achievement which Augustine has failed adequately to understand, was to create a new conception of the being of God, in which God's being was seen to consist in personal communion. Underlying this is the most fundamental ontological question of all, that concerning the nature of the world in which we live. What kind of world is it? Is it one fitted for the development of persons and personal values? The Western world has for the most part decided that it is not, or at any rate that such foundation as it has is at best the product of an unknown deity. Augustine has given us little reason to believe that God is to be known *as he is* from his manifestation in the economy. All the drive of his thought is away from that to a knowledge derived from and based in the structures of human mentality: to an essentially singular deity for whom community is epiphenomenal or secondary. It is that which is at stake in the argument about whether and to what extent he is a modalist.

The question can be put in other terms. Is the basis of Augustine's deity personal? What is finally real about him, the community constituted by the relatedness of Father, Son and

Spirit to each other, or something else? We return to the question of substance. Wolfson puts his finger on the essential difference between Augustine and his predecessors without fully appreciating its significance. (Like so many Western thinkers, he regards the matter as largely one of solving philosophical puzzles about the oneness and threeness of God, rather than of fundamental ontology.) He comments that whereas for Tertullian, Nicaea and Basil the *substratum* of God is the Father, with Augustine the analogy works differently. For him the other two persons do not derive their godhood from the Father (they derive only their existence, not their divinity, from him).[22] The only conclusion can be that, in some sense or other, it is divine substance and not the Father that is the basis of the being of God, and therefore, *a fortiori*, of everything else.

This matter of the derivation of things is of crucial importance for two reasons. The first is that if something other than the Father is the ontological foundation of the being of God, the world and everything in it derives from what is fundamentally impersonal. What under (or over-) lies is some*thing* other than the God made known in the economy. The second is that a doctrine of God as essentially and in all senses unknown is the inevitable result, at least if we go by the economy of salvation. For it is the function of the Spirit to realise through the Son the knowledge of the Father. But if the Father is not the substratum of the Godhead, what is? What is it that the Spirit makes known through the Son? We are thrown back on to some unknown and unknowable substance underlying the economy. Both the platonic and aristotelian doctrines of *hypo-* and *hyperkeimenon* presuppose that fundamental reality is other than that by which it is made known: it underlies as other, in the sense of being essentially foreign to the material world through which knowledge is sought. The conceptual and ontological revolution achieved by the Cappadocians is that God is as he is made known by the Son and the Spirit: he is other – distinct – in person, to be sure, but not in being as God – for he is made known *as he is*. The danger of Augustine's failure to maintain that revolution is that the insight will be lost, as indeed it has

[22] Wolfson, *Philosophy*, p. 357.

been for much of Western theological history, certainly in recent centuries.

It is not being suggested that Augustine is propounding straightforward versions of the various heresies to which he is near. That is perhaps the problem, for the subtlety of his approach disguises its underlying problematic. Thus, for example, he is aware of the danger of Eunomianism, as he is of Arianism and modalism. The question which this chapter is designed to ask is whether he has the conceptual equipment to avoid a final collapse into something like them, and the answer must be that he has not. And if he has not, then how are we to avoid the conclusion that the road which he took did in fact lead, albeit by many twists and turns, to that deep-seated problematic about the knowledge of God with which we now so anxiously wrestle?

CHAPTER 4

THE COMMUNITY
The Trinity and the being of the church

I *The drive towards monism*

'What on earth is the church for?' In Lent 1986 there took place an inter-church study programme under that heading. The question, however, appears to carry a remarkable assumption: that we know what the church is. At one level, of course, we do, and can answer fairly accurately the question of what it is in a number of ways, in the terms of sociological and historical analysis, for example. But at another level there is a case for saying that the question of the being of the church is one of the most neglected topics of theology. We speak of the church as 'one, holy, catholic and apostolic', but disagree on how the concepts should be understood because their meaning is determined by different assumptions and theologies. Similarly, while the choice of metaphors does make a difference – classically in the case of the Second Vatican Council's use of the notion of the people of God as a control on the metaphor of the body – there is little doubt that they too can be used in different ways and therefore with varying ontological content.

The case to be argued in this chapter is that the manifest inadequacy of the theology of the church derives from the fact that it has never seriously and consistently been rooted in a conception of the being of God as triune. Here, certainly in the British context, the deficiencies of ecclesiology are matched only by a failure to give due place as a matter of general practice to trinitarian theology. There is a widespread assumption that the doctrine of the Trinity is one of the *difficulties* of Christian belief: a kind of intellectual hurdle to be leaped before orthodoxy can be acknowledged. Some of the reasons

56

for this have emerged from the study of Augustine in the previous chapter. In fact, we shall find that the problems with the theology of the church run in parallel with some of the chief weaknesses of Augustine's theology of the Trinity, among which lies his failure to establish adequate distinctions between the modes of action of Father, Son and Spirit. Because the differences between the persons become effectively redundant, they no longer bear upon the shape of thought about the realities of life in the world, and in this case are not able to shape ecclesiological thinking. If all divine actions are actions of the one God, so that the actions of the Trinity towards the world are undivided in an absolute sense, the persons are irrelevant for thought, and a kind of monism results. We may say, then, that because the Trinity has been divorced from other doctrines, it has fallen into disrepute, except as the recipient of lip service. But because it has been neglected, the church has appropriated only a part of its rich store of possibilities for nourishing a genuine theology of community.

The first evidence for the thesis is that Harnack, who, unlike some others, devotes much space in his *History of Dogma* to the development of ecclesiology, can find little systematic reflection upon it in Eastern theology, and points out – accurately – that there is no dogmatic treatment of it in John of Damascus' *On the Orthodox Faith*.[1] In the West, attention centred, as it has ever since, on the clergy, and it is not much of an oversimplification to say that ecclesiological discussion in our time nearly always centres on, or degenerates into, disputes about clergy or bishops, the result being that the question of the nature or being of the church is rarely allowed to come into sight. What then is missing? The answer can be approached by way of a contrast. The efforts of early work on christology were devoted to an examination of the question of the being of Christ: of who and what kind of being he is in relation to God the Father and the Holy Spirit, on the one hand, and, on the other, to the rest of the human race. Similarly, trinitarian reflection centred on the nature of God and of his relation to the world. Together, the two central strands in early Christian

---

[1] Adolph Harnack, *History of Dogma*, E.T. by Neil Buchanan and others of 3rd edition, London: Williams and Norgate, 1897, Vol. III, p. 235.

thinking have some claim to have generated an ontology that was distinctively different from those prevailing in the ancient world and, though in greater continuity, yet different also from the ontology (-ies?) implicit in the Old Testament writings.

Did anything similar take place in ecclesiology? There is some case for saying that, at the very least, a process of similar rigour was not carried through; and in some cases that here was a sphere where, far from developing a distinctive theology of community, the theologians mainly conformed their views to those of the world around, with baneful consequences. Here, if anywhere, the thesis associated with the name of Harnack, that the implications of the gospel came to be overlaid with an ideology foreign to them, is more than amply confirmed. Evidence in the East for the development of ecclesiology is not easy to find, chiefly for the reason that there appears to be none. Harnack, without giving references, asserts the East's acceptance of 'the fancy that the earthly hierarchy was the image of the heavenly'.[2] 'The idea of the church that had the most vitality in the East was that of something which, regarded as active was "the lawful steward of the mysteries ..." and conceived of as passive, was the image of the "heavenly hierarchy".'[3] Too much should not be made of unsubstantiated allusions to hierarchy. But may it not at least be suggested that in a world where neoplatonism was influential, the urge to think in terms of degrees of reality, of a hierarchically structured world, was compelling in the absence of a drive to think otherwise? And is it not also true that a major achievement of ancient christological and trinitarian theology was that it did call in question that very way of thinking about reality?

The development in the West is both more explicit and more dismal, for the theology of the church appears to have derived in large measure by analogy from the conception of an earthly empire.[4] A crucial phase in the development is to be observed in 'Cyprian's idea of the church, an imitation of the conception

---

[2] Harnack, op. cit., Vol. II, p. 85.

[3] Harnack, op. cit., Vol. IV, p. 279.

[4] In explicit contradiction of dominical command and example, as in their anti-papal polemics Puritans like John Owen were not reluctant to point out. See his *Of Toleration*, in *Works*, ed. W. H. Goold, Edinburgh: T. & T. Clark, 1862, Vol. VIII, pp. 163–206.

of a political empire, viz., one great aristocratically governed state with an ideal head'.[5] There is, in the letters of Cyprian to which Harnack refers, little if any direct comparison of the church with an empire. He prefers the analogy of the military camp.[6] But Harnack's comment is justified, in that the letters breathe a spirit of authoritarian commitment to the unity of the church above all else. Appeals to Scripture are allegorised or arbitrary (Cyprian likes texts which can be employed against heretics and schismatics – i.e. anyone outside the 'enclosed garden', 69.2), and, so far as I can see, rarely to the texts which express the nature of the church as a community. The theological basis is equally jejune, with Cyprian's God operating mainly as a principle of unity.[7] As von Campenhausen has shown, such remnants of the primitive ecclesiology as do survive are found in Cyprian's conception of the relationship of mutual love of the bishops, who accordingly become the 'real' church.

When we come to Augustine, the picture is more complicated. A conception of the church as the community of believers is undoubtedly important for him, but it is overlaid by developments deriving from the church's change of status after Constantine. The official recognition of the church meant that it was no longer certain whether it was a community of believers at all, so that it appeared rather to be a mixed community of the saved and the lost. This in turn led to two developments: the first a strong stress on the institutional nature of the church, which fostered a tendency, with us to this day, to see the clergy as the *real* church. The church does not have its being from the congregating of the faithful – because not all of the faithful *are* faithful! – but from its relation to a hierarchical head. The mixed nature of the church necessitates in turn an imposed, rather than freely accepted, discipline. The second is the platonising distinction between the visible and invisible church. The real church – represented by the clergy? – is the invisible church, those known only to God, the elect. It is ironical, but

[5] Harnack, op. cit., Vol. II, p. 85, note 1. Harnack recognises, as should we, the constraints under which Cyprian was operating, but that is not the point here.

[6] Cyprian, *Letters* 46.2, 54.1.

[7] See especially the approving quotation in *Letters* 49.2 of the confession 'that there is one God and that there is one Christ the Lord ..., one Holy Spirit, and that there ought to be one bishop in the Catholic Church.'

not surprising, that such a conception, too, required increasing stress on the institutional and clerical organisation of the body.

The conclusion must be that the conception of God as a triune communion made no substantive contribution to the doctrine of the church. It is a semi-Harnackian conclusion in the sense that it shares Harnack's view that the original teaching of Christianity was overlaid with a philosophy that was foreign to it, but qualifies it in an important respect. Harnack's view, which is apparent throughout his great *History of Dogma*, was that the whole apparatus of early dogmatic theology was the imposition of a false metaphysic upon the gospel. I would hold rather, with John Zizioulas,[8] that the development of the doctrine of the Trinity was the creation, true to the gospel, of a distinctively Christian ontology; but would add that its insights were for the most part not extended into ecclesiology. What happened was that the vacuum was readily filled by rival ontologies. There appear to have been two complementary influences. The first is the neoplatonic doctrine of reality as a graded hierarchy. From where, if not from such an influence, did the notion of hierarchy derive? There is scarcely biblical evidence worthy of the name. But Aquinas implies, without ever spelling the matter out, that the hierarchy of the church – that there is in the church an ontological grading of persons – is modelled on that of heaven.[9]

The second is the legal-political, which we have already met in Cyprian and will meet again. It is sometimes claimed that up to and including Aquinas in the West the conception of the church was largely legal. The outcome can with little exaggeration be said to have been catastrophic, for the essence of a political institution, defined by its law, is that it employs constraint in order to maintain its unity. It can therefore be argued – with much support from the actual course of historical events – that the monistic drive with which this ideology has imbued the church has, far from being the cement of church unity, in fact been its solvent, because rebellion against its constraints has had its inspiration in Christian sources. It is

[8] John D. Zizioulas, *Being As Communion. Studies in Personhood and the Church*, London: Darton, Longman and Todd, 1985.

[9] Aquinas, *Summa Theologiae*, 1a.108.4, cf. 108.2.

then quite reasonable to speculate whether things might have been otherwise if the advice of Gamaliel in Acts (5.38f) and Paul to the Corinthians had been heeded. In his *Of Toleration* and in dispute with Bellarmine, John Owen points out that according to 1 Cor. 11.19 'heresies' are 'for the manifesting of those that are approved, not the destroying of those that are not ...' Quoting 2 Tim. 2.25, 'Waiting with all patience upon them that oppose themselves, if at any time God will give them repentance ...', Owen comments: 'Imprisoning, banishing, slaying, is scarcely a patient waiting.'[10] The point of this citation of past controversy is not to raise old spectres, but to argue that bad ecclesiastical practice is at least in part the outcome of bad theology, and that awareness of this is a necessary step for modern ecclesiology.

II *The 'heretical' contribution*

The reference to heresy and its treatment brings us to the next stage of the argument, and the claim that there is much wisdom to be found in the history of those who have been called heretics because their teaching and behaviour endangered not so much the creed as the seamless unity of the institution. If the effect of Constantine's settlement was a movement towards the clericalism of the invisible-visible polarity, the waning of that social order is calling attention again to the need to rethink the structures of the church as a community. If we look at some representative figures, we shall see a pattern beginning to emerge. First among them is Tertullian, whose denial that the church consists in the number of its bishops is often cited. But its context is also important. The polemic of the *De Pudicitia* concerns in large measure the abuses consequent upon the arrogation of the power of the keys to the clergy. Tertullian realises that the other side of the coin is the need to call attention to the fact that the church is first of all a community:

> The church itself is, properly and principally, the Spirit himself, in whom is the trinity of the one divinity, Father, Son and Holy Spirit. [The Spirit] gathers (*congregat*) that

[10] Owen, *Works*, VIII, p. 202.

church which the Lord has made to consist in 'three'. And so
... every number which has combined together into this faith
is accounted a church by its author and sanctifier.

The point is obscure, and the Latin almost untranslatable. But
its point is clear in drawing links between three terms: the
Trinity, the community of faith and its free act of congregating.[11]

Harnack's remarks on Novatian are equally illuminating,
because they make a comment about the institutionalising of
the church and the relation between church and gospel.
Novatian appears to be in a measure of continuity with the
Tertullian of the *De Pudicitia* on the question of the forgiveness
of sins. He has a different ecclesiology from his opponents
because he has a different soteriology and eschatology. According to Harnack, he operates, on the one hand, with a theology
that limits the power of the bishop to absolve because he
believes that gross sin must be left to the eschatological
judgement of God; and, on the other, with a view of the church
not so much as the place where people are prepared for
salvation (the 'orthodox' conception) as the community where
salvation is now being realised – in both cases, positions which
arguably have greater biblical support that those of his opponents. 'To the Novatians [*sic*] ... membership of the Church
is not the *sine qua non* of salvation, but it really secures it in
some measure'. Harnack's comment reaches the heart of the
matter:

His proposition that none but God can forgive sins does not
depotentiate the idea of the Church; but secures both her
proper religious significance and the full sense of her dis-
pensations of grace: it limits her powers and extent in favour
of her content. Refusal of her forgiveness under certain
circumstances – though this does not exclude the confident

[11] Tertullian, of course, operated before the temptations of state support
had come to wield their corrupting appeal. But his arguments for toleration
maintain their validity: Nec religionis est cogere religionem, quae sponte
suscipi debent, non vi. Quoted by Owen, op. cit. p. 184, to whom the argument
that religion requires free adoption would naturally appeal. The use of
Tertullian here should not be taken to imply adoption of that less attractive
side of his thought chronicled by Hans von Campenhausen, *Ecclesiastical
Authority and Spiritual Power in the Church of the First Three Centuries*, E.T. by J. A.
Baker, California: University of Stanford Press, 1963, pp. 231ff.

hope of God's mercy – can only mean that in Novatian's view this forgiveness is the foundation of salvation and does not merely avert the certainty of perdition.[12]

As Harnack represents it, therefore, Novatian's position is a denial of the Constantinian view of the church that we have met in this connection: it is not a mixed community existing in some contingent relationship to the 'real' church but 'As the assembly of the baptised, who have received God's forgiveness, the Church must be a real communion of salvation and of saints ...' (ibid.). In that respect, we can see a real link between this early protester against the development of ecclesiology and the concern of, for example, the Puritans with church discipline. It is surely not a historical accident that Western Christendom has thrown up a series of movements whose extremes have sometimes dabbled in millenialist violence, but whose more orthodox branches, labelled as heretical because of the extreme narrowness of the institutional definition of orthodoxy, have dedicated themselves to the same kind of community ecclesiology that seems to underlie the arguments of both Tertullian and Novatian.[13]

What is theologically at stake in this contradistinction of 'orthodox' and 'heretics'? The heart of the matter is pneumatological. Somewhere between the disputants is a major difference on the way in which the Spirit is conceived to constitute the church. On the one side is a drive for unity, and a corresponding and growing emphasis on the structure of the institution; on the other a rebelliousness deriving from a different priority. To each corresponds a difference in the temporal framework, the conception of history, of the two sides. The one is increasingly dualistic: this life is a preparation for the next, a training ground for a future destiny. The other stresses more strongly the community as the place where the conditions of the life to come may be realised in the here and now. The reason for the divergence is the major deficiency in

[12] Harnack, op. cit., Vol. II, p. 119. Harnack's diagnosis is confirmed by a similar report made by von Campenhausen of Cyprian's position, that 'the assurance of real here-and-now forgiveness was replaced by a mere likelihood and possibility of salvation', op. cit., p. 288.

[13] For numerous instances, see Norman Cohn, *The Pursuit of the Millennium*, London: Secker and Warburg, 1957.

the development of pneumatology in the West, certainly in so far as it is measured against the New Testament. In the latter, there is considerable emphasis on the eschatological dimensions of the Spirit as the one by whose agency the life of the age to come is made real in the present. When that is lost, the Spirit tends to be institutionalised, so that in place of the free, dynamic, personal and *particular* agency of the Spirit, he is made into a substance which becomes the possession of the church. It can be argued, then, that the criticism of the mainstream common to many of the 'heretical' movements of European church history is that they see the institution as *claiming* too much of a realisation of eschatology,[14] while *expecting* too little of the community as a whole. It is significant that the extreme millenarian sects are like the official institution in claiming on their side too a realisation of the last things. Both alike deny the freedom of the Spirit and the contingency and fallibility of their embodiment of the church. Corresponding to the imbalance in ecclesiology and pneumatology that this reveals there is, inevitably, an equally problematic christology. How that may be conceived to be is the subject of the next stage of the enquiry.

III *Christ, the Spirit and the church*

When we seek the christological dimensions of ecclesiology, the enquiry is complicated by the fact that there are two interlocking factors in operation. There is first the matter of what can be called the historical determination of the church, the way in which we may suppose that in the economy of things the church was instituted by Jesus, and that, of course, means a Jesus conceived to have been invested with divine power or authority. Most would hold to the fact of the instituting; disagreements arise over the manner and character of the action, and how it affects the present. Second, distinguishable but not separable from the first, is the way the church is conceived to be patterned or moulded by the shape and

[14] The underlying theological problem is that historical churches make dogmatic claims on the basis of an appeal to a history whose actual course often appears to contradict the claims.

direction of Jesus' life and its outcome: here the stress is as much on the dogmatic as on the historical significance of Jesus.

The effect of a belief in the christological determination of the church according to the first, historical, category, is to be found in a number of places. Its force is determined by what it is believed that Jesus is doing in, for example, choosing twelve disciples. If, on the one hand, the twelve represent a reconstituted Israel,[15] the emphasis will be on the creation of a historical community – as, for example, it is understood in Schleiermacher; if, on the other hand, the disciples are the first of an order of clergy, to whom is transmitted authority over the community, a more strongly clerical ecclesiology will – and did – emerge. Even at this stage of historical enquiry we are presented with a dogmatic question, that of the end and direction of Jesus' exercise of instituting authority. Both of the interpretations we have noted can be employed to create or to attempt to create direct causal and therefore ontological and logical links between past historical events and present conditions. But both are questionable. There is considerable doubt whether direct links should be drawn between past historical happenings and consequent ecclesiologies. The attempts of denominations to trace their church order to dominical institution are now discredited, though not in such a way as to prevent the continuation of the practice. Worse, such a procedure runs the danger of introducing a rent in the fabric of history, overstressing the newness of the church and underplaying its continuity with Israel. It is worth noting here that in connection with his point that Jesus institutes the church John Zizioulas has remarked that even Jesus has to be freed from past history.[16]

Dogmatically – and now we move directly into the second of the factors which operate in this sphere – the point develops as

[15] R. Newton Flew, *Jesus and his Church*, London: Epworth Press, 1960 (first ed. 1938), p. 38.
[16] Zizioulas, op. cit., p. 130: 'Now if *becoming* history is the particularity of the Son in the economy, what is the contribution of the Spirit? Well, precisely the opposite: it is to liberate the Son and the economy from the bondage of history. If the Son dies on the cross, thus succumbing to the bondage of historical existence, it is the Spirit that raises him from the dead. The Spirit is the *beyond* history, and when he acts in history he does so in order to bring into history the last days, the *eschaton*.'

follows. Christology's tendency is to universalise, and the way in which christology universalises ecclesiology determines the way in which we conceive of the createdness and, consequently, catholicity of the church. Something of the force of the matter can be seen with the eyes given us by the doctrine of election. The logic of Barth's claim that 'God is none other than the One who in His Son or Word elects Himself, and in and with Himself elects His people'[17] has often been taken to imply a doctrine of universal salvation. The moment of truth in the contention is that if election is ordered christologically, and with greater emphasis on the divine Christ than on the human Jesus of Nazareth, the fate of us all appears to have been pre-determined in eternity. A like ordering of ecclesiology to a monophysite or docetically tending christology has even more disastrous effects, and if I discern such monophysite tendencies in the christology underlying the *Dogmatic Constitution of the Church* in the documents of the Second Vatican Council, it is not to suggest that the error is only found in the Catholic tradition. 'As the assumed nature . . . serves the divine Word as a living organ of salvation, so, in a somewhat similar way, does the social structure of the church serve the Spirit of Christ . . .'.[18]

What kind of ecclesiology would derive from a greater stress on the fact that the ecclesiological significance of Jesus derives equally from the humanity of the incarnate? To hold, with Chalcedon and the Letter to the Hebrews that Jesus is without sin does not imply that he is omniscient, or even infallible. 'But of that day . . . no one knows, not even the angels in heaven, nor the Son, but only the Father' (Mk. 13.32). It is part of the being of a human person to be contingent and fallible (though not, of course, to be sinful). If our christology take on board the full implications of the contingency and fallibility of Jesus, what of the church? In view of the temptations and the trial in Gethsemane, may we claim even indefectibility of Jesus? He did, indeed, escape defection. But how? Not through some inbuilt divine programming, though that is the way it has often been made to appear, but by virtue of his free acceptance of the

[17] Karl Barth, *Church Dogmatics*, translation edited by G. W. Bromiley and T. F. Torrance, Edinburgh: T. & T. Clark, 1956–69, Vol. II/2 (1957), p. 76.
[18] Vatican II, *The Conciliar and Post Conciliar Documents*, ed. A. Flannery, Leominster: Fowler Wright, 1975, p. 357.

Spirit's guidance. How far then may the church, consisting as it does of still sinful people, claim more for itself than it claims for him?

A second area in which we may examine the effect of the christological determination of ecclesiology is in the area of authority. The modern church must acknowledge with due penitence that it has rarely exercised authority after the manner of Jesus of Nazareth. To discover whether there is any theological reason for this – any reason, that is, other than attributing it to human sinfulness alone – we return to the question of the relation of christology and pneumatology. What is the relation between the Spirit and the church? Sometimes it has appeared that because a *logical* link has been claimed between Spirit and institution, the institution has made too confident claims to be possessed of divine authority. The outcome, as we saw in the previous section, has been too 'realised' an eschatology of the institution, too near a claim for a coincidence of the church's action with the action of God. Against such a tendency it must be emphasised that, as christology universalises, the direction of pneumatology is to particularise. The action of the Spirit is to anticipate, in the present and by means of the finite and contingent, the things of the age to come. This is true even christologically: it is only through the Spirit that the human actions of Jesus become ever and again the acts of God. Has the historical church made the mistake of claiming a premature universality for her works and words instead of praying for the Spirit and leaving the outcome to God?[19] Certainly, as James Whyte has argued, untenable and circular claims have been made for the operation of the Spirit in relation to the church. He summarises the logic of the statement of the Anglican-Roman Catholic International Commission on authority:

> The decisions of councils or pope on fundamental matters of faith are not true because they are authoritative. They are authoritative because they are true. They are true because they are authentic interpretations of apostolic faith and witness. They are authentic interpretations of apostolic faith

[19] See John Howard Yoder, *The Politics of Jesus*, Grand Rapids: Eerdmans, 1972.

and witness because the Holy Spirit guards from error those who have been given the authority to make such pronouncements.

He points out that such arguments are not only circular and self-justifying, but are dogmatically flawed, in making too much of the divinity of the church, too little of its humanity.[20]

What is required, therefore, is a reconsideration of the relation of pneumatology and christology, with a consequent reduction of stress on the church's institution by Christ and a greater emphasis on its constitution by the Spirit. In such a way we may create fewer self-justifying and historicising links with the past and give more stress to the necessity for the present particularities of our churchly arrangements to be constituted by the Spirit. Such a reconsideration would begin by re-examining the relation of christology and pneumatology in general. The persistent vice of Western theology has been, because it is so christologically oriented, a tendency to premature universalising, and in that respect the authors of *The Myth of God Incarnate* are at one with the tradition to which they take exception. The form that the universalising has taken has been docetic in direction, producing a tendency to conceive the motive force, so to speak, of Jesus' life as being the eternal Word. The outcome, as we know so well, is that his humanity becomes problematic: it appears to be almost conceptually inevitable that it is either loosely joined to the Word as in classic Nestorianism or overridden by it. Modern critics of the whole tradition, attempting to correct the balance by an appeal to the historical Jesus have made the mistake of generalising too soon from the supposed historical base, and have turned Jesus into an instance of some universal characteristic. What is needed is, rather, a greater emphasis in the action of the Holy Spirit towards Jesus as the source of the *particularity* and so historicity of his humanity.[21]

In view of the fact that the ecclesiology of John Owen will

[20] James Whyte, 'The Problem of Authority', *King's Theological Review* 7 (1984), pp. 39, 38.

[21] It seems to me no accident that Schleiermacher, the father of modernist christology, was profoundly uncomfortable with the concrete Jewishness of Jesus. He was hurrying on to higher things. See *The Christian Faith*, E.T. by H. R. Mackintosh and J. S. Stewart, Edinburgh: T. & T. Clark, 1928, p. 384.

concern us later, it is not inappropriate to note here that his christology, in this respect anticipating by a century and a half that of Edward Irving, attempts precisely that reordering. In the first place, Owen *limits* the direct operation of the Word on the human reality of Jesus, in some contrast to Athanasius' incautious talk of the Word's 'wielding his body' and of using it as an 'instrument',[22] talk that was, of course, formalised by Apollinaris to rather different effect. In answer to those who would in effect make the Holy Spirit redundant in christology Owen holds that 'The only singular immediate act of the person of the Son on the human nature was the *assumption* of it into subsistence with himself.' One implication of this is an assertion of the hypostatic union which does not entail 'a transfusion of the properties of one nature into the other, nor real physical communication of divine essential excellencies unto the humanity'. The humanity remains authentically human and is not subverted by the immanently operating Word. Wherein, then, consists its capacity to do the work of God? 'The Holy Ghost ... is the *immediate, peculiar, efficient* cause of all external divine operations: for God worketh by his Spirit, or in him immediately applies the power and efficacy of the divine excellencies unto their operation ...'[23]

Such a conception does much to create space for a conception of the humanity of Jesus which gives due emphasis to his freedom, particularity and contingency: they are *enabled* by the (transcendent) Spirit rather than *determined* by the (immanent) Word. It also has important implications for the doctrine of the church, which has, in most times and places been tempted – and, unlike Jesus, has usually succumbed – to behave as if she were immune from error. And if the Spirit which constitutes the church is the one who was responsible for the shape of Jesus' life, we are still free to teach that he will give the church a christomorphic direction. But it will be a different shape from the authoritarian one of the past, because it will be more oriented to the humanity of the saviour. It is some such concern which, despite its relative lack of pneumatological content, has informed the ecclesiology of John Howard Yoder.

[22] Athanasius, *De Incarnatione*, 17, 42.
[23] Owen, *Works*, op. cit., Vol. III, pp. 160–162. I owe these references to my student, Alan Spence.

In *The Politics of Jesus* his concern was to argue that the church's exercise of power should take its direction from the way in which Jesus bore himself in face of the political forces of his day.[24] In more recent times he has turned his attention more explicitly to ecclesiology, arguing for a voluntary community which lives from the historical particularity of its origins.[25] All such enterprises enable us to reappropriate an ecclesiology of the humanity of Christ. That is the first and crying need if responses to the collapse of Christendom are not to take the form of new authoritarianisms, as they are indeed doing. Christology, then, is the starting point. But of itself it does not take us far enough along the road, because we are seeking an ontology, some understanding of the nature of the church, that is rooted in the being of God. Christology is only the starting point, because it is so closely related to the question of the status of the events from which the church originated. If we wish to say something of what kind of sociality the church is we must move from a discussion of the relation of christology to pneumatology to an enquiry into what it is that makes the church what it is. And that first necessitates a move from the economic to the immanent trinity: or from the ontic to the ontological.

IV   *Towards an ontology of the church*

The argument stands as follows: that on 'economic' grounds one source of the weakness of the ecclesiological tradition has been identified. An overweighting of the christological as against the pneumatological determinants of ecclesiology together with an overemphasis on the divine over against the human Christ has led to a 'docetic' doctrine of the church. To recapitulate the argument of previous sections, it can also be said that much ecclesiology has been dominated by monistic or hierarchical conceptions of the church, whose ontological basis is to be found in either neoplatonism or some other non-personal metaphysic. Where there is no explicitly Christian

[24] John Howard Yoder, op. cit.
[25] John Howard Yoder, *The Priestly Kingdom. Social Ethics as Gospel*, Notre Dame University Press, 1984.

theological ontology, an implicit and foreign one will fill and has filled the vacuum. The contention is, accordingly, that a more satisfactory ontological basis will be found if we pay attention to the doctrine of the Trinity, which was, when first formulated, the means to an ontology alternative to those of the intellectual worlds in which Christianity once took shape, and must now reshape its form of life if it is to be adequate to the challenge of modern conditions. The doctrine of the Trinity, as it comes to us from the Cappadocian theologians, teaches us that the first thing to be said about the being of God is that it consists in personal communion. Communion is for Basil an ontological category. The *nature* of God is communion.[26]

Suppose, then, that we begin with the hypothesis that the sole proper ontological basis for the church is the being of God, who is what he is as the communion of Father, Son and Spirit. Where does it lead us? Great care must be taken in drawing out the implications of such a claim, and in particular the temptation must be resisted to draw conclusions of a logicising kind: appealing directly to the unity of the three as one God as a model for a unified church; or, conversely (and, I believe, more creatively, though still inadequately) arguing from the distinctions of the persons for an ecclesiology of diversity, along the lines of the expression currently popular in ecumenical circles of 'reconciled diversity'. That would be to move too quickly, playing with abstract and mathematically determined concepts and exercising no theological control over their employment.

1. The crucial intermediate stage involves a trinitarian theology of creation. As many great thinkers, Coleridge prominent among them, have realised, a theology of the Trinity has important implications for the ontology of the creature. First, it forbids all monistic or pantheistic identification of the creation with the creator. More important, perhaps, in refusing to develop a logical link between creator and creation, it prevents back-door collapses into monism. The reason for this is to be found in the second, more positive, point, that the doctrine of the Trinity replaces a *logical* conception of the relation between

[26] John Zizioulas, op. cit., p. 134.

God and the world with a *personal* one, and accordingly allows us to say two things of utmost importance: that God and the world are ontologically distinct realities; but that distinctness, far from being the denial of relations, is its ground. Such relation as there is is personal, not logical, the product of the free and personal action of the triune God. The world is therefore contingent, finite and what it is only by virtue of its continuing dynamic dependence upon its creator; or, to say the same thing in another way, by the free action of the Spirit on and towards it.

An inescapable characteristic of the church in this context is that as part of the creation it, too, is finite and contingent. That is to repeat the point that was made in the previous section as an implication of conceiving the church in the image of the humanity of Christ. The gospel is that the Father interrelates with his world by means of the frail humanity of his Son, and by his Spirit enables anticipations in the present of the promised perfection of the creation. What, then, is it for the church to reflect, as part of the creation, the being of God? The answer, as John Zizioulas has shown, lies in the word *koinonia*, perhaps best translated as community (or perhaps sociality, and compare the Russian *Sobornost*). One implication of the threefold community that is God is its dynamism: the being of God is a community of energies, of perichoretic interaction. As such, it is difficult to conceive its consistency with any static hierarchy. Such a hierarchy tends to generate or justify an ideology of permanent relations of subordination, as is instanced by Richard Roberts' telling use of the Hegelian phenomenology of the relation between lord and bondsman. Commenting on Kenneth Kirk's ecclesiology, he writes:

> The ministry has a final status in relation to the church; the Essential Ministry of the Episcopate creates and has contingent upon it a Dependent Ministry of the Presbyterate and then, beyond that are the distant, dependent laity.[27]

We may glimpse behind such a conception further echoes of

[27] Richard Roberts, 'Der Stellenwert des kirchlichen Amtes', *Zeitschrift für Theologie und Kirche* 83 (1986), pp. 382f. Alan Sell similarly questions the Lima document's assertion that the ministry is constitutive of the church's life and ministry. 'This would be to place the ministry above the gospel', 'Ecclesiastical Integrity and Failure', Society for the Study of Theology, 1987, p. 15.

the imperial analogy, and there may also be traces of a misuse of trinitarian appropriations. But that takes us to a further stage in the argument.

2.   We have seen that a central feature of the conception of the church is the way in which its historical shape is formed by its (supposed) relation to the economic Trinity: to the Spirit-led Jesus in its past and to the Christ-shaped Spirit in its present. But caution has also been advised about arguing directly to the church from the immanent Trinity. That is particularly important when appropriations are attempted from supposed patterns of relationship between persons of the Godhead. Moves of that kind can be used to justify theologically the dependent status of the laity because it is supposed that the hierarchy is in some way more directly a reflection (ikon?) of the Father or Son.[28] The point can be illustrated by Derrick Sherwin Bailey's perceptive criticism of Paul's argument in 1 Cor. 11.7 that 'a man ought not to cover his head, since he is the image and glory of God; but woman is the glory of man'.[29] Paul's exegesis and theology are both questionable. According to Genesis 1.26, it is man and woman together who are the image of God, a point which is itself of profound ecclesiological significance. Moreover, on a duly apophatic treatment of the trinitarian relations, it is illegitimate to attribute Fatherly, and so apparently superordinate, functions to man; but Son-like, and so subordinate, functions to woman, as Barth continues to do.[30] Rather, we should not claim such detailed knowledge of the inner constitution of the godhead that we can attempt direct and logical readings-off of that kind.

What kind of analogy between God and church, Trinity and community, may there then be? If there is one, it should be of an indirect kind, in which the church is seen as called to be a, so to speak, finite echo or bodying forth of the divine personal dynamics. How might this operate? Let me introduce the topic by noting a contrast between the Cappadocian and Augustinian

[28] Henri de Lubac, *The Splendour of the Church*, London: Sheed and Ward, 1956, p. 71, alludes to the possibility of deriving the hierarchy from the trinitarian processions.
[29] Derrick Sherwin Bailey, *The Man-Woman Relation in Christian Thought*, London: Longmans, 1959, pp. 294ff.
[30] Karl Barth, *Church Dogmatics*, op. cit., Vol. III/4 (1961) pp. 188–202.

conceptions of the Trinity. The latter is modalist in direction, if not actually modalist, in the sense that the three persons of the Trinity tend to be conceived as posterior to an underlying *deitas* or being of which they are, so to speak, outcrops. By contrast, the Cappadocian development, which Augustine so signally failed to appropriate, is that there is no being anterior to that of the persons. The being of God is the persons in relation to each other. The different theologies of the Trinity generate correspondingly different ecclesiologies. Corresponding to the Augustinian conception there is an ecclesiology which conceives the being of the church as in some sense *anterior* to the concrete historical relationships of the visible community. Such a conception is recognisable by two symptoms. The first is a platonising conception of the invisible church which operates as ontologically prior – because it is the *real* church – to the 'mixed' historical community. The second is the correlative teaching that an order of persons or ecclesiastical structure in some way undergirds or frames the personal relationships of the community: that the real being of the church is to be found underlying the relations of the people rather than being a function of them. Such a conception is illustrated by a point made by de Lubac: 'no constituted assembly without a constitution, which includes a hierarchy ... no realised community (*Gemeinschaft*) without a society (*Gesellschaft*) in which and through which it is realised'.[31] That gives the ontological game away. Why should there be no community without a society? May not the actual relations of concrete historical persons constitute the sole – or primary – being of the church, just as the hypostases in relation constitute the being of God?

That things might conceivably be so is suggested by the ecclesiology of the seventeenth century Puritan, John Owen. Owen is interesting because he is clearly seeking, as perhaps one of the first to do so, an ontology of the church as a community. He is aware that he is breaking new ground, for he remarks that the Reformers, believing that the reformation of doctrine was all that was needed, failed to develop a theology of the community.[32] That for Owen the being of the church

---

[31] de Lubac, op. cit., p. 75.

[32] John Owen, *The True Nature of a Gospel Church, Works*, op. cit., Vol. XVI, p. 20. Note the title's aspiration to ontology.

consists in its communion is clear from the use he makes of the terminology of Aristotelian causality. Speaking of what he calls the 'visible church-state', he distinguishes between

> (1) The material cause of this church, or the matter whereof it is composed, which are visible believers. (2) The formal cause of it, which is their voluntary coalescency into such a society or congregation, according to the mind of Christ. (3) The end of it is, presential local communion, in all the ordinances and institutions of Christ ...[33]

That is from an early essay, and in the later *True Nature of a Gospel Church*, he expands the idea slightly;

> By the matter of the church we understand the persons whereof the church doth consist, with their qualifications; and by its form, the reason, cause, and way of that kind of relation among them which gives them the being of a church ...[34]

What is interesting about the later formulation is the fact that the Aristotelian terminology now takes a back seat so that terms deriving from Cappadocian trinitarian theology – *person, cause, relation* – may come into the lead. The result is that Owen's definition of the church is an echo of their theology of the Trinity. The being of the church consists in the relations of the persons to each other.

A more speculative concern is whether we may develop an analogy between the free relations of the persons of the Godhead and the resulting conception of the church as a voluntary society, if one whose voluntary coalescence is also and first conceived as the work of God the Spirit. The basis would again be the Cappadocian teaching that God is what he is in virtue of what the Father, Son and Spirit give to and receive from each other. There is, hardly surprisingly, in Owen a strong note of the voluntary exercise of membership in the visible church. Is it possible to discern behind this the influence of the theology of the Trinity, for he is undoubtedly a deeply trinitarian thinker? At the very least, it is clear that ecclesiology is for him rooted in the freedom of obedience to the gospel.

[33] John Owen, *Works*, op. cit., Vol. XV, p. 262.
[34] John Owen, *Works*, op. cit., Vol. XVI, p. 11.

'Wherefore *the formal cause of a church* consisteth in an obediential act of believers ... jointly giving themselves up unto the Lord Jesus Christ, to do and observe ...'.[35] Nor is the resulting conception of the church a static one. The church is the work of the eschatological Spirit and so there is in Owen an emphasis, derived from the New Testament, on the newness of what is happening:

> If [the church] constitute new relations between persons that neither naturally nor morally were before so related, as marriage doth between husband and wife; if it require new mutual duties and give new mutual rights among themselves ... it is vain to imagine that this state can arise from or have any other formal cause but the joint consent and virtual confederation of those concerned unto those ends ...[36]

For obvious historical reasons, Owen repeatedly emphasises the voluntary nature both of membership of the local church and of the federating of local churches with each other. All the most interesting developments in theology have come under the constraints of some historical pressure, and the fact that under the impact of his particular circumstances he moved so far towards a conception of the church as a community of freely relating persons must be accepted for what it is: an ecclesiology which echoes God's eternal being in relation. It is also to be observed that Owen uses what can be called the more subordinate of the Aristotelian causes to account for the voluntary combining of the people. It is clear that for him the 'efficient' and 'moving' causes of the church – though he does not use such terminology – are the 'two hands' of God (Irenaeus), the Son who institutes and the Spirit who constitutes. We shall return to the point raised by that observation.

Another more recent essay in ecclesiology has produced some similar results. Edward Farley's *Ecclesial Man* is primarily an attempt to produce a phenomenological study of the church as a community of redemption. On the face of the matter, phenomenology is the foe of ontology, in appearing to bracket ontological questions in order to describe appearances. But the way in which it is done in Farley's study appears to achieve not so

[35] Ibid., p. 29.
[36] Ibid., p. 26.

much ontological agnosticism as a shedding of the weight of traditional ontological assumptions so that the structure of the visible community may be seen. The result is a description of the actual relations in which members of the community have their being, an ontology of the community which lives by its own descriptive strength rather than needing the support of – say – an ideal invisible background. A crucial passage is as follows:

> [Ecclesia] is not an exclusive form of social organization such as a nation or tribe. … It does, however, involve a determinate intersubjectivity. … [I]n its concrete, everyday actualization, ecclesia involves interpersonal relationships and reciprocities which occur in conjunction with its characteristic activities such as worship. These reciprocities presuppose an intersubjective structure in which participants constitute each other as believers.[37]

Once again, there are echoes of the Cappadocian Trinity. The participants constitute each other as believers, as the persons of the Trinity constitute each other as persons.

It is in the final clause of the extract from Farley that is to be found also the weakness of the phenomenological approach, and it corresponds to its strength. In saying that the participants constitute each other as believers, Farley appears to be ascribing to members of the church the work that belongs to God the Spirit. By so doing he appears to have developed a rather idealising picture of visible church, and in two respects. First he has claimed too much for what is, as we are constantly reminded, a company of sinners, albeit of sinners forgiven and on the Christian way; and, second, he has read too directly from the being of God to that of the church. He has, in sum, failed to distinguish satisfactorily between the divine and human determinants of the being of the church.

Farley's phenomenology calls attention to the perils of attempting a theology of the church, prominent among which is the danger of what could be called a constructing of social reality in blithe disregard for the way things happen to be. Any ecclesiology must accordingly attempt to hold together two conflicting pulls. On the one hand if, with the New Testament,

---

[37] Edward Farley, *Ecclesial Man. A Social Phenomenology of Faith and Reality*, Philadelphia: Fortress Press, 1975, p. 152.

we are to speak of the church of God, the being of the church must be rooted in the being of God. On the other, however, a resulting ecclesiology must make due allowance for the fact that even as such the church belongs to the created world, and that all finite organisms may fail to be nourished by their roots or may even be torn away from them. The church remains this side of eternity a highly fallible community existing in a measure of contradiction of what it is called to be, and if as a matter of fact it has maintained a measure of integrity through the vicissitudes of its history, that may not be attributed to some inherent indefectibility. To be honest about our own history, there is need to bear constantly in mind the temptations, by no means always resisted, to regression into a fallen past.

Too much is therefore not being claimed for the theology of the church that is being attempted in this chapter. The hope is to have created the framework by which a link may be drawn between the being of God and that which is from time to time realised by the Spirit. It is a kind of analogy of echo: the church is what it is by virtue of being called to be a temporal echo of the eternal community that God is. What, then, is the point of such theoretical activity? 1. An attempt is being made to develop concepts with the aid of which the things we say about the church may be understood. One simple example will suffice. Much has been made of the metaphor of the body of Christ, but, as the differences within Christendom reveal, it is by no means clear how it should be construed. It is an organic metaphor, and as such could be taken in a number of ways, totalitarian or pantheistic for example. There is much talk of organic unity of the churches, but the equally much used text from the Fourth Gospel (17.11), 'that they may be one, even as we are one' should give us pause, especially if we are aware of the trinitarian control. It is speaking not so much of an organic as of an interpersonal unity: the personal unity of distinct but freely related persons. It is in some such light that we should approach the interpretation of the Pauline metaphor of the body, for we shall be aware that it is used in a number of senses: not only as a warning against disunity, but to stress the plurality of the church's gifts and graces (1 Cor. 12.14ff, Rom. 12.4ff). The trinitarian ontology helps us to appropriate something of the richness and openness of that central ecclesial model.

2. Paul's misuse of trinitarian attributions has already been mentioned, and in fairness to him we should refer to another point made this time with his help by Sherwin Bailey, who in general refutes decisively the myth of Pauline misogyny.[38] Drawing on and correcting Barth's trinitarian anthropology, he concludes:

> Man ... is in the image of God in its Manward aspect primarily by virtue of his essential structure as a bi-personal male-female unity in which (relationally ... not numerically) the coinherence of Father, Son and Holy Spirit is reflected in terms of finite existence.[39]

Bailey's anthropology brings with it important ecclesiological implications, for if the image of God is primarily or even only largely realised in terms of the unity of the sexes, a major aspect of the church's calling is to be a community of women and men:

> Against all one-sex institutions and orders ... as against all vows of celibacy (compulsory, and even voluntary), there is set an insistent question mark; they are only justified if they do not hinder free and healthy partnership between the sexes. ... Nor are celibacy and monasticism alone in question; there are numerous Church societies, guilds and associations which are constituted on a single-sex basis, and are hardly calculated to uphold the obligation of partnership.

What that implies for the argument about the ordination of women should not be too difficult to realise. At the very least, it must be seen that the ecclesiology of community relativises, and not before time, the whole question of an ordained caste. More positively, as Bailey proceeds to argue, renewal in the image of God is essentially directed to 'harmonious creative relation between man and woman'.[40]

That final point serves to introduce a more general consideration. Relations in the church have so often been construed in terms of the permanent subordination of one group

[38] D. S. Bailey, op. cit., ch. II.
[39] Ibid., p. 271.
[40] Ibid., pp. 284, 286 and 289.

to another, even though the superordinate group has for the sake of appearances dignified its position with the rhetoric of 'service'. If, however, the attribution of particular positions to particular groups or orders is to be replaced by a pattern more reflective of the free personal relations which constitute the deity, should we not consciously move towards an ecclesiology of perichoresis: in which there is no permanent structure of subordination, but in which there are overlapping patterns of relationships, so that the same person will be sometimes 'subordinate' and sometimes 'superordinate' according to the gifts and graces being exercised? And would that not more nearly echo the relationships of which Paul is speaking in 1 Corinthians 12–14, from which the notion of a permanent order of leadership is completely absent? The concept may be thought to be hopelessly idealistic, but is that because we have so long been in thrall to the inherited stereotype? Whether that be so, the chief point of this section remains: that to base a theology of the church in the Trinity is of great practical moment, because ancient questions tend to receive different answers if the primary control on ecclesiology is the tri-personal community of God. If it is true, as the opening sections of this chapter held, that early ecclesiology failed to exercise appropriate control, and as a result produced authoritarian and monistic doctrines of the church, it is important that the whole matter be reconsidered.

V   *The visible community*

In the previous section there has been attempted an ontology of the church, in which it was suggested that a movement, carefully controlled by an apophatic doctrine of the immanent Trinity, can be made between a doctrine of God and a doctrine of the church. The relation between the latter and the former has already been described as an 'echoing': the being of the church should echo the dynamic of the relations between the three persons who together constitute the deity. The church is called to be the kind of reality at a finite level that God is in eternity. Can further account be given of this analogy? Most obviously, it can be said that the doctrine of the Trinity is being used to suggest ways of allowing the eternal becoming of God – the eternally interanimating energies of the three – to provide the basis for the personal dynamics of the community.

Unless, however, everything is simply to hang in the air, there is need of some intermediate linkage, and this will be sought with the help of a return to some of the matters treated in the third section. What is the relation between the ontology of the church – the so to speak theoretical framework with the help of which it is thought – and its actual being? That is to say: the source of our *ontology* of the church is a doctrine of the Trinity; but how is God the three in one related to the actual historical and visible community? In what sense is our ecclesiology any more than a theory which is abstractly derived from an equally theoretical concept of God?

An essential intermediate step is that we ground the being of the church in the source of the being of all things, the eternal energies of the three persons of the Trinity as they are in perichoretic interrelation. The primary echoes of that being are to be heard in the ways of God to the world in creation and the perfection of that creation in both Jesus and the Spirit. It is noteworthy that both of the supposedly deutero-Pauline letters to Colossae and Ephesus ground the being of the church in the purpose of the Father to reconcile all things to himself through the Son and in the Spirit: that is to say, in the fulfilment of the destiny of creation. Scholars have sometimes argued that Col. 1.18a, 'He is the head of the body, the church', is an interpolation into the logic of a hymn otherwise dedicated to a celebration of the cosmic Christ. But the text as it stands is precisely to the point: the church is the body called to be the community of the last times, that is to say, to realise in its life the promised and inaugurated reconciliation of all things. It therefore becomes an echo of the life of the Trinity when it is enabled by the Spirit to order its life to where that reconciliation takes place in time, that is to say, to the life, death and resurrection of Jesus.

The concrete means by which the church becomes an echo of the life of the Godhead are all such as to direct the church away from self-glorification to the source of its life in the creative and recreative presence of God to the world. The activity of proclamation and the celebration of the Gospel sacraments are temporal ways of orienting the community to the being of God. Proclamation turns the community to the Word whose echo it is called to be; baptism and eucharist, the sacraments of incorporation and *koinonia*, to the love of God the Father towards his world as it is mediated by the Son and Spirit. Thus there is no timeless church: only a church then and now and to be, as the Spirit ever and again incorporates people into Christ and in the same action brings them into and maintains them in community with one another.

To return to where we began, with an attack on the monism of the church and its dominance by an ontology of the invisible, it must be said that there is no invisible church – at least not in the sense in which it has usually been understood – not because the church is perfect, but because to be in communion with those who are ordered to Jesus by the Spirit is to be the church.[41] Whether a community of those who claim the name of church is justified in its claim is a question which may always be asked. But should our criteria be those of monistic, legal and 'organic' structures, or the trinitarian ones concerned with whether a community freely orders and disciplines its life so as to echo the community of Father, Son and Spirit? It is with that directedness to the Trinity that this endeavour to understand something of what the church is should appropriately come to an end.

---

[41] It is always illuminating to interpret such expressions as those of Paul's about being 'in Christ' in a social rather than an individualistic or mystical way. It is because Paul has such a strong sense of the fact that to be related to the community is to be related to Christ that he can make remarks like that of 1 Cor. 7.14, that 'the unbelieving husband is consecrated through his wife, and the unbelieving wife is consecrated through her husband.'

CHAPTER 5

THE CONCEPT OF THE PERSON
The One, the Three and the Many

As human persons we are, in large measure, what others have made us. Readers of that fashionable genre, the novel of modern academic life, will have gained a not altogether favourable impression of the interaction of people in the world of learning. But, however exaggerated the picture, it does remain true that the quality of a university institution has much to do with the way we treat and are treated by each other. Too many Howard Kirks and the system would collapse. The same is true of all the other societies and institutions, the structures of conviviality, in which human life takes shape, including, but by no means limited to, the two institutions beloved of political rhetoricians, the family and the state. In this context, too, we become what others enable us to be.

To provide the framework of this chapter, I want to take the matter already touched on, the importance of the person: that what we and our institutions are is largely a matter of persons in relationship. In doing so, I hope to take further some of the topics adumbrated in the final section of chapter one above. For the heart of the argument, I want to throw some light on that important matter by propounding two theses. The first is that there exist in the Western tradition two distinct though sometimes overlapping views of the person, one of them believed almost everywhere, but wrong; the other neglected but right; and that they have importantly different theological backgrounds. The second thesis is closely related to the first, and will suggest the falsity of at least aspects of another fashionable doctrine, that gods are simply or mainly the projection of human needs and values. The evidence I shall review suggests that the opposite also happens, and that our views of what it is to be human are projected from what we believe about God.

I   *Persons and individuals*

First, then, a review of some features of the way the person has been understood in recent centuries. I begin with René Descartes, the fountainhead of most recent discussions of the nature of the person. For Descartes, the person is the thinking thing, the intellectual reality to which all other human experiences ultimately reduce. I am a mind, possibly, unless philosophical justification for an alternative position can be found, alone in a world which is an illusion. Two points can be made about Descartes' legacy to the tradition. The first is that to identify the person with the mind, and in particular a mind rather loosely related to a body, is to generate a strongly individualist and dualist view of what we are. It is dualist because it operates with a view of mind as essentially non-spatial and of body as equally essentially spatial and material. And what are put asunder in virtue of the way they are defined it is very difficult, even for God, we might say, to join together. Likewise, Descartes' view of the person is individualist because the conception of the human being as a mind encased in matter gives rise to a necessarily problematic relation with other persons. How do we know, he asks at one stage of his argument, that what I think are other persons are not simply machines wearing hats and coats?[1] The human being is thus defined in such a way that relations with the other are rendered essentially problematic.

The second point to be made about Descartes' formulation of the question is that philosophical discussion of the person since his time has been dominated by questions directly related to his ontology. The aspect that concerns us directly is the matter of personal identity: what am I and how do I know that I am the same individual as the one born so many years ago? It would not be appropriate to review here the history of the

[1] René Descartes, *Meditations on the First Philosophy*, in *The Philosophical Works of Descartes*, E.T. by Elizabeth Haldane and G. R. T. Ross, Cambridge University Press, second ed., 1931, Vol. I, p. 155.

debate, only the inadequacy of its dualist and individualist approach to the ontological question. Is the real 'I' a mind pushing around a lump of matter, or a lump of matter in some way organised in a way suggesting mind? In recent years Ayer has reviewed the problem, inconclusively, though he is 'inclined' to see personal identity as dependent upon bodily factors.[2] In contrast, Professor H. D. Lewis has been most consistently associated with a traditionally Cartesian position.[3] An interesting attempt to tread a middle path is that of P. F. Strawson, who argued that we should consider the concept of the person to be logically prior to that of individual consciousness, and that a person is an entity of which both mental and material characteristics are predicated.[4] The strength of Strawson's position is to be found in his assertion of the logical priority of the term *person*; to this matter we shall return. The weakness is that of the mainstream debate as a whole, as is suggested by the title of Strawson's book, *Individuals*. To treat the person and the individual as the same thing – to define the person as an individual – is to lose both person and individual.

Evidence for such a claim is to be found in Derek Parfit's recent study, *Reasons and Persons*. Arguing for a reductionist view, he holds both that there is no personal identity, and that the loss of the concept is a liberation. 'Instead of saying, "I shall be dead", I should say, "There will be no future experiences that will be related, in certain ways, to these present experiences". Because it reminds me what this fact involves, this redescription makes this fact less depressing.'[5] It is an attempt to escape from self, but the vision remains egocentric and individualist. In adopting what he sees to be a Buddhist kind of position, Parfit shows that when personal identity is sought in the way it has been in post-Enlightenment philosophy, it disappears, and that when it does, the smile remaining on the Cheshire cat is a bleak one indeed.

If this were merely a matter of discussions between linguistic

---

[2] A. J. Ayer, 'The Concept of a Person', *The Concept of a Person and Other Essays*, London: Macmillan, 1963, p. 116.

[3] H. D. Lewis, *The Elusive Self*, London: Macmillan, 1982.

[4] P. F. Strawson, *Individuals. An Essay in Descriptive Metaphysics*, London: Macmillan, 1982.

[5] Derek Parfit, *Reasons and Persons*, Oxford University Press, 1984, p. 281.

philosophers, little would be at stake. But the fact that a parallel development has taken place in social and political thought should give us pause. If the person is lost, then so are we, ripe for being swallowed up into an undifferentiated mass, the many absorbed into the embrace of the one. Just as philosophically a stress on the individual loses the person, so is it socially. Many are the laments to be heard about modern individualism, and they are justified. But the outcome of individualism is even more lamentable. There is a case for saying that a far greater danger in modern mass societies is what that expression implies: the loss of the manysidedness of our humanity in the undifferentiated unity of the whole. It is surely significant that Kierkegaard, the most perceptive of the observers of Europe's developing liberal institutions, protested the importance of the individual on grounds which showed a concern for proper social relationships. In *Two Ages* he shows how the present age exhibits a levelling process in which the proper dynamics of human relationships are submerged. We talk about relationships instead of living them, and 'count ... each other's verbal avowals of relation as a substitute for resolute mutual giving in the relation'.[6]

However inadequate may appear Kierkegaard's prescription – 'the idolized positive principle of sociality in our age ... can be halted only if the individual, in individual separateness, gains the intrepidity of religiousness'[7] – there can be little doubt that he had identified the enemy with unerring accuracy. Hegel, with his tendency to make the human person the pawn of the process of history, was immediately in his sights. But what he has to say applies equally to those movements which are today most strident in their rejection of individualism, but also most deficient in their conception of the person. 'Most sociologists', writes Andrew Walker, himself a sociologist, 'hardly ever

[6] Soren Kierkegaard, *Two Ages. The Age of Revolution and the Present Age*, E.T. and ed. by H. V. and E. Hong, Princeton University Press, 1978, p. 79. See also John W. Elrod, *Kierkegaard and Christendom*, Princeton University Press, 1981.

[7] *Two Ages*, p. 86. Kierkegaard's individualism shares many of the features of Augustine's. In *The Sickness unto Death*, E.T. by Walter Lowrie, in *Fear and Trembling and the Sickness unto Death*, Princeton University Press, 1954, p. 147, he writes in language much of which could come from the *De Trinitate* of 'the condition of the self when despair is completely eradicated: by relating itself to its own self and by willing to be itself the self is grounded transparently in the power which posited it'.

use the word "person" at all. A quick look through the 14 volumes of the *International Encyclopedia of Social Science* reveals that "person" is not in the index ..."[8] Nor, it can be added, does it appear to be present in indexes to the works of Karl Marx. Marx, writing only two years before the publication of Kierkegaard's *Two Ages*, showed a similar concern for the importance of right relations in our life together. But he jumped in a different direction. His response to the same phenomenon – modern liberal Europe – was to assert what Kierkegaard most feared, the priority of the universal. It is as a species-being that humankind is free. And that means insofar as he treats himself as a universal.[9] Kierkegaard was to show the inadequacy of such a proposal: the idea of a pure humanity is simply a 'higher negativity':[10] an impersonal abstraction, we might say. And however much Marx's later thoughts changed, the point remains: that a species-being, a universal, is impersonal, and it is not possible to base the freedom and society of persons on what is impersonal. The conclusion must be – and this is where Kierkegaard himself falls most short – that modern individualism and modern collectivism are mirror images of one another. Both signal the loss of the person, the disappearance of the one into the many or the many into the one, and the reason is that there is no mid term between the two features of our life, no way of ensuring the proper being and *hypostasis* of both the universal and the particular. It is fortunate that we do not entirely model our lives on the theories of the dominating philosophies of our times.

II   *The alternative tradition*

Alongside the main stream there is an alternative tradition of philosophising about the person, and it is to be found in the

[8] Andrew Walker, 'The Concept of the Person in Social Science', paper prepared, 1985, for the British Council of Churches' Study Commission on Trinitarian Doctrine Today, p. 1. I believe that today Dr Walker would wish to qualify this judgement a little.

[9] Karl Marx, *Works, March 1843 to August 1844*, in Karl Marx, Frederick Engels, *Collected Works*, Vol. 3, London: Lawrence and Wishart, 1975, p. 275. I am grateful to Kenneth Surin for guidance in approaching the works of Marx in this area.

[10] *Two Ages*, p. 87.

works of those whose names are entirely absent from the bibliography and index of Derek Parfit's mammoth exercise in deconstruction. This time, I shall begin with a recent figure and move, speculatively, back into the past. In the second volume of his Gifford Lectures, *Persons in Relation*, the Scottish philosopher John Macmurray presented a radically different view of the person from anything we have met so far. In the first place, his ontology is different. Where Descartes began with the mind and its distinction from the body, Macmurray begins with the concept of action. As agents, we are unities. Against the Enlightenment's dualism of mind and matter, Macmurray argues that 'both matter and spirit are misconceptions' and that dualism arises from a fragmentation of human experience into 'on the one hand, an "I think" and, on the other, an "it happens"'.[11] Whatever we make of this radical rejection of a long tradition, there is no doubt that it makes possible a view of the person that is distinctively and importantly different.

That brings me to the second feature of Macmurray's treatment, and it is that for him the concept of the person is logically prior to the other notions that are associated with it. It is that upon which the rest of our knowledge and being depends. And that leads directly to the third and main point. *As persons we are only what we are in relation to other persons*: '... the Self exists only in dynamic relation with the Other ... [T]he self is constituted by its relation to the Other, ... it has its being in its relationship'.[12] We must therefore centre our attention first not on the identity of the individual, but on the matrix within which individuality takes shape. 'Since mutuality is constitutive for the personal, it follows that "I" need "you" in order to be myself.'[13] One benefit of this view is immediately apparent, and it is that the individual is on such an account relativised without being legislated out of existence. A social philosophy emerges which avoids the objectionable features of both the main products of the Enlightenment, individualism and collectivism. For Macmurray, community and society are to be distinguished. A society is an external, impersonal unity, a means to some end

[11] John Macmurray, *Persons in Relation*, London: Faber and Faber, 1961, p. 213.
[12] Ibid., p. 17.
[13] Ibid., p. 69.

other than itself, and therefore a grouping of isolated individuals.[14] A community, on the other hand, is 'a unity of persons with persons ... Each remains a distinct individual; the other remains really other. Each realizes himself in and through the other.'[15]

The latter point is the one I wish to pursue here. What is the origin and meaning of the claim that as persons we realise our individuality only in and through each other? We might think that ultimately it has its roots in the Fourth Gospel's profound meditations on the way Jesus and the Father exist only 'in' each other, the extended exposition of the claim that from eternity and in the incarnation the Word is with God and the Word is God. But at this stage I want to suggest ways in which such biblical ways of thinking have enabled and fertilised two millennia of thought about the person.

Macmurray, it must be remembered, was Scottish, and heir to a number of influences that tend to have passed us English by. It has been suggested by Professor T. F. Torrance that a crucial link in the development of a relational view of the person is the nineteenth-century Scottish philosopher, Sir William Hamilton, who was directly or indirectly influenced by John Calvin.[16] However the tradition operated, there is to be found a remarkable likeness between some of the arguments used by Macmurray about the human person and those used eight centuries before of the persons of the Trinity by Richard of St Victor. In *Of the Trinity*, Book 3, Richard has an interesting if rather *a priori* argument for the propriety of the threeness of God. Unlike Augustine, the fountainhead of most Western theology of the Trinity, he looks not at the inner soul for his clues to the nature of God, but at persons in relation. His argument goes something like this. For there to be love, it must be directed towards another.[17] But the love of two for each other is inadequate, likely on its own simply to be swallowed up in itself, like, we might say, the love of Vronsky and Anna Karenina in

[14] Ibid., ch. 6.

[15] Ibid., pp. 157f.

[16] T. F. Torrance, *Transformation and Convergence in the Frame of Knowledge. Explorations in the Interrelations of Scientific and Theological Enterprise*, Belfast: Christian Journals, 1984, pp. 229f.

[17] Richard of St Victor, *De Trinitate*, ed. G. Salet, *Sources Chrétiennes*, 63, Paris: Les Editions du Cerf, 1959, Book 3, xix.

Tolstoy's novel. If it is truly to be love, the two will seek a third in order to be able to share their love. 'Shared love is properly said to exist when a third person is loved by two persons harmoniously and in community.'[18] That is exactly the same kind of argument that was repeated, presumably unknowingly and in a related context by John Macmurray:

> ... to obtain this analysis, we isolated two persons from their relation to all others. If their relation to one another is exclusive of the others, then its relation to the others is negative ... To be fully positive, therefore, the relation must be in principle inclusive, and without limits.[19]

Could it be that although there is no direct reference to a God conceived as triune in Macmurray's work, in some way there is a measure of dependence; that in some way Macmurray's thought about the human person derives from Christian thought about God? That brings us to the third main section of the chapter.

III   *Theology and anthropology*

I said earlier that my first main thesis was that there are in the Western tradition two different ways of thinking about the person. In Descartes and his successors we have the individualist, which collapses so easily into the collectivist. In Macmurray we have the first evidence for a more relational view of the matter, that we truly find ourselves neither as individuals nor as parts of collectives, but as persons in free relations to each other. Towards the end of the previous section, I began to advance the second main thesis, that Macmurray's view of the person appears to derive from Christian thought about God. If this is so, it casts doubt upon the modern thesis that theological doctrines are the projections of anthropological theories. Feuerbach's view that the doctrine of the Trinity really means that 'participated life is alone true, self-satisfying divine life'

---

[18] Ibid., 3.xix.927B. 7–9. Taking more account of this point would revolutionise discussion of the nature of human sexuality, especially the widespread assumption that everything has effectively been said when the relations of pairs have been treated.

[19] Macmurray, p. 159.

begs the question of the origin of our belief in the importance of participated life.[20] The way things have happened historically suggests that the dependence is otherwise: that anthropology stems from theology, and not the other way round. To support such a view we can, by glancing at some features of the history of thought about the person, show how the influences operated, and that it is thought about God that is determinative.

First of all there is the fact that Richard of St Victor not only precedes the use made of his argument by John Macmurray, but precedes it in a particular way. Whereas Macmurray's concern is with the human person, Richard and his predecessors were almost entirely preoccupied with the doctrine of God. For this reason we must qualify Professor Torrance's claim that a relational view of the person is to be found in such theologians as Richard of St Victor and Calvin, and qualify it in two ways. In the first place, it is rather misleading to say that Richard has a relational view of the person. His definition, when he comes to give it, is not very different from that to be found in more individualistic strands of the Western tradition.[21] What appears to have happened is that ways of thinking about God relationally have survived in the West in almost subliminal manner, continuing to find a place in an otherwise inhospitable tradition, and that both strands, the individualistic and the relational, have existed side by side, sometimes in the same thinker. What we find in Richard is an approach to the doctrine of the Trinity that contains possibilities for the development of a relational view of the person.

The second qualification is that made necessary by the difference of context. In our passage, Richard is not concerned with the nature of the human person. Preoccupation with that is a characteristically modern phenomenon, a positive if by now over-worked outcome of the Enlightenment's anthropocentrism and Kant's Copernican revolution. What we can say then is not that there is to be found in these pre-modern thinkers a relational view of the person, but that with the change of interest in the modern era different ways of thinking about God

---

[20] Ludwig Feuerbach, *The Essence of Christianity*, E.T. by George Eliot, New York: Harper and Bros., 1957 ed., p. 67.

[21] Richard of St Victor, 4.xxii.24: *naturae intellectualis incommunicabilis existentia.*

came to underlie and fertilise different conceptions of the human person.

Support for such a view comes from the history of Western thought about the nature of God. There are, indeed, two discernible strands, and the source of the individualistic tradition is to be found in two of the dominant influences from early centuries. First, there is Boethius. His famous definition of the person as *naturae rationabilis individua substantia*, an individual substance of rational nature, is the heart of the troubles.[22] Not only is there stress on individuality – *un*relatedness – but the tendency that was to play so important a part in modern individualism, of defining our humanity in terms of reason (Descartes again!), is given strong prominence.[23] But Boethius was anticipated in certain important respects in Augustine's treatment of the Trinity, deeply influenced as it was by neoplatonic rationalism. As we have seen in chapter three, Augustine is at his weakest in his treatment of the *persons* of the Trinity, flattening out their distinctiveness, partly because he does not appreciate the weight being borne by the Cappadocian concept of *hypostasis* or person, partly because the concept of relation is simply inadequate as an equivalent – only a person can be personal; and a relation is not a person – and partly because in distinction from Richard of St Victor he seeks the human analogue of the Trinity not in the loving relation of persons to each other but inside the head of the one individual, in the structures of the mind's intellectual love of itself.[24] The syndrome of intellectualism and individualism found in Boethius is thus anticipated in a slightly different form. But the effect is the same, and it is not surprising that Eastern Orthodox thinkers are consistently critical of this side of the Western way of conceiving the Trinity. Again and again in the *De Trinitate* the

[22] Boethius, *Contra Eutychem*, III, 4f.

[23] Even Tertullian, who shows otherwise a movement towards a relational view of the person, falls into this trap, perhaps because like so many others he does not transfer his theological insights to his anthropology. See *Against Praxeas* 5 for the anthropology, 10 and 24 for the relational view of the person in God.

[24] See chapter three above for the evidence that although Augustine says in *De Trinitate* XIV, xii (15) that the real image of God is to be found in the mind's love of God, there can be no doubt that the conception plays little part in his overall discussion, which is determined rather by the analogy derived from the inner configurations of the mind.

godlikeness of the human person is located in the mind, and there is in this respect a direct link between Augustine and the modern tradition stemming from Descartes.[25] Christopher Kaiser's judgement must therefore be deemed fundamentally correct that in Augustine 'the complete dissociation of [the] eternal intra-trinitarian relations from ordinary human relations forced him into a rather static concept of deity, on the one hand, and an individualistic concept of humanity, on the other'.[26] We shall return to Augustine in greater detail later.

IV *Person and relation*

The argument so far, then, is this. Behind the individualistic concept of the person, whose development has had such disastrous effects on modern Western thought, there lies a correlative concept of God. Behind the development of an alternative way of thinking lies a decisively different theology. What is its distinctive character? The answer can first be sought in the differences between Augustine and other Western theologians. In his discussion of the persons of the Trinity in Book I of the *Institutes*, John Calvin engages in a discussion with the Western tradition, calling in evidence the theology of Tertullian and Hilary of Poitiers against Jerome, and, indirectly, Augustine.[27] It is significant that Hilary is in this respect true to those concerns of Tertullian which place him closer to the theology of the East than to Augustine. Tertullian's stress on the monarchy of the Father and the distinctive characters of the persons within the godhead is continued in characteristic fashion by Hilary. Two features are particularly significant. The first is a concern to avoid what we can fairly call individualism in a repeated denial of the loneliness and isolation of God,

[25] The fundamental analogy of memory, understanding and will is heavily platonic, and is related to the theory of knowledge as recollection. See again chapter three above.

[26] Christopher B. Kaiser, *The Doctrine of God. An Historical Survey*, London: Marshall, Morgan and Scott, 1982, p. 81.

[27] John Calvin, *Institutes of the Christian Religion*, I.xiii.5f. His praise of Augustine, one of the major authorities of the *Institutes*, is here carefully qualified: 'With what great freedom does Augustine *sometimes* break forth?' (my italics).

something Aquinas noted but did not develop.[28] The second is a correlative concern for the particularity of the persons in God as a way by which there is expressed that distinctiveness in unity which is such a marked feature of the biblical characterisation of the divine being and action.[29] The general point to be made is that there is in these thinkers a movement towards a relational concept of the persons in God which maintains their distinctness in a way that is absent from Augustine. It is this which appears to have been taken up by Calvin in his clear preference for some parts of the Western tradition against others, and which feeds also the thought of those who have kept alive a relational view.

But it is, of course, to the Cappadocians and particularly to Basil that the real development of a relational conception of the person is owed. By giving priority to the concept of person in their doctrine of God, they transform at once the meaning of both concepts. The being of God is not now understood in the way characteristic of Greek metaphysics, but in terms of communion. God *is* 'a sort of continuous and indivisible community' says the letter usually attributed to Basil of Caesarea. The writer realises the implications of what he is doing: he is changing the meaning of words and so the way we understand the reality of God. It is, he says, 'a new and paradoxical conception of united separation and separated unity'.[30] The being of God consists in the community of *hypostaseis* who give and receive their reality to and from one another.

Another way of putting the matter would be to say that by centring their attention on the seriousness with which the Bible expresses the unity and diversity of God's action, the Cappadocians have brought the concept of the person into the position of logical priority that modern thinkers like Macmurray and Strawson would give it. The significance of their move can be appreciated if a contrast is made with what Augustine makes of the same concepts. The contrast is almost total, and

---

[28] Hilary of Poitiers, *De Trinitate*, IV.17.23f; 24.3f (CCL LXII, pp. 120, 126). In the latter passage it is explicitly stated that the distinction of persons is mentioned *ne solitarii error subesset.* Aquinas' allusion to Hilary is in *Summa Theologiae* Ia.30.3.

[29] Hilary, IX.42.42 cf. VI.8.4 (pp. 149, 203).

[30] Basil of Caesarea, *Letters* 38, 4 (MPG 32, 332a17f and 333d20).

has two marked features. First of all, Augustine does not really know what to do with the concept of the person, and says, in a well known passage, that he uses it only 'in order not to remain silent'.[31] Because, as he admits, he does not understand the Greek usage,[32] and because he can only speculate that perhaps they preferred the term *hypostasis* because it is more in accordance with their linguistic usage,[33] he is unable to appreciate that they are in the business of *changing* language to perform new functions. It is therefore not surprising that Augustine's own attempts to come to terms with the matter are marked by an extreme woodenness in the use of logical categories, so that *relation* remains a concept owing more to Aristotelian logic than to attention to concrete and personal realities. The second marked feature of the contrast is that Augustine says the opposite of what the Cappadocians say about two essential matters. On the one hand he cannot escape an individualistic concept of the person. 'The Father', he says, 'is called person in respect to himself, not in relation to the Son or the Holy Spirit.'[34] Consequently, on the other hand, his concept of God escapes transformation, and he denies what for Basil was the heart of the matter: that 'three somethings subsist from one matter (*materia*) which, whatever it is, is unfolded in these three'.[35] He denies, in other words, that the being of God 'unfolds' in the relations of the persons.

But it is this point – that the being of God lies in the relation of persons – that is so important for us. The contemporary Greek theologian, John Zizioulas, has elaborated something of its meaning:

> In God the particular is ontologically ultimate because *relationship is permanent and unbreakable*. Because the Father, the Son and the Spirit are always together, the particular beings are the bearers of the totality of nature, and thus no

[31] Augustine, *De Trinitate* V.ix (10).
[32] Ibid., V.viii (10): *nescio quid volunt interesse inter* ousian *et* hypostasin ...
[33] Ibid., VII.vi (11): *quod forte secundum linguae suae consuetudinem.*
[34] Ibid., *Ad se ... dicitur persona, non ad filium vel spiritum sanctum.*
[35] Ibid., *Nec ... dicimus ... unum deum tamquam ex una materia tria quaedam subsistant, etiamsi quidquid illud est in his tribus explicatum sit.* In that respect, Aquinas' view that the Father or the Spirit could have been the one to become incarnate (op. cit., IIIa.3, 5) is the logical outcome of Augustine's trinitarian theology.

contradiction between 'one' and 'many' can arise. In trying to identify a particular thing, we have to make it part of a relationship, and not isolate it as an *individual.*

In God, that is to say, there is no ultimate breach between the 'one' and the 'many' because of the part played by the person conceived relationally. Accordingly, there is 'a reality of communion in which each particular is affirmed as *unique* and irreplaceable by the others'.[36] The Cappadocian tradition is saying about the persons in God what John Macmurray said about (human) persons in community: 'the other remains essentially other. Each realises himself in and through the other.'[37] The uniqueness of each person is thus preserved, but without the destructive lapse into individualism.

The logically irreducible concept of the person as one whose uniqueness and particularity derive from relations to others was developed by the Eastern Fathers in the heat of their concern for the loyalty of the Christian church to the biblical understanding of God. It has continued, like an underground stream, to water the Western tradition, and continues to be desperately needed in our fragmented and alienated society. A person, we must learn and relearn, can be defined only in terms of his or her relations with other persons, and not in terms of a prior universal or non-personal concept like species-being, evolution or, for that matter, subsistent relation (and the list could be much extended from current political debate).

V   *Two modern theologians of the person*

But how shall we learn the lesson? Let me bring this chapter to a close by paying intellectual debts to two nineteenth century theologians who, like John Macmurray, represent an alternative tradition in Western intellectual life. The first – to show that there is theological life in England, too – is to Samuel Taylor Coleridge. Coleridge is a pivotal figure in the alternative tradition in Western thought. So far as I know, he is the first to

[36] John Zizioulas, 'The Ontology of Personhood', paper prepared, 1985, for the British Council of Churches' Study Commission on Trinitarian Doctrine Today, p. 9.
[37] Above, note 15.

have developed both a trinitarian understanding of God and a relational view of the human person. His concept of the person, as it emerges in the *Essay on Faith*, is relatively unformed, and convoluted even by his standards. But it is worth hearing his words because they echo some of the things we have heard and in their own way anticipate Macmurray's more accessible formulation:

> Now the third person could never have been distinguished from the first but by means of the second. There can be no He without a previous Thou. Much less could an I exist for us, except as it exists during the suspension of the will, as in dreams ... This is a deep mediation, though the position is capable of the strictest proof ...[38]

I shall not go into Coleridge's proof here, but move immediately to a dominating feature of his theological work. As Daniel Hardy and others have shown, a concern for the conditions of a rich and free personal life on earth is at the heart of Coleridge's preoccupation with trinitarian thought.[39] Who are we – the many; and who – or *what* – is the one to whom we owe our being? Upon the answer to the second question – the question about God – depends the answer to the first. Coleridge was concerned with the Trinity because he was concerned with the fashionable mechanical philosophy of his day, a philosophy which still underlies the worries of so many contemporary theologians. If the one, the reality which makes the world what it is, is not merely one – impersonal, mechanical, mere nature – but persons in relation, a unity of free *hypostases* taking their being and particularity from each other, then we may understand how it is that we have a world fit for the creation and redemption of persons. In other words, we learn from Coleridge not simply that there are analogies to be drawn from the divine to the human person, but that the question of the three in one is also the question of the kind of world we live in. We return to the question from the beginning

[38] S. T. Coleridge, 'Essay on Faith', in *Collected Works*, ed. W. G. T. Shedd, New York: Harper and Bros., 1853, Vol. 5, p. 559. See also Owen Barfield, *What Coleridge Thought*, Middletown, Connecticut: Wesleyan University Press, 1971, pp. 163–165.

[39] Daniel W. Hardy, 'Coleridge on the Trinity', *Anglican Theological Review* LXIX (1988), pp. 145–155.

of the chapter. Modern culture, as it is dominated by the individualism of the Enlightenment and the reaction against it, cannot find room for both the unity of mankind and the free, particular plurality of the many. We must therefore take seriously the thought of our alternative tradition, for it contains resources of inestimable value.

But it is not simply a matter of a quest for intellectual resources. The question also arises of the concrete means by which our human unity in plurality is to be realised. Here Coleridge is relatively weak because, like many a Western thinker, Augustine included, he is deficient in the incarnational dimensions of his theology (though he was not bound to be, given other features of his thought). Therefore my second debt is to his friend, Edward Irving. Irving held that the concrete link between the one and the many, the eternal God and his erring creation, is Jesus Christ, who is both the one and the many: the historic *hypostasis*, Jesus Christ, utterly human, tempted as we are; and yet through the Holy Spirit the basis from all eternity of a personal and communal relationship with God. The *cantus firmus* of Irving's christology, and, more than that, the intellectual and ontological basis of it, is a trinitarian conception of God, and indeed one owing more to the East than the West. It was his unerring grasp on the distinctive *hypostasis* of the eternal Son in relation to those of the Father and Spirit that enabled Irving to risk the daring christology for which he was condemned, but which now has so much to teach us.[40] It is the utter and complete self-giving of the eternal Word,

[40] Edward Irving, *The Collected Writings of Edward Irving*, Vol. V, ed. G. Carlyle, London: Alexander Strahan, 1865. The distinctiveness of the *hypostases* is seen in a passage like the following. 'He submits Himself to the Father to be made flesh; his Father sendeth the Holy Spirit to make him a body ... he came by that part, not through connection with Adam, but by his own free will, and his Father's free will, and the free will of the Holy Ghost ...' (p. 159). And yet nowhere does Irving approach tritheism. The incarnation takes place 'by creative act of Father, Son and Holy Ghost', while, more significantly, all that is done is the work of the Father, a mark of a duly conceived 'monarchy'. This is particularly evident in Irving's rejection of Western forms of atonement theory which separate the Father from the Son in their understanding of the cross: 'This most unsound view of the matter ... doth in effect make altogether void the Father's activity in the sufferings and death of Christ' (p. 147). See my 'Two Dogmas Revisited: Edward Irving's Christology', *Scottish Journal of Theology* 41 (1988), pp. 359–376, and now in *Theology Through the Theologians*, Edinburgh: T. & T. Clark, 1996, pp. 151–168.

obedient to the Father and dependent upon the Spirit, that makes the particular historic person, Jesus Christ, at the same time the way of the many to God. Thus Irving develops his christology of the one who is also the many by returning to the classical patristic theme that Coleridge had reworked for the modern age. The world and all in it takes its creation and recreation from the trinitarian relatedness of Father, Son and Spirit.

There remains one thing to be said, and it is intended to reinforce the conclusion of chapter two. If only a part of the argument is justified, trinitarian theology is interesting and important. We have suffered too long the paralysing effects of myth and projection theory and the years of positivist over-simplification, and must realise that theological factors influence at a deep level the products of human culture, not only philosophy, but also art and science. In this chapter, first given as an inaugural lecture, I have not sought to defend the teaching and research of Christian doctrine in a modern university. Who needs to be defensive about a discipline so rich in possibilities for intellectual exploration and debate? What I have sought to do, rather, is to show something of the way in which the immense riches of the Christian revelation and tradition may be brought to bear on matters of urgent and universal importance.

CHAPTER 6

THE HUMAN CREATION
Towards a renewal of the doctrine of the *Imago Dei*

I *Some problems of theological anthropology*

Two interrelated questions face the enquirer after a theological anthropology: the ontological and what can for want of a better term be called the comparative. The ontological question is the question about what kind of entity is the human, and has traditionally been answered in terms of a duality: of matter and spirit, body and soul, or the like; most radically perhaps in Descartes' famous dualism of intellectual mind and mechanical body. In Descartes, the ontological dimension is apparent: the human constitution reflects the dual structure of the universe as matter and (divine) idea. Mind, the godlike part of the person, is able by virtue of its equipment with innate ideas to comprehend by the use of pure reason the rational structure of the machine. In terms of anthropology, the outcome is that despite Descartes' attempts to show that his mind is more intimately related to his body than is a pilot to a ship, we are inescapably presented with the image of a mind pushing around a mechanical body. Ryle's characterisation of this as the 'ghost in the machine' is not so far from the mark.

The comparative enquiry concerns the way in which the human being is and is not like other entities supposed to people the universe: God on the one hand and, on the other, the non-human creation in all its various forms. The two questions are sometimes conflated, if not confused, by supposing that an argument for the distinctive ontology of the human might be derived from a comparison and contrast: by means of a quest for ways in which the human is different from other entities. Thus it might be held that God is infinite reason and the non-human creation is without reason, so that, on the one hand, the human is different from the divine by virtue of its finitude, and, on the other, from the non-human by virtue of its possession of reason. We are here very near to the traditional form of the doctrine of the image of God, which by being located in reason provides an answer to both of the questions with which we began. It is the possession of the image as reason which at once determines being and makes possible a comparative judgement both 'above' and below. Again, Descartes provides a fairly extreme example. The human mind, by virtue of its rationality, provides evidence both of a kind of image of God and at the same time a criterion of radical discontinuity from the rest of creation. The animals are merely machines, and it is said that some of the enlightened believed that their cries of pain were no more than the squeaks of unlubricated machinery.

But it is important to realise that the two questions do not have to be conflated. There are other ways of doing ontology than a process of speculative comparison and contrast: what Barth would call natural theology. Perhaps, as I shall argue, it is better to root contrast in ontology, and not the other way round. Moreover, it is in the long-lived tradition of rooting the image of God in reason that we see the deficiencies endemic in the tradition, deficiencies of which Descartes' anthropology provides but an example. A stress on reason elevates one characteristic of the human above others which have equal claim to consideration as part of our being. In particular, it encourages the belief that we are more minds than we are bodies, with all the consequences that that has: for example, in creating a non-relational ontology, so that we are cut off from each other and from the world by a tendency to see ourselves as imprisoned in matter. (Spelled out, the two dimensions would lead us into the problems of individualism and ecology.)

The weakness in theological anthropology which is now so often observed can, accordingly, be seen to derive from errors of both method and content. Historically, the roots of the syndrome can be found in Irenaeus, whose anthropology in other dimensions takes so different a direction. In his famous distinction between image and likeness there began the process of making reason both a chief ontological characteristic and a criterion of difference between human and non-human.[1] By the time of Aquinas the tendency had hardened into a dogma. Perhaps most revealing is his citation of John of Damascus: 'being after God's image signifies his capacity for understanding, and for making free decisions and his mastery of himself'.[2] While that definition has the merit of not limiting the image to reason, it is to be noted that all of the characteristics are static possessions of the human as individual, rather than (say) characteristics implying relation. There remains, too, the problematic nature of the human relation to the rest of creation.

The theological dimension of the problems can be discerned in Augustine. From the outset, there is in Augustine a tendency to develop anthropology in terms of neoplatonic categories. For him the human likeness to God must be in the mind or soul, so that other possibilities are excluded from the outset.[3] One implication is that our embodiedness cannot be the place where the image, and hence our true humanity, is found. That is a foreclosing of the ontological question which has a number of consequences. The first is a tendency to overstress the inner dimensions of the person. (I avoid here the words *intellectual* and *psychological* because their employment would prejudge questions about Augustine's meaning.)[4] The second is equally important. Augustine's quest for the Trinity within the soul, the inner Trinity, risks reducing the Trinity to theological irrelevance, for it becomes difficult to ask in what way the doctrine of the Trinity may in other ways throw light on the human condition. The heart of the matter is perhaps in the doctrine of relations. Since relations are qualifications of the inner Trinity, and not relations between persons, it becomes difficult to see how the triune relatedness can be brought to bear on the central question of human relatedness. God's relatedness is

---

[1] See Emil Brunner, *Man in Revolt. A Christian Anthropology*, E.T. by Olive Wyon, London: Lutterworth, 1939, p. 504.

[2] Aquinas, *Summa Theologiae*, 1a.93.5.

[3] See especially *De Trinitate* XI.

[4] That the same kind of anthropology is with us still is evident from the number of modern attempts to ground humanity in such features of our experience as consciousness, inwardness and subjectivity.

construed in terms of self-relatedness,[5] with the result that it is as an individual that the human being is in the image of God, and therefore truly human. The outcome is another, theologically legitimated, version of the tendency to individualism which arises in every dimension of what has been said so far.

II *Cosmologies and anthropologies*

It is considerations such as those outlined in the previous section that give credence to Barth's critique of the theological respectability of natural theology. Certain approaches to theological anthropology have as a matter of fact been foreclosed because of *a priori* philosophical decisions. The difficulty with Barth's approach, however, is that it leaves out certain stages of argument which seem to be advisable in the modern context if an appearance of authoritarianism is to be avoided. The time has therefore come to ask whether an approach that is different from either the traditional or the straighforwardly 'Barthian' can be attempted. The question can be approached indirectly, with the observation that different theories about the kind of entity that the world is bring in their train different conceptions of what it is to be human. That is to say, we can observe the way in which as a matter of fact cosmologies have been correlative with anthropologies. At its most simple level, the matter can be illustrated with the help of the distinction often made between Old Testament cosmologies and others of the Ancient Near East. While the latter tended to conceive the world as born from the womb of deity or developed from deity's defeated body – thus suggesting the at least potential deity of aspects of the world – the former, by distinguishing more definitely between God and what he had made, suggested a different view of the place of the human creature: more unified, and with fewer pretensions to deity. In later thought, a similar distinction emerges between broadly Greek and Hebrew views of the person.

[5] In that respect, Kierkegaard's anthropology bears many of the marks of Augustine. See *Sickness unto Death*, E.T. by Walter Lowrie, Princeton University Press, 1954, p. 147: 'by relating itself to its own self and by willing to be itself the self is grounded transparently in the power which posited it.'

While not wishing to give simplistic views of their distinction, I want to begin with an account of a general difference. In *The Greeks and the Irrational*, E. R. Dodds traces the origins of Greek cosmological anthropology to the myth of the Titans. These were the giants who slew, cooked and ate the body of the infant Dionysus. In revenge, Zeus slew the Titans, from whose smoking ruins there derived the human race. Underlying that legend are the roots of an essentially dualistic ontology which can be said to be almost universal in Greek thought and, through Augustine, though with qualifications, highly influential for Christian anthropology. The duality suggested is to be found on the one hand in the evil matter from which the human race arises; and from the fragment of deity deriving from the ingested divinity ('the horrid tendencies of the Titans, tempered by a tiny portion of divine soul-stuff').[6] Therein, undoubtedly is to be found the basis of the doctrine that the defining characteristic of humanity or the place of the image of God is reason.

A more developed philosophical treatment of the dualism is to be found in Plato. In the *Republic*'s discussion of the tripartite soul, Plato is not far from suggesting that embodiment is in itself a form of fallenness.[7] Physical desires and appetites are for the most part a bad thing, to be sternly controlled by reason. But for our purposes, the interesting discussion comes in the *Phaedo*. There we find the repeated assertion that the body is a prison, and death the liberation from it. The true philosopher abstains from pleasures and pains, each of which fastens the soul to the body with a kind of rivet, contaminating the soul in the process. Similarly, the soul is naturally immortal, because it resembles the divine, while the body resembles mortal things.[8] Overall, the message is clear: with a dualistic cosmology, a dualistic anthropology is likely to be correlative.

But it is a mistake simply to contrast a Greek dualism with a more Hebrew or unitary approach. Monism is a problem, too. Something more sophisticated and complex than a simple opposition is required, and that is why Carver Yu, whose recent

---

[6] E. R. Dodds, *The Greeks and the Irrational*, University of California Press, 1951, p. 155.

[7] Plato, *Republic*, 436ff.

[8] Plato, *Phaedo*, 83b, 80a.

diagnosis of Western individualism is so good, cannot solve the problem by simply opposing to it a biblical and relational ontology, as he tends to do in the final chapter of his book.[9] For a more subtle diagnosis of the possibilities we turn to Coleridge. In 'On the Prometheus of Aeschylus' he offers an immensely valuable threefold typology of world-views. There are, he says, three available cosmologies, not just two. (That is to say, he will not simply oppose 'Greek' and 'Hebrew', monist and dualist.) The first he calls the 'Phoenician'. According to this, 'the cosmogony was their theogony and *vice versa*'. That is to say, the origin of the cosmos and the origin of the divine are one and the same process. What emerges is a conception of the world as a kind of undifferentiated unity. We have an equation containing only two terms: 'a self-organising chaos' and '... nature as the result'.[10]

Moving on from Coleridge, or rather moving on to concerns he expressed in other writings than this, we might see in pantheism the typical modern version of this form of cosmology. According to Spinoza, for example, the coming to be of God and of the world are one and the same thing, except of course that in Spinoza's timeless system to speak of a cosmogony is perhaps not easy: nonetheless, his cosmogony is his theogony. The Coleridgean objection to such cosmologies can be seen in Spinoza's view that we can no more do other than we in fact do than the angles of a triangle can choose to be less or more than 180°. The outcome is the absolute necessitarian determinism that Coleridge saw to be enemy of human personality and freedom. Similarly, if we consider the description of the chaos as 'self-organising' we may think of the implications for anthropology of an effective divinisation of the process of evolution. The authoritarian tendency of some of Teilhard de Chardin's work has sometimes been suggested, and in this context we can see why. In a 'Phoenician' cosmology, the person is not separable from the world, and so lacks the space to be free.

[9] Carver T. Yu, *Being and Relation. A Theological Critique of Western Dualism and Individualism*, Edinburgh: Scottish Academic Press, 1987.
[10] Samuel Taylor Coleridge, 'On the Prometheus of Aeschylus', *Complete Works*, ed. W. G. T. Shedd, New York: Harper and Brothers, 1853, Vol. IV, pp. 353, 354f.

Coleridge's second cosmology, which he names the Greek, differs in that it has three rather than two terms. It is midway between the Phoenician and the Hebrew. It does assume a divinity 'antecedent to the matter of the world. But on the other hand it coincides with the Phoenician in considering this antecedent ground ... not so properly the cause of [corporeal matter], as the occasion and the still continuing substance. ... The corporeal was supposed co-essential with the antecedent of its corporeity.' That is where Prometheus comes into Coleridge's conception of things. The 'fire' Prometheus steals from heaven is mind, the 'form', the incipient or potential divinity, which shapes human nature. (A modernised equivalent, we might say, of the fragment of divinity remaining in the immolated Titans.) There are important and positive anthropological implications, of which Coleridge is aware: mind, being stolen from heaven, is 'no mere evolution of the animal basis', and reveals the distinction between the human and the other creation. But that, as we have seen, is also the beginning of danger. In some respects, as Coleridge points out, 'the Greek philosopheme does not differ essentially from the cosmotheism, or identification of God with the universe ...'.[11]

In general, the Greek cosmology has a number of problems. John Zizioulas has pointed one. 'In platonic thought the person is a concept which is ontologically impossible, because the soul, which ensures man's continuity, is not united permanently with the concrete "individual" man ...'.[12] Platonic thought cannot handle concrete relatedness: the godlike part of us excludes relations with others through the medium of our embodiedness, because our bodies *separate* what is really ourselves – the 'inner' – from others of us. (The concept of love in the *Symposium* is the logical outcome.) Similarly, the continuity with the divine that is implied brings problems for the divine-human relationship. As relations with other finite creatures are too distant through lack of relationship, here there is a danger that the relation will be too close. To be godlike in the wrong sense is a great burden, and the nature of the human image of the divine has to be handled very carefully

[11] Coleridge, op. cit., pp. 354 and 360.
[12] John D. Zizioulas, *Being as Communion. Studies in Personhood and the Church*, London: Darton, Longman and Todd, 1985, p. 28.

if the burden is to be avoided. We require space as well as relation: to be both related to and other than those and that on which we depend.[13]

III   *Space to be human: the Trinity*

Coleridge believes the Hebrew view of things to be related to the Greek, which, as we have seen, he regards as a mid-point between the Phoenician and Hebrew, but superior. It is, first of all, mathematically superior, in that it has four terms in contrast to the preceding two and three. (Coleridge was perhaps too enamoured of mathematics, but at least the point can be taken that the greater possibilities of the four term conceptuality allows for greater ontological richness and openness.) The four are as follows: the self-sufficient immutable creator; the antecedent night; the chaos; the material world resulting from the divine fiat. It is not very clear what is meant by all this, but some light can be shed by moving from the 'Prometheus' to a consideration of Coleridge's theology of the Trinity in general. That is to say, we reach the place where we must go beyond the general matter of celebrating the Hebrew over against other cosmologies, and ask more particularly about the doctrine of God.

The idea of the Trinity was for Coleridge the transcendental of transcendentals, that which served as the supreme mark, determinant perhaps, of being. The Trinity is 'that Idea Idearum, the one substrative truth which is the form, manner and involvement of all truths ...'.[14] Nor by 'idea' did he simply mean, as so many of his British predecessors had done, simply a mental construct or concept. As he shows in *On the Constitution of the Church and State*, an idea is antecedent to a conception, and has an (almost?) ontological status. It is, indeed, a kind of conception, but one 'which is not abstracted from any particular state, form, or mode, in which the thing may happen to exist at this or at that time; nor yet generalized from any

[13] I owe the concept of space used in this context to Daniel Hardy, 'Coleridge on the Trinity', *Anglican Theological Review* LXIX (1988), pp. 145–155.

[14] Coleridge, 'Notes on Waterland's Vindication of Christ's Divinity', *Complete Works*, op. cit, Vol. V, p. 407.

number or succession of such forms or modes; but which is given by the knowledge of *its ultimate aim*'. Interestingly for our purpose, Coleridge, in discussing one instance of idea, that 'of an ever-originating social contract', argues that it is dependent on 'the yet higher idea of person, in contra-distinction from *thing*...'.[15] Person is somewhere near the top of the hierarchy of ideas. Yet, remarkably, all such ideas are in some way or other subordinate to the transcendental of transcendentals, the Trinity.

In his paper 'Coleridge on the Trinity', Daniel Hardy has spelled out some of the developments in Coleridge's doctrine of the Trinity after the 'Prometheus' essay. Attempting to free himself from the 'restrictive notion of space-like being' to be found in that essay, Coleridge turned to the will as the clue to the Trinity. What he was seeking was a ground for reality without any of the anti-personal implications that follow from the rejected alternatives. Hardy quotes from the *Opus Maximum*: 'If then personeity, by which term I mean the source of personality, be necessarily contained in the idea of the perfect will, how is it possible that personality should not be an essential attribute of this will, contemplated as self-realized?'[16] The Augustinian and individualistic form of that formulation is manifest, but so also is its instinctive feeling for the right questions. Coleridge knew that if there was to be personality, there had to be both relatedness and space at once between God and the world and within the world between finite persons. He was not here concerned with narrowly pragmatic matters, but with the real, which 'had to be seen in its connection to its foundation'.[17] His quest for the idea of the Trinity was a quest for that which would enable him both to think the real and to show the bearing of that reality on life in the world. At the very least, there is a concern for conceptualising a kind of space between God and the world, a space in which personal freedom operates.

I have suggested by frequent use of the concept that under-

[15] Coleridge, *On the Constitution of the Church and State, The Collected Works of Samuel Taylor Coleridge*, ed. John Colmer, London: Routledge, 1976, Vol. 10, pp. 20, 12, 15.
[16] Hardy, op. cit., p. 155.
[17] Hardy, op. cit., p. 148.

lying Coleridge's schematism is a concern for space in which the human can be human. According to the Phoenician scheme, there is no space between God and the world, and so no human freedom. According to the kind of Hellenism we have viewed, the space is placed in the wrong place: between mind and matter, so that there is too little space between the human mind and God, too much between one person and another: space is here at the expense of relation. In the third, Hebrew, scheme, there is space, because of the freedom of the immutable God to create *ex nihilo*. But we need more than space. Indeed, from one point of view, space is the problem: individualism is the view of the human person which holds that there is so much space between people that they can in no sense participate in each other's being. There is clearly space and space, and our requirement now is to find a conception which is correlative with that of relation.

IV   *In the image of God*

On a more articulated account of the Trinity than Coleridge in practice allowed, we shall give prominence to the concept of the person rather than personeity. Only thus shall we avoid the monism that Coleridge so rightly feared, but risked by his emphasis on the will. *Person* is here difficult to define: if it is indeed one of those *ideas* which are logically primitive because they reflect what is ontologically primitive, that is what we should expect. Such concepts cannot be defined in other terms, because they are the *ideas*, and I continue to use the italics to indicate Coleridge's technical sense, in terms of which other concepts can and must be understood. But that is not to say that they can in no way be *thought*. They can, for example, be thought when they are found to be concretely instantiated in particular forms of life. Classically, they came to be thought *theologically* under the impact of the Christian gospel. As a result the Greek theologians came to understand God as a communion of persons, each distinct but inseparable from the others, whose being consists in their relations with one another. As Barth said, but in a rather different way, person means primarily what it means when it is used of God.[18] But before we take up this suggestion, asking what the theological concept of person contributes to the understanding of the finite person, we must first ask a preliminary question: how, in the light of Coleridge's third possibility, the trinitarian, are we enabled to see the world and human life within it? Is there here too a kind of cosmology within which anthropological possibilities may be articulated?

What flows from the conception of God as three persons in communion, related but distinct? First, there is something of the space we have been seeking. We have a conception of *personal space*: the space in which three persons are for and from each other in their otherness. They thus confer particularity upon and receive it from one another. That giving of particularity is very important: it is a matter of space to be. Father, Son and Spirit through the shape – the *taxis* – of their inseparable relatedness confer particularity and freedom on each other. That is their personal being.

What is the outcome when we turn in the light of such a doctrine of God to the theology of creation? Creation becomes understood as the giving of being to the other, and that includes the giving of space to be: to be other and particular. Much is made in recent cosmology of the singularity – particularity – of our universe. It is what it is and not another thing because of the unique conditions that give it the space-time shape that it has. But we should also note that recent science has much to say about the interrelatedness of all that is. We need not claim that such teaching necessarily derives from the doctrine of creation or even that it is in some way related to it, although claims, frequently made, that modern science is in some way causally related to the Christian doctrine of creation

---

[18] Karl Barth, *Church Dogmatics*, II/1, E.T. by G. W. Bromiley, Edinburgh: T. & T. Clark, 1975, p. 272. Compare Wolfhart Pannenberg, 'The Question of God', *Basic Questions in Theology*, Volume Two, E.T. by G. H. Kehm, London: SCM Press, 1971, p. 230: 'If the concept of the personal is originally based upon a religiously determined experience of reality ...' The famous and futile Western quest for analogies of the Trinity in the created world (such as those listed by Barth in *Church Dogmatics* I/1, pp. 343f) can in this light be understood as an attempt to follow up some of the possibilities of the logical primitiveness of trinitarian thinking. Their weakness is their employment as attempts to illustrate the divine Trinity: the world is used to throw light on God, rather than the other way round, so that attention falls on irrelevances like the number three rather than on the personal nature of the triune God.

may have some justification. (Note that some of Einstein's difficulties with quantum theory derived from his own rather Spinozistic concept of God.) The point is that the world's otherness from God is part of its space to be itself, to be finite and not divine. But as such it also echoes the trinitarian being of God in being what it is by virtue of its internal *taxis*: it is, like God, a dynamic of beings in relation.

Yet to claim creation's particularity and contingency, even its own kind of freedom, is not the same as to say that it is made in the image of God, unless with the philosophers of Process we are to conclude that those beings in relation are all in some sense personal. Rather, creation's non-personality means that it is unable to realise its destiny, the praise of its creator, apart from persons. It is not personal, but requires persons in order to be itself. That is why it awaits with eager longing the revealing of the children of God (Rom. 8.19). It is in some such context as this that we have to seek for the outlines of a theological anthropology.

One of the sources of recent controversy in cosmology has been the anthropic principle, which at the very least suggests a necessary relatedness of the cosmos to human intelligence. It would be a mistake to try to take this speculative principle to be evidence that the world is created for the production of human life, though that may as a matter of fact be the case. But at the very least, recent discussions encourage us to conceive a positive relation between human rationality and the structure of the universe. On its own, such an approach leads only to a repetition of the problematic which I outlined at the outset: of an attempt to read off from some naturally observed feature of the world a difference – and, indeed, a difference consisting in reason – between human and non-human, which then becomes definitive of the difference between not only the two but also the human and the divine. If, then, we are to pursue theologically the question of the way in which the cosmos provides a context for anthropology, further intermediate steps are needed in the argument.

To put the question another way: what in all this are we to make of the doctrine of the image of God? Given the rejection of the view that the image is to be found in reason, or any merely internal characterisation of the individual, there seem to be two recent contenders for the title, both dependent upon readings of the first two chapters of Genesis. The first locates it in the human stewardship of the creation.[19] There is much to be said for this approach, especially in view of the close relationship in Genesis between the creation of humankind and the command to shepherd the earth. Such a theology is, however, too literalistic and too restricted, especially in the light of the New Testament reorienting of the doctrine to Christ. Is the image of God as realised in Christ to be expressed in terms of his stewardship of the creation – indeed, part of the matter – or must other things also be said? We must here remember that the concept of image has in this respect very little biblical employment, and if it is to be used theologically must draw upon a wider range of biblical background than such explicit talk of image as there is in Scripture.

The second candidate for the interpretation of image interprets it with Genesis' 'male and female created he them'. Barth, famously, creatively and controversially pursued this approach, which was developed in somewhat less literalistic style by Derrick Sherwin Bailey.[20] The weaknesses of this approach, Barth's particularly, have often been pointed out. Two should be rehearsed. The first is its tendency to be binitarian: the anthropology reflects a Father-Son duality reflected in that of male and female, rather than expressing a theology of communion. That is not to say that there is nothing of anthropology of communion in Barth. The anthropology of mutuality in *Church Dogmatics* III/2 is immensely illuminating, as are many of the things he says about man-woman relations, despite their unpalatability to a certain kind of feminism. The second weakness is a tendency to anthropocentrism in Barth. Andrew Linzey's analysis of Barth's treatment of the creation sagas has shown that Barth underplays the way in which Genesis brings the non-human creation into the covenant.[21] We need more

[19] Hans Walter Wolff, *Anthropology of the Old Testament*, E.T. by Margaret Kohl, London: SCM Press, 1974, ch. xviii; Douglas John Hall, *Imaging God. Dominion as Stewardship*, Grand Rapids: Eerdmans, 1986.

[20] Barth, *Church Dogmatics* III/1 and Derrick Sherwin Bailey, *The Man–Woman Relation in Christian Thought*, London: Longmans, 1959, pp. 268ff.

[21] Andrew Linzey, 'The Neglected Creature. The Doctrine of the Non-human Creation and its Relation with the Human in the Thought of Karl Barth', PhD, University of London, 1986.

than an extended exegesis of Gen. 1.26f, and in particular a broader treatment of the topic, if we are really to make more satisfactory use of the concept of the *imago dei*.

Where, then, is the image of God to be found? Interesting about the two alternatives we have reviewed is that while one of them relates humankind to the cosmos, the other is chiefly concerned with relations within the human species. It is an unsatisfactory theological anthropology which requires a choice between the two, which are both right insofar as they discern in relatedness a clue to the solution of the problem. The weakness of both approaches can be obviated by finding a concept which bases them – and any other dimensions – in a theological ontology. Insofar as we are concerned with human being and not particular qualities or tasks there is a missing conceptual link to be found: it is, of course, that of the person. To be made in the image of God is to be endowed with a particular kind of personal reality. To be a person is to be made in the image of God: that is the heart of the matter. If God is a communion of persons inseparably related, then surely Barth is thus far correct in saying that it is in our relatedness to others that our being human consists.

That relatedness takes shape in a double orientation. In the first place, we are persons insofar as we are in right relationship to God. Under the conditions of sin, that means, of course, insofar as the image is reshaped, realised, in Christ. But since we are here enquiring about human createdness, we shall leave that in the background, as a very real background, nevertheless. The relation to God takes shape through the Son and the Spirit. To be in the image of God is to be created through the Son, who is the archetypal bearer of the image. To be in the image of God therefore means to be conformed to the person of Christ. The agent of this conformity is God the Holy Spirit, the creator of community. The image of God is then that being human which takes shape by virtue of the creating and redeeming agency of the triune God.

The second orientation is the 'horizontal' one, and is the outcome of the work of the first. What is the shape that the image of God takes in time? The human person is one who is created to find his or her being in relation, first with other like persons but second, as a function of the first, with the rest of the creation. This means, first, that we are in the image of God when, like God but in dependence on his giving, we find our reality in what we give to and receive from others in human community. One way into the content of the image, its concrete realisation, is through the concept of love. It seems likely that we shall be content here neither with the unitive concept of love which has tended to reign in the West, nor with the strong reaction signalled in Nygren's one-sided assertion of agape against eros. While it seems to me that agape does indeed reflect the biblical expression of the divine self-giving in Christ, to stress that alone can lead to an almost individualistic unrelatedness. Barth here is better when he sees our humanity as realised in the mutual giving and receiving of assistance with gladness.[22]

But if we are to speak of realising our being in relations, something more than that has to be said. Of crucial importance is the matter of the way in which the structure – the *taxis* – of human community constitutes the particularity, uniqueness and distinctness of persons: their free otherness in relation. To be a person is to be constituted in particularity and freedom – to be given space to be – by others in community. *Otherness* and *relation* continue to be the two central and polar concepts here. Only where both are given due stress is personhood fully enabled. Their co-presence will rule out both the kind of egalitarianism which is the denial of particularity, and leads to collectivism, and forms of individualism which in effect deny humanity to those unable to 'stand on their own feet'.

It is important also to realise that this being in the image of God will embrace both what we have been used to call spiritual and our bodiliness. The merit of the approach to anthropology by means of the concept of person is that it relativises so many inherited dualisms. Relations are of the whole person, not of minds or bodies alone, so that from all those created in the image of God there is something to be received, and to them something to be given. When the image is located in reason, or for that matter in any internal qualification like consciousness, problems like those of 'other minds' are unavoidable. The person as a being in relation is one whose materiality is in no

---

[22] Karl Barth, *Church Dogmatics*, III/2, pp. 265ff.

way *ontologically* problematic, whatever problems derive from the way in which we relate in actual fact to others.

The contention that our realising of the image of God embraces our embodiedness as much as our intellect and 'spirituality' leads into the further point that we are not human apart from our relation with the non-personal world. Much current misuse of the creation, with its attendant ecological disasters, derives from a lack of realisation of human community with the world. It is not the same kind of community, that of equals, as that with which we were concerned when speaking of the community of persons. But it is a fact that we receive much of what we are from the world in which we are set and from whose dust we come. It is the context within which we become persons, and it, too, is in a kind of community with us, being promised a share in the final reconciliation of all things. Although it is not itself personal, the non-human creation is bound up with that of the human, and depends upon us for its destiny. It is not something we stand over against in the sense that it is at our arbitrary disposal, as 'technocracy' assumes. It is rather, to use Polanyi's metaphor, the reality which we indwell bodily, intellectually and spiritually. Here, being in the image of God has something to do with the human responsibility to offer the creation, perfected, back to its creator as a perfect sacrifice of praise. It is here that are to be found the elements of truth in the claims that the image of God is to be found in the human stewardship of the creation.

In all of this, John Zizioulas' point that *person* is an eschatological concept must constantly be borne in mind. To say that is to say that personhood is being that is to be realised, and whose final realisation will come only when God is all in all. And yet, as Graham McFarlane has argued, that need not be taken to undermine the fact that it is also, and without inconsistency, a protological concept.[23] It is a way of conceptualising the origins of human being in the creating goodness of God, though without prejudice to the dynamic orientation of this being to a purposed end. Irenaeus' theory that Adam and Eve were

[23] Graham McFarlane, 'Strange News from Another Star. An Anthropological Insight from Edward Irving', *Persons, Divine and Human. King's College Essays in Theological Anthropology*, edd. Colin E. Gunton and Christoph Schwöbel, Edinburgh: T. & T. Clark, 1991.

created childlike is not in every way satisfactory, but it does suggest that human life in the image of God is human life directed to an end. The image is not a static possession, but comes to be realised in the various relationships in which human life is set. The New Testament's reorientation of the concept to Jesus makes the point well. It is because Jesus is 'the image of the invisible God' that God is 'through him to reconcile all things, whether on earth or in heaven ...' (Col. 1.15, 20). The one through whom all was created is also the means of the re-establishment of the image in humanity. The image, therefore, created through the Word and in the Spirit, has in like manner to be realised through them, between the resurrection of Jesus and his return in glory.

V   *Conclusion*

The chapter began with the linking of two questions: the ontological and the comparative. What kind of being is the human? In what ways is the human species like and unlike God? We have come to answers rather unlike those of much of the tradition. *Ontologically*, it has been argued that where the latter tended to stress the non-bodily, a trinitarian theology will stress the relations which involve all dimensions of our reality. Where the tradition tended to see our imagedness to consist in the possession of certain faculties, here the stress is on the ontology of personhood. To be in the image of God is at once to be created as a particular kind of being – a person – and to be called to realise a certain destiny. The shape of that destiny is to be found in God-given forms of human community and of human responsibility to the universe.

The *comparative* question also finds a different kind of answer. Human difference from the rest of the creation does not lie in some absolute ontological distinction, but in an asymmetry of relation, and therefore a relative difference. As created beings, human persons are bound up closely with the fate of the rest of the material universe, as stewards rather than absolute lords. And the difference between God and those made in his image? The interesting point now is that the question of our difference from and likeness to God becomes less pressing. It is not found in some structural difference, but in the most basic one of all: God is the creator, we are of his creation. The triune God has created humankind as finite persons-in-relation who are called to acknowledge his creation by becoming the persons they are and by enabling the rest of the creation to make its due response of praise.

CHAPTER 7

IMMANENCE AND OTHERNESS

Divine sovereignty and human freedom in the theology of Robert W. Jenson

I *Freedom in the Reformation tradition*

A Christian is a perfectly free lord of all, subject to none.
A Christian is a perfectly dutiful servant of all, subject to all.[1]

Luther's famous paradox can form our starting point, if only because it is in such manifest contradiction of the wisdom of our age, which in truly undialectical fashion prefers to accept the first without the second, and, indeed, that without its basis in the gospel. We prefer to find freedom grounded in ourselves rather than lying in the gift of the creator. Beneath the surface of Luther's formulation, however, there lies far more than an appealing paradox: there is a theology of human life under God. It has at least two dimensions. The first is to be found in another much quoted dictum, that we are not born for freedom: we must be slaves either of God or of the devil. Freedom, that is to say, is not an innate possession – quite the reverse – but has to be given. The gospel is a gospel because it is a setting free, from the slavery that is indeed slavery to the slavery which is the freedom of the Christian. There is for Luther no freedom without redemption through grace from the law, sin, death and the devil.

The second dimension is that in which the liberation is spelled out, and is the subject of a recent study by Eberhard Jüngel.[2] Jüngel's aim in his short treatise is to defend Luther

---

[1] Martin Luther, *The Freedom of a Christian*. In *Three Treatises*, Philadelphia: Fortress, 1960, p. 277.

[2] Eberhard Jüngel, *Zur Freiheit eines Christenmenschen. Eine Erinnerung an Luthers Schrift*, München: Christian Kaiser, 1987.

against charges that his is a dualistic and non-worldly conception of freedom, and in particular against the criticism which holds that it leads to social unfreedom (pp. 61ff). Against criticisms of that kind, Jüngel argues that when Luther speaks of freedom as a qualification of the inner rather than the outer person, he does not mean that it has nothing to do with our outward social reality. It is not a doctrine of pure inwardness, but a way of showing how our freedom has to be seen as a liberation which takes place by the action of God 'from within'. Its basis is a movement from old to new by virtue of our relation to Christ. Faith is dependent upon the prior 'joyful exchange' in Christ, which it receives and ratifies (p. 88). He is the king and priest who, far from lording it over his subjects, makes them into kings and priests themselves. That is their liberation, which then gives rise to those 'outer' acts which are the service of others.

This means that Christian liberty is, so to speak, completed by its orientation to the neighbour. There is, Jüngel claims, no individualism here, but talk of 'the societal structure of the Christian life' (p. 108). However, in Jüngel's exposition of what this means, the content is rather exiguous. Apart from Luther's claim that we are now able to see the neighbour as Christ, and a citation from Gollwitzer saying the same thing in rather more words, no content is given to the allusion to the societal structure, and it has to be said that such appears to be of relatively small moment in Luther's theology.

When we come to Calvin, the matter is more formalised, but clearly in much the same tradition. Calvin shares with Luther a strong doctrine of the bondage of the will, which is fiercely articulated without concession to secular conceptions of freedom as indifference. He also shares a view that freedom is the gift of God and in particular the fruit of justification, so that it is treated as an 'appendix' of justification.[3] Therefore the first of the three 'parts' of freedom consists in the freedom from seeking justification through the law, a freedom Calvin articulates with extended use of the Letter to the Galatians (ibid. xix.2f). The second part of Christian freedom runs parallel with that which Jüngel found in Luther, and it consists in the inner

---

[3] John Calvin, *Institutes of the Christian Religion*, III.xix.1.

transformation which results from the new relation to God in Christ, so 'that consciences ... voluntarily obey the will of God' (xix.4). 'Christian liberty is in all its parts a spiritual matter, the whole force of which consists in giving peace to trembling consciences ...' (xix.9).

The third part does not concern us here, but something does need to be said about that *skandalon* of later Calvinist history, the doctrine of predestination. It should be observed that Calvin treats of election in the chapters almost immediately following those on justification and freedom. It, too, serves the cause of human liberation, because in expounding it 'the apostle attributes all to the mercy of the Lord, and leaves nothing to our wills and exertions' (xxiv.1). It is another of the doctrines whose function is to turn our eyes to God, the source of our freedom from the law:

> But if we are elected in him, we cannot find the certainty of our election in ourselves; and not even in God the Father, if we look at him apart from the Son. Christ, then, is the mirror in which we ought, and in which, without deception, we may contemplate our election (xxiv.5).

When it comes to the exposition of the nature of freedom, Calvin will, no more than Luther, limit his doctrine to merely inward or religious matters. The chapter with which we are concerned spends much time on the resulting behaviour to the neighbour.[4] It must be remembered also that Calvin had an interest in the political dimensions of freedom. In the final chapter of the *Institutes,* in which he articulates some of the social and political implications of his theology, Calvin's discussion is far more nuanced than is sometimes noticed, and certainly far more so than are some recent political theologies. Not needing to look over his shoulder at Marxists anxious to accuse him of quietism, he is happy to assert that 'spiritual liberty is perfectly compatible with civil servitude' (IV.xx.1). Yet this is not to suggest that the kingdom of God and worldly

---

[4] Calvin's concern for the social implications of the law of God is evident in, for example, his exposition of the eighth commandment. The commandment not to steal has a positive function, and 'obligates us to care for others' good'; 'to make only honest and lawful gain; ... not ... to become wealthy through injustice, not ... to strive to heap up riches cruelly wrung from the blood of others ...' (II.vii.46).

politics are in no relation to each other. Indeed, political liberty is one of the things for which magistrates are responsible in Calvin's scheme of things: 'there is no kind of government happier than where liberty is framed with becoming moderation ...' (xx.8).

In both Luther and Calvin, then, the source of freedom is the liberation that only a sovereign God can give. Even the form of what they have to say has much in common, despite Höpfl's view that liberty was of less importance to Calvin than to the other Reformers.[5] Most significant, perhaps, for the parallel with Luther is Calvin's tendency to conceive freedom in terms of inner and outer:

> There is a twofold government in man: one aspect is spiritual, whereby the conscience is instructed in piety; the second is political, whereby man is educated for the duties of humanity and citizenship ... These are usually called the 'spiritual' and 'temporal' jurisdiction ... by which is meant that the former sort of government pertains to the life of the soul, while the latter has to do with the concerns of the present life. ... Now these two, as we have divided them, must always be examined separately; and while one is being considered, we must call away and turn aside the mind from thinking about the other (III.xix.15).

It is in that latter feature that the problems are to be found. Despite Calvin's political concerns, and despite the defence which Jüngel makes against the less subtle dismissals of Luther's views, there seem to me to be three closely related areas in which that dualism of inner and outer does betray serious theological weakness. They are all a function of the West's Augustinian heritage. What seems to have happened is that the Reformers drew upon aspects of Augustinian thought to equip them to face the urgent need of the day, the reappropriation of a liberty deriving from the gospel in face of the contemporary tendency to Pelagianism. While it would be unjust to expect them to have solved all the accompanying problems, we can

---

[5] Harro Höpfl, *The Christian Polity of John Calvin*, Cambridge University Press, 1982, p. 35. This statement is rather odd in view of the fact that one of the only six chapters of the 1536 edition of the *Institutes* bears the title 'Christian Freedom, Ecclesiastical Power, and Political Administration'.

with benefit of hindsight see that other dimensions of their Augustinianism bequeathed serious problems for future generations.

The first concerns the relative individualism of both of their formulations. As has already been suggested in connection with Luther, very little attention is paid to the way in which freedom might be conceived to take shape in community. That, of course, is a pneumatological concern, and there is in Calvin's chapter on freedom very little direct reference to the Holy Spirit, in surprising contrast to other areas of his theology. The weakness can best be seen in the above extended quotation from Calvin. Is there really no link to be made between the spiritual freedom of the Christian and the liberty in which people are for and with each other in society? If the Holy Spirit is truly the creator of community wherever it is to be found, should it not be possible to say something about the way in which Christian freedom and political liberty may be supposed to bear upon each other?[6]

The second area concerns the way Christian liberty involves our embodiedness, our concrete reality as material. It is the same weakness viewed in another dimension. Too much stress on our spiritual natures – where 'spiritual' tends to mean 'inward' rather than 'in relation to God the Holy Spirit', however carefully that inwardness is qualified, as Jüngel shows Luther's conception to be – will lose sight of the fact that we are related to one another through the medium of our bodies. In this respect, there is, it seems to me, a tendency to spiritualising to be found in both of the Reformers, and that is why the questions must inevitably appear to be different in the times after the Enlightenment. Is there not something lacking in the Reformation legacy – deriving perhaps from Augustine's platonism – which later led to the feeling that an important element, particularly that concerning the material and social dimensions of human living, had been omitted?

---

[6] Here, too, care is required. As Christoph Schwöbel has pointed out to me, there are to be found in the early Luther indications of a less dualistic and individualistic theology. A good account is to be found in Martin Rade, 'Der Sprung in Luthers Kirchenbegriff und die Entstehung der Landeskirche', *Ausgewählte Schriften*, Band 3, ed. Christoph Schwöbel, Gütersloh: Gerd Mohn, 1988, pp. 151–166.

A similar theological concern underlies the third point. Does not the discussion of freedom largely in terms of justification, or more generally in terms of redemption or salvation rather than of creation, predispose to a 'spiritualising' of the concept? Of course, the order of salvation must bulk large in view of the fact that human people by sin enter a state of slavery. The Reformers are right to hold that we are not free unless we are set free. But, even allowing for that, should it not be possible to conceive our freedom as a function of our *createdness*, of the relation we have to our creator by virtue of being made in the image of God, for example? Such an approach can itself succumb to a 'spiritualising' tendency. But if it is remembered that the doctrine of creation has much to say about the human continuity with the rest of the world in which we are set, the outcome is less likely to be a spiritualising of redemption as a process in which the Christian is taken out of the world into a 'religious' sphere. And that takes me to the real subject of the chapter.

Robert Jenson is, as he once remarked – thus giving me the idea for the topic of the chapter – a Lutheran who has devoted a good proportion of his theological life to the exposition of the thought of two Reformed theologians. In the process, he has engaged, from a position firmly within it, with the weaknesses of the Reformation tradition: with the bearings of theology on human political reality, especially in relation to American social life; with the implications of the gospel for the concrete human person as embodied;[7] with the positive relation between creation and redemption; and, in all his work, with the perils of a false spiritualising of reality. Time will not permit all of these dimensions to be treated in one chapter, although we shall constantly stumble across aspects of them. But I hope that by taking a central topic, the doctrine of the God of the gospel and the conception of human freedom to emerge in its light, we shall be able to go to the heart of the matter.

[7] See especially *Visible Words. The Interpretation and Practice of Christian Sacraments*. Philadelphia: Fortress Press, 1978, pp. 21–25. It must always be remembered that if we are *related* to other persons, it is through the medium of our bodies. Without that emphasis, there is bound to be an individualistic conception of the person, because our embodiedness becomes a barrier between one person and another. Community is, as we learn from the Trinity, of persons in relation, and freedom a function of that community: when persons give to and receive from each other the space to be themselves.

II   *The God of the gospel*

We begin with one aspect of Jenson's theology which has close
links to the common Reformation tradition: a concern for
freedom conceived as freedom from the bondage of the law.
That theme is treated by him in a characteristically modern
way, and here Karl Barth is the catalyst. One of the best known,
and disputed, features of Barth's *Commentary on Romans* is that
wherein Paul's critique of the law is interpreted as a critique of
religion. The law from whose bondage we need to be freed by
the God of the gospel is religion, by which is meant a certain
kind of human enterprise in face of the world. It is an
appropriate theme for one who is a self-consciously American
theologian to adopt. Religiosity is America's, and also her
church's, modern slavery: 'a different divine offering on every
street corner'. Religion functions as the law that enables us to
evade the just demands of God. Therefore: 'the Western
Church must either renew its trinitarian consciousness, or
experience increasing impotence and confusion'.[8] On such a
view of things, one major dimension of freedom is liberation
from religion by means of the trinitarian gospel.

But that is not the only way in which Jenson's theology can
claim direct descent from the Reformers' theology of freedom.
It is also possible to observe, from the very beginning of his
theological writing, the development of a theme parallel to that
of the Lutheran paradox with which we began. It is that
wherein human freedom is located within a strong assertion of
the lordship of God over history. In *Alpha and Omega* the
critique of Barth centres on his inadequate treatment of
predestination. 'Our topic is God's control of history. That
is what is meant by "predestination".'[9] But, the criticism
implies, the way in which Barth loads everything on to a pre-
temporal electing decision has its problems. These centre on
the question of the relation of creation and reconciliation, but
clearly the matter of freedom is not far from the centre of

[8] *The Triune Identity. God According to the Gospel.* Philadelphia: Fortress Press,
1982, p. ix. See also 'The Triune God'. *Christian Dogmatics*, edd. C. E. Braaten
and R. W. Jenson, Philadelphia: Fortress Press, 1984, Vol. I, pp. 83–191.
[9] *Alpha and Omega. A Study in the Theology of Karl Barth.* New York: Thomas
Nelson & Sons, 1963, p. 141.

interest. Here two points can be made with the help of later works.

The first is Jenson's realisation that the doctrine of predestination, for all of its current rejection by the unthinking, is liberating, in the sense that it liberates human effort. 'Given Christianity's record of legalisms, it is hard to credit but it is true nevertheless: the gospel's specific morality is a morality of *freedom*.' And the freedom is bound up with election: 'Modern denominations descended from the Calvinists have gotten over such theological hard sayings as double predestination – and have also gotten over any world-transforming energies.'[10] The second is that election's modern historical contradiction, Arminianism – in Jenson's understanding the denial of the divine lordship of history – is at the heart of America's present day problems:

> Broadly, 'Arminianism' was New England's name for a kind of religion that appears in all times and places of the church, and has other times been known as 'semi-Pelagianism,' 'synergism,' etc. 'Arminianism' is our self-serving interpretation of human responsibility over against God's mercy, according to which if we are blessed it is at least partly because we have chosen and labored to be, while when we suffer God is suddenly invoked for our unilateral rescue. But what Edwards called 'Arminianism' should also be seen as a somewhat more specific phenomenon, the peculiarly American form of this religion ... in Bonhoeffer's phrase, 'Protestantism without the Reformation.'
>
> Edwards' 'Arminianism' was the Christian version ... of the American culture religion.[11]

Arminianism, then, is the religion of those who 'find a doctrine of total dependence on God's will uncongenial' (p. 55); or, we might say, of those who prefer a 'secular' conception of freedom to the kind of concept we have found in Luther and Calvin. Against this Edwards asserted not only the doctrine of justification in something like traditional Reformation form,

[10] *Story and Promise. A Brief Theology of the Gospel about Jesus.* Philadelphia: Fortress Press, 1973, pp. 81, 84.
[11] *America's Theologian. A Recommendation of Jonathan Edwards.* New York and Oxford: Oxford University Press, 1988, pp. 53f.

but a God whose lordship of history is unequivocal. Jenson
introduces his discussion of this aspect of Edwards' theology
with a summary of his own:

> Throughout Christian history, it is the linked doctrines of
> providence and election by which God's actuality is insisted
> upon. To know that all things, and particularly human
> creatures' destinies, happen within the will of God, and to
> believe that there is indeed and in fact God, are obviously the
> same thing exactly – at least, if with 'God' we refer to
> anything like what the Bible refers to with that word. ... [I]t
> is the doctrines of providence and election in which also the
> offence of God's actuality is most immediate (p. 99).

American political thought is almost unanimously opposed to
such a theology: it has gone Arminian. We do not need to go
into the detail of Jenson's subtle defence of Edwards' thought
against the kind of over-simplification it suffers in its popular
understanding. The chief point here is to note the continuity of
thought between *Alpha and Omega* and *America's Theologian*,
twenty-five years apart as they are. What is presented is a
doctrine of the sovereignty and priority of God over against the
comfortable accommodations of modernity. And that is precisely Edwards' relevance. Now that the '"heavenly city of the
eighteenth-century philosophers" has broken walls', Edwards'
God comes into his own: '"after Auschwitz" the merely moral
universe and its gentlemanly God are simply and trivially
implausible' (p. 110).

It is also to be observed, of course, that one of Edwards' great
expositions of the theme comes in a treatise on the freedom of
the will. Aspects of that work will come into view later. But this
section on the sovereignty of God must end with a return to
Barth, between whom and Edwards Jenson sees some community of interest (p. 106). The point of turning now to *God After
God*, Jenson's second book on Barth, is that it brings to the fore
the eschatological dimensions of our subject, for that is where
Jenson seeks a doctrine of God which will encompass a 'reli-
gionless' theology of sovereignty. The book's subtitle gives the
clue to the its direction: 'the God of the past and the God of the
future, seen in the work of Karl Barth'. The questions to Barth
concern the way in which the sovereignty of God is conceived.

Simply expressed, as the discussion of predestination in *Alpha and Omega* has already shown, it is a matter of whether its orientation is to the past or the future. The contention of the later book on Barth is that there is something in the *Church Dogmatics* that compels us to read it as 'the most perfect eternalizing yet achieved of the gospel's themes and story', although we are reading it wrongly if we do so.[12] That is to say, there is in Barth a tendency to conceive all the effective divine agency to have taken place 'already' in timeless eternity.

Both the problem and Jenson's proposed alternative are found in the doctrine of the Trinity. Barth's weakness is to be traced to his postulating 'a reality of God in himself distinct from God-for-us'. There is a legitimate theological reason for the distinction between the immanent and economic Trinity, insofar as it represents an attempt to establish the freedom of God.[13] The error in the distinction is that, certainly in Barth's hands, it re-establishes the very relation between time and eternity that is the essence of religion. In Barth, the weakness emerges in the concept of the eternal Trinity as the prototype of the temporal manifestation of God. 'Such a comparison can only be between timelessness and time' (p. 153). The notion of analogy between time and eternity must therefore be dropped, and instead 'We will have to understand the radicalness of God's temporality as a certain pattern of that temporality itself.'[14]

The resurrection of Jesus of Nazareth from the dead is the heart of Jenson's reformulated doctrine of the Trinity, because what he believes to be required is a shift in orientation from past – that timeless eternity into whose embrace religion invites us – to future. If God is conceived to exercise his sovereignty from open future rather than closed past, the whole doctrine of God is changed. The reformulation brings about a closer relation of God to time and history: 'the Trinity is simply the

[12] *God After God. The God of the Past and the God of the Future, Seen in the Work of Karl Barth*, Indianapolis and New York: Bobbs-Merrill, 1969, p. 152.

[13] 'The Triune God', p. 154. We shall see later that more than the freedom of God is at stake.

[14] *God After God*, p. 155. An important discussion of the development of the analogy between time and eternity, with particular reference to Origen and Aquinas, is to be found in Jenson's *The Knowledge of Things Hoped For. The Sense of Theological Discourse*, New York: Oxford University Press, 1969.

Father and the man Jesus and their Spirit as the Spirit of the believing community. This "economic" Trinity is *eschatologically* God "himself," an "immanent" Trinity' ('The Triune God', p. 155). As a consequence, the being of God is conceived in direct relation to the saving history that is Jesus of Nazareth. 'The "a person" that God is, is the human person Jesus, the Son. The triune event that God is, is by its triunity a person, this one. ... We will say, all there is to being God the Father is being addressed as "Father" by the Son, Jesus; all there is to being God the Spirit is being the spirit of this exchange' (pp. 170f). Jenson rejects all doctrines of a *logos asarkos*, a ' "not (yet) incarnate Word," ', Jesus' metaphysical double' as a collapse into timelessness. 'Instead of interpreting Christ's deity as a separate entity that always *was* – and proceeding analogously with the Spirit – we should interpret it as a final outcome, and just so eternal, just so as the bracket around all beginnings and endings' (p. 155). How goes it with human freedom in such a context?

III   *God, otherness and freedom*

Freedom is to be found in the space in which persons can be themselves in relation with other persons. That is the lesson of the doctrine of the Trinity. Father, Son and Spirit constitute each other as free persons by virtue of the shape their inter-relationship takes in the trinitarian perichoresis. Otherness is an essential feature of the trinitarian freedom, because without otherness the distinctness, particularity, of a person is lost. But, in trinitarian terms, the otherness is not the freedom of the *individual* – a freedom *from* others, as we so often make it in the West – because it is a freedom that is a function of relatedness: it is given and received, because personal being is constituted by relatedness. We should say, then, that the essence *of* the being in relation that is the Trinity is the *personal space* that is received and conferred.

Does Robert Jenson appropriate in his own theology the full significance of the trinitarian revolution? An approach to that question will be the burden of this section of the chapter. He undoubtedly recognises the extent of the achievement of the early trinitarian theologians: 'The doctrine of the Trinity was the creation, if one will, of a *new ontology* of "God" on the basis of the gospel. The doctrine of the Trinity is the ancient church's victory over the timeless Presence of Greek religion ...' (*God After God*, p. 47). What he does not say so much about is its contribution to the concept of the person, and that may be more crucial to the whole topic with which we are concerned than he everywhere realises. We approach the question through the concept of space.

For there to be freedom, there must be space. In terms of the relation between God and the universe, this entails an ontological otherness between God and the world. The necessity for ontological otherness is best illustrated in Coleridge's attempts to extricate himself from the mechanistic and pantheistic cosmologies which he believed to be the enemies of human freedom. Kierkegaard once observed that the only real alternative to Christianity is pantheism,[15] and Coleridge's view was very similar. Atheism and deistic mechanism are in effect identical with pantheism, for all of them swallow up the many into the one, and so turn the many into mere functions of the one.[16] There is, that is to say, no basis in any such unitary conception of God for freedom because there is in it no space between God and the world. Putting it another way, we can say that the logic of all unitarian thought is immanentist in the sense that it finally brings God and the creation too closely together: either the world is swallowed up in deity, or its reality is the logical, and so necessitated, outcome of the way God is. By contrast, the doctrine of the Trinity allows for such space because it enables us to conceive the world as other than, while yet in relation to God. It thus generates a conception of contingency, in both senses of the word: the contingency of the

---

[15] Soren Kierkegaard, *Concluding Unscientific Postscript*, E.T. by D. F. Swenson and W. Lowrie, Princeton University Press, 1941, p. 202. Kierkegaard's words could have been designed for the argument of this chapter: 'For the only consistent position outside Christianity is that of pantheism, the taking oneself out of existence by way of recollection into the eternal, whereby all existential decisions become a mere shadow-play beside what is eternally decided from behind.'

[16] S. T. Coleridge, 'Notes on Waterland's Vindication of Christ's Divinity'. *Complete Works*, edited by W. G. T. Shedd, New York: Harper and Brothers, 1853, Vol. 5, pp. 404–416 (pp. 405f).

world on God, and its contingent, non-necessary reality: a kind of ordered freedom which in turn becomes the basis for the human freedom which is the concern of this chapter.

For there to be *human* freedom, there needs be something more than this, what I have already called *personal* space. This, too, is the gift of God the creator, because, in distinction from but relation to the rest of the created order, the human species is made in the image of God: that is, is created to exist in the freedom that is being in relatedness, in community. The notion of freedom as realised in community is by no means absent from the theology of Robert Jenson. It emerges in a remark made in connection with Jonathan Edwards. '*Freedom of the Will* diagnoses in advance the pathology of any society in which freedom becomes freedom *from* the community' (p. 143). Moreover, there is an echo in his thought of the essentially trinitarian notion that freedom and the distinctness of particularity mutually require one another. Father, Son and Spirit are equally God, while expressing their divinity in different functions, and so, from one point of view, unequally. As if on this basis, Jenson rejects with Edwards' help certain features of modern individualistic egalitarianism which involve a false conception of freedom. 'Gifts and authorities of different sort and equal weight, and of the same sort and unequal weight establish the community's freedom by their mutual interplay' (p. 142). The matter is that of 'equality without egalitarian myths' (p. 153). Similarly, he asks: '. . . can faith, interpreted as an event exclusively between God and each soul separately, be plausibly presented also as the base of humans' true community with each other?' (p. 176). That, as we saw, is a question to be asked of the great Reformers also.

There is, however, yet more to say about the nature of human freedom in community: and in particular that it is an eschatological reality, in that it consists in realising that otherness in relationship of one person to another that is the life of the age to come. The gospel promises anticipations of that future reality in the here and now; and the agent of that community of the free is the eschatological Spirit who, by relating us to the Father through the Son, brings us into communion with each other. Now, it is important in all this to realise that the Holy Spirit is not some immanent and impersonal causal force but a free and personal other. To make some such point was the burden of the critical aspects of Jenson's treatise on the Holy Spirit in *Christian Dogmatics.* Because Augustine held, he argues, that the three persons of the Trinity were 'functionally indistinguishable', he was unable to give form to a truly trinitarian conception of the relation between God and the creature, so that he 'was left with the standard position of Western culture-religion: on the one hand there is God, conceived as a supernatural entity who acts causally on us; and on the other there are the results among us of this causality'. The outcome is the causal conception of grace to be found in Aquinas and later theology.[17]

Over against that causal conception of grace there is required, I would argue, a conception of the personal relationship of God the Spirit to the human agent, according to which the Spirit is the Spirit of the Father as our *other* electing us into communion with him through the Son. The model for the otherness of the Spirit is, of course, the relation of Jesus to the Spirit in the Gospels, where the Spirit is portrayed as over-against Jesus, driving him into the wilderness to be tempted, supporting him through the temptation and empowering the ministry that follows. All this demands a doctrine of the personal distinctness of the Holy Spirit in relation to both Son and Father, and that in turn demands an abandonment of the Western *Filioque* doctrine whose chief function is to prevent such an individuation. That leads me to the chief question I would like to ask of Robert Jenson's trinitarian theology. Does it enable the emergence of an adequate conception of the otherness and particularity of the Holy Spirit?

The omens are favourable. For example, there is the point made in connection with our recurring concern, predestination. The bane of historic formulations of this doctrine, as we have seen, is orientation to the eternal past and its apparent denial of human freedom. By appropriating the doctrine to the Spirit, election is conceived as that which happens in the present – liberation into the community of faith – and some of the deterministic connotations are avoided ('The Holy Spirit',

---

[17] 'The Holy Spirit', *Christian Dogmatics*, op. cit., pp. 101–178 (pp. 126, 128).

pp. 136ff). Similarly, in a paper on ecclesiology, 'The Community of the Resurrection', we read the following:

> By no means only in Scripture, *spirit* is the articulation of personhood and community. Spirit is life as breath or wind, life as received from and re-exerted upon the other. It is subjectivity not as self-contained in mere cognition of the other, but as intrusion upon and self-discovery in the other. ... [T]he mutuality of spirit and communication ... also belongs to the phenomenon.[18]

But this is also the place where questions begin to arise. In a relation of 'intrusion ... and self-discovery' is there really community, or are we dangerously near a Hegelian conception of self-realisation through the other? In other respects also I think that there can be discerned in Jenson's theology survivals of Western conceptions which at once deprive the Spirit of particularity – especially in relation to the Son – and at the same time run the risk of abolishing the space between God and the world. 'The Spirit is the power of the eschaton ... this Spirit is identified as Jesus' spirit, as every human being has spirit' ('The Triune God', p. 101). There are two chief problems with that formulation. The first is that it is very nearly a natural theological projection from a supposed meaning of *spirit* to a theological conception. The second is the use of the expression the 'Spirit of Jesus'. Here there is undoubtedly an element of Western pneumatological subordinationism.

Let me explain what I mean by unpacking a little the concept of the spirit of Jesus. Is it enough to speak of Jesus as having spirit as human beings have spirit? We have already seen that the Spirit is Jesus' other who empowers his life and ministry. It could also be argued that the first two chapters of the Gospel of Luke express a certain priority of the Spirit over the Son, as the one who acts as the agent of the incarnation. There is also a long and respectable tradition which holds that it is the Spirit by whom Jesus is raised from the dead. The fact that after the resurrection Jesus becomes the one who pours out the Spirit does not take away from the fact of an equality-within-difference of function which cannot be given sufficient weight by talk

---

[18] 'The Community of the Resurrection'. Paper read to the Society for the Study of Theology, Leeds, England, 1988, p. 6.

of the Spirit as the spirit of Jesus. Indeed, one of the objections to the Western *Filioque* is that it prevents us from realising that, although the risen Jesus is indeed the agent of the pouring out of the Spirit, the incarnate Son is equally the gift of the Spirit. We have to speak of the Spirit's Jesus as much as of Jesus' Spirit.

A direct result of the failure to give to the Spirit personal distinctness is a problematic conception of freedom. 'Genuine freedom is the reality of possibility, is openness to the future. Genuine freedom is Spirit' ('The Triune God', p. 156). I do not like that because of its tendency to substitute an abstraction – the future – for a concrete: community with other persons. Once we say, however, that genuine freedom is the gift of the Spirit, the whole game changes. The Spirit is on such an account a person, inseparably related to the other persons of the Trinity, indeed, but the one whose distinctive function is to bring other persons into relationship while maintaining their otherness, their particular and unique freedom. It is for that kind of reason that more must be said than that the Spirit is Jesus' spirit.

My question to what I believe to be a major contribution to the church's trinitarian tradition centres, accordingly, on the matter of space. I have argued for a greater 'space' – otherness – between the persons of the Trinity than Jenson's theology appears to allow. I return to the point made with the help of Coleridge. The contention was that conceptions of the undifferentiated unity of God bring God too close to the world, and so close off the space which is needed for there to be human particularity, freedom and otherness. I do not want to suggest that Jenson's Trinity is in any way an undifferentiated unity. But there are pressures in it working for such an outcome, pressures deriving from a relative failure to give to the persons of the Godhead particularity and distinctness.

Let us look again at a statement cited at the end of the previous section. 'The "a person" that God is, is the human person Jesus, the Son. The triune event that God is, is by its triunity a person, this one. ... We will say, all there is to being God the Father is being addressed as 'Father' by the Son, Jesus; all there is to being God the Spirit is being the spirit of this exchange' ('The Triune God', pp. 170f). That seems to me to come dangerously close to Augustine's abolition of the real functional distinctions between the persons – and so of tending to reduce the Spirit to a kind of link between Father and Son – and therefore to being a repetition of the single-person deity of the Western tradition. In the terms used in the paper's title, it is in danger of making immanence the enemy of the true otherness without which freedom is not truly freedom in relation, in community.

For the same kind of reason I would want to argue for the necessity of a stronger distinction between economic and immanent Trinity, between God in eternity and God in time. I would not want to use the language of prototype and ectype, but would hope to avoid connotations of timelessness by appeal to the personal dynamism of *perichoresis*, albeit one conceived on the basis of the economy of salvation. The question to be asked concerns the kind of talk of an immanent Trinity – if any – that is licensed by our knowledge of God in the economy of salvation. Is there no alternative to a God of timeless eternity reached by negative abstraction from the action in time? It may be – and here we can only be speculative – that what is needed is the holding in tension of concepts developed with the help of both temporal and spatial phenomena.

The economy makes known not a timeless prototype but an eternity characterised by the dynamism of freely related persons. I have tried in this paper to outline a conception of personal space as the space in which persons give to and receive from each other what they are. Are there any possibilities that we may save talk of the immanent Trinity from timelessness by speaking, after Barth but in a different way, of an eternity which is neither timelessness nor everlasting time but a function of the personal space in which Father, Son and Spirit are related to each other? I have already mentioned the concept of *perichoresis*: a metaphor of spatial motion which introduces a dynamism into the eternity in which the persons are what they are in and through one another. In such a way concepts taken from both space and time are used to express the dynamics of a kind of eternal personal relatedness, the interanimation of divine energies in eternity, a kind of theological equivalent of the space-time of relativity physics.

But, it may be asked, what is the point of such speculation

about the inner being of God? The answer is that the distinction between economic and immanent Trinity achieves more than a concept of God's freedom. It is, as we have seen, a matter of human freedom as well. The personal otherness, the self-sufficiency, of God is the basis on which freedom depends because it is the ground for the otherness of the human in relation to God. That freedom derives from the gift in both creation and redemption of the God who has and is personal space, and so can be the creator of such space. If God is not and has not personal space 'in advance', in eternity, the danger remains that human freedom will be overwhelmed by a sovereignty of immanence. Our freedom is based in, derives from, God's sovereignty. But unless it is at least in part a sovereignty of transcendence, of personal space, it threatens to overwhelm us.

IV *Conclusion*

Through my disagreement with one who has taught me much, I have arrived at an alternative, perhaps in part complementary, diagnosis of a central problem of Christian theology in the modern world. Over against a contention that the disarray derives from an eternalising of God, I have argued that divine immanence is equally problematic. Over against a stress on timelessness, I have suggested that pantheism and its equivalents are the real enemy. Both approaches have much in common, and in particular share a concern to establish human freedom theologically without placing unbiblical limits on the sovereignty of God. In other words, by re-conceiving the sovereignty of God in a trinitarian way both wish to establish genuine human freedom without making the choice that the Enlightenment and its successors – Edwards apart – sometimes try to force upon us, between eternity and time, God and freedom.

The chapter began with an outline of the Reformation's attempt to save human life from the slavery of self-salvation. That need is as pressing now as it was then, except that things have become worse with the widespread assumption of theology's irrelevance to the whole topic. Robert Jenson's achievement, in the light of this situation, is twofold. In the first place, he has provided a theological diagnosis of the malaise which yet stands in true continuity with the Reformation's concerns. Second, he has isolated a number of respects in which the Reformation, in common with much of the tradition of Augustine, has been weak: its dualism, its tendency to other-worldliness, its false eternalising of the gospel. The weaknesses, as he again sees so clearly, have something to do with the failure to think trinitarianly enough. It is as one of those who have in our generation renewed trinitarian theology that I wish to affirm Robert Jenson's achievement; beside that, our differences, though important in themselves, pale into relative insignificance.

CHAPTER 8

RELATION AND RELATIVITY
The Trinity and the created world

I *Words and the world – again*[1]

Discussion of the relation between the world and the words with which we attempt to describe, characterise or generally come to terms with it are as old as philosophy itself. Plato's proposal presents one clear option: the world, if properly – that is, rationally – approached is found to contain, embodied more or less adequately within its shifting and temporal materiality, the objective and timeless ideas or forms which give it its structure and reality. The mind's task is to discover what they are by thought, by abstraction. They are to be found by reflection on certain of the general words from the vocabulary of thought. Kant's programme contains a second option, and it is an inversion of Plato's. The concepts are, indeed, both timeless and, in a sense, objective. But their locus is not reality, 'out there', so much as the structures of human rationality. The human mind replaces exterior eternity as the location of the concepts by means of which reality is understood.

Both proposals, insofar as so crude a summary can begin to do justice to their subtlety, are idealist, and, indeed, systems of transcendental idealism. The difference between them lies in the nature and location of their transcendentality. Plato's ideas are absolutely objective, constituting as they do the eternal structure of the universe. It is therefore a realistic idealism. Kant's concepts

[1] A previous and differently oriented treatment of this topic is to be found in my *Actuality of Atonement. A Study of Metaphor, Rationality and the Christian Tradition*, Edinburgh: T. & T. Clark, 1988, chapter 2. The present version is reprinted from C. Schwöbel, editor, *Trinitarian Theology Today*, Edinburgh: T. & T. Clark, 1995, Chapter 5.

are subjectively objective, inhering in the structures of human rationality, and therefore tend to generate a more subjective idealism, calling into the question the very possibility of our being able to speak in our words of the world as it actually is.

Despite the claims, sometimes heard, that the philosophies of both men, and particularly Plato, have been refuted beyond hope of salvation, there is much to be said for aspects of both systems, and in particular their common quest for trans-cendentality. May they not both be right in holding that there are concepts without which we cannot make sense of our world – or rather, more positively, that enable us to *think* our world? Put more carefully, may it not be suggested that inherent within certain words there lies the possibility of *conceiving* things as they are? Here, of course, the choice is for aspects of Plato's realistic programme: to seek concepts which are in some way or other rooted in or indicative of the deep structures of reality. At this point, however, one of Kant's objections to the platonic quest must be faced. Does not the history of metaphysical speculation present to us a spectacle of empty battles, battles fought without hope of victory?

The answer to Kant's question is a Yes, but. Yes indeed, but (1) what else is to be expected? Does the propriety of the quest for transcendentals depend on an expectation of the kind of final solutions that Kant rather arrogantly claimed that he had himself found? But (2) even within the inconclusive skirmish-ing, do we not find a wide general agreement on the kind of concepts we are looking for, even if there is much disagreement on how we are to understand them? The example given by Tom Stoppard's philosopher, George, in opposition to relativistic theories of ethics is as good as any:

> Certainly a tribe which believes it confers honour on its elders by eating them is going to be viewed askance by another which prefers to buy them a little bungalow some-where, and Professor McFee should not be surprised that the notion of honour should manifest itself so differently in peoples so far removed in clime and culture. What is surely more surprising is that notions such as honour should manifest themselves at all. For what is honour?[2]

[2] Tom Stoppard, *Jumpers*, London: Faber, 1972, pp. 54f.

But that takes us to a further consideration. It is to Hegel and some of those who influenced him that we owe the injection into the debate of a category that played no constitutive part in the thought of either Plato or Kant. It is that of history. If we take the history of thought seriously, we are bound to concede that such transcendentals as there are can be read timelessly neither off the structure of the world nor from the shape of human rationality. They emerge, rather, in the commerce, the interaction, between the two. There is thus more of a dynamism involved than either of those two philosophers were able, in their place in the history of thought, to incorporate in their philosophy. To understand this dynamism requires attention to the fact that the same, or the same kinds of, concepts may appear in different cultural contexts and may be related but not identical in meaning. We shall note examples later in the chapter. It follows that the battles of which Kant was so scornful may not be empty battles at all, but part of the intellectual process. Because combatants are disagreed about some, even many, features of the concepts of God or of beauty, it does not follow that nothing about the way things are can be discovered in the dialectic of ideas.

The fact that the transcendentals emerge in the interaction between mind and world means that neither a straight platonic not a pure Kantian approach to the problem is right. We are rather in the realm of what Sabina Lovibond has called the parochial transcendental, concepts which are not absolutely transcendental in the platonic sense but which in some way or other belong in our embodiedness in the world.[3] The interesting question then becomes not simply which transcendentals are the right ones and so enable us to understand or indwell our world the better, but also how we light upon them at all. We are here close to the questions of revelation and discovery: not of what is known as particular divine revelation, so much as of the more universal question of whether things make themselves known to us in such a way that our concepts are not simply constructed by our minds – as the Kantian picture has it – but are a response to something prevenient. But the theological question also raises its head. Whence come the prevenience and the capacity

---

[3] Sabina Lovibond, *Realism and Imagination in Ethics*, University of Minnesota Press, 1983, pp. 210ff.

for response? Where do the concepts come from in the first place?

Let me take as an example a passage, which I have already used in a different though related context, from Michael Faraday's famous paper on electricity and the nature of matter. Faraday's paper is part of the process whereby nineteenth century science moved away from the conception, beloved of mechanistic atomists, of the universe as a collocation of mutually impenetrable parts, to a more relativistic notion. He suggests a concept of atoms as fields of force rather than discrete substances, and develops a theory of the 'mutual penetrability of atoms'. His way of putting the matter is remarkable, that 'matter is not merely mutually penetrable, but each atom extends, so to say, throughout the whole of the solar system, yet always retaining its own centre of force'.[4] Physics has, of course, come a long way since then, in extending Faraday's 'solar system' to the whole of the universe and in the vast extension and mathematizing of the concepts he suggested. But I begin with him for a very good reason. He speaks of the solar system rather as the classical trinitarian theologians did of the Trinity. What we have in Faraday is a kind of doctrine of the *perichoresis*, the interpenetration, of matter. As the three persons of the Trinity interpenetrate the being of the others, so it is with the matter of which the world is made.

I am not suggesting that the doctrine of the Trinity is in any way responsible for the way that Faraday came to think – at least not directly – although it cannot be denied that there are theological determinants in many systems of thought, certainly in modern science, however much it may think that it has outgrown its parentage.[5] Rather, I want to ask whether concepts generated by theology, and particularly trinitarian theology, bear any relation to those employed in conceiving the world as it is presented to us

[4] Michael Faraday, 'A Speculation touching Electric Conduction and the Nature of Matter', *On the Primary Forces of Electricity*, ed. Richard Laming, 1938, pp. 7f. For a use of Faraday in christology, see my *Yesterday and Today. A Study of Continuities in Christology*, London: Darton, Longman and Todd, 1983, p. 117.

[5] Since first writing that, I have come to learn that the suggestion may not be so wide of the mark. See Geoffrey Cantor, *Michael Faraday: Sandemanian and Scientist. A Study of Science and Religion in the Nineteenth Century*, London: Macmillan, 1991, p. 172, suggests that Faraday's conception of the notion of unity in diversity reveals 'a clear echo of the Christian tri-unity'.

in some of the discoveries of modern science. That is to say, I am going to ask some questions about conceptual similarities, and raise the question of whether the concepts developed in trinitarian theology enable us not only to conceive the reality of God, but also have transcendental possibilities, and so enable us to come to terms with the fundamental shape of being.

The question, necessarily involved in such an enquiry, of whether the world is *like* the God conceived to be triune, is an odd and difficult one. Faraday's words suggest that in some respects it is. But if it is taken to suggest that the world is in some way in the image of God, it causes two problems in particular. The first is that it makes it difficult to distinguish between the being of the world and that of the human creature. In avoiding such a difficulty, it must be argued that to be in the image of God is to be personal, and that is the distinctive mark of the human creation over against the rest of the creation. The second, and it is the same point made from a different angle, is that if the being of the world is conceived to be in the image of God – as it undoubtedly is in some systems of metaphysics – it becomes impossible to conceive adequately the character of the non-human creation. Rather, I should want to hold that the distinctive being of the world is that it is itself in relation to persons, but that is not itself personal. The pitfalls of personalising the world are many, and shown by the otherwise interesting attempts of Process philosophers like Hartshorne to use relational language of all dimensions of being. Against that, the thesis to be argued here is that the world is like God not in being in his image, but in the more limited sense that there are some conceptual parallels between the concepts in which the being of God is expressed and the ways in which we may conceive the world. I shall illustrate the parallels by appeal to some modern scientific conceptuality. The claim to be argued is that some trinitarian concepts appear to bear a certain likeness to some of the concepts that have been either appropriated or developed by modern scientists.

II   *Outlines of a trinitarian theology of creation*

Before, however, I engage directly in that enterprise, I want to outline, as background and support, the basic content of a trinitarian theology of creation. The advantage of a trinitarian approach to the theology of creation is that it enables us to say a number of important things, chief among them that the world is 'good', a distinct reality with its own being, and yet only so by virtue of its dependence upon and directedness to God. The basis of a trinitarian theology of creation was already marked out by Irenaeus in his engagement with the world-denying theologies of his opponents. He argued that because the world was created through the Son, it is real and good; and that because the Son became incarnate, there is a continuity between creation and redemption, between all the will and works of God in and towards the world. According to Irenaeus it is therefore the material world as a whole which is destined for redemption, and indeed already participating in it by virtue of the work of the eschatological Spirit.

Later trinitarian theology enables us to see more clearly the importance of the doctrine of the immanent Trinity. Because God is, 'before' creation took place, already a being-in-relation, there is no need for him to create what is other than himself. He does not need to create, because he is already a *taxis*, order, of loving relations. In some recent theology it has been suggested that such a theology is to be rejected on the grounds that, if God does not need the creation in some way or other, he must be a distant and unfeeling monarch. Such an objection confuses two points. The first is the proper objection to the form that doctrines of aseity have sometimes taken, suggesting as they do the total uninvolvement, of an Epicurean kind, of a completely immutable and unfeeling deity. Yet it does not follow that for God to enter into relation with the world he must need it in some way.

And the second point is that far from suggesting an unrelatedness of God to the world, trinitarian theology is based on the belief that God the Father is related to the world through the creating and redeeming action of Son and Spirit who are, in Irenaeus' expression, his two hands. The doctrine of the Trinity, certainly in the form advocated in this volume, is derived from the involvement of God in creation, reconciliation and redemption. But what it also enables us to say is that far from being dependent upon the world God is free to create a world which can be itself, that is to say, free according to its own order of being. It is the relation in otherness between God and the world that is conceived with the help of the doctrine of the Trinity, and probably cannot adequately be conceived in any other way. The world is itself, not God, but worldly according to its own measure of being. Yet it is so by gift of the God who creates and sustains it in such a way that it is itself.[6]

III *Some trinitarian concepts*

What, then, are the features of the doctrine of the Trinity of which echoes are to be found in recent scientific thought? A number of them arise out of the discussion of a trinitarian theology of creation in the previous section, but another will need to be added. Central among them are two, the concepts of relation and of freedom. The former has a chequered history. In the Cappadocians, it was developed to be able to speak of the way in which the persons of Father, Son and Spirit are to each other. The relation of Father and Son was centrally expressed by means of an analogy from human reproduction, in terms of begetting; that between Father and Spirit in the distinct but more vague and less personal concept of breathing or procession. Overall, the relations of the three are summarised in the concept of love, which involve a dynamic of both giving and receiving. The persons are what they are by virtue of what they give to and receive from each other. As such, they constitute the being of God, for there is no being of God underlying what the persons are to and from each other. God's being is a being in relation, without remainder relational.

But, and here we come to the second central concept, the fact that the relations are relations of love entails their freedom, which at least means their non-necessity. We have already met the claim that a trinitarian theology of creation involves the non-necessity of the world. The world does not have to be,

---

[6] It is one of the merits of Hartshorne's analysis to show that the logic of an inadequately relational account of the God-world relation so easily collapses into pantheism: that there is not a very great distance from the causal definition of relation in the *Summa Theologiae* to the outright pantheism of Spinoza. Whether he can himself escape a form of pantheism is another matter. See especially Charles Hartshorne and W. L. Reese, editors, *Philosophers Speak of God*, University of Chicago Press, 1953.

because it is the outcome of the free creating act of the God who is already a relational being. But that is spoken of an action of God towards that which is not himself. What can it mean that the inner relations of the eternal God are free? Is God not always what he is, and therefore necessarily so? Bound up with that question is that of whether God's eternity entails a form of necessity. Is it possible to speak of an eternal freedom?

One limit which is set for the discussion of this question is that in using concepts like relation and freedom of the being of God it must be emphasised that we are not attempting a map of the inner reality but to say what we can of the God made known in Christ. In this case, it is being claimed that the freedom of the divine being is at the very least reflected in the freedom with which he enters into relation with that which is not himself. One conceptual link is to be found in the free obedience of Jesus, who is enabled by the Spirit to do the Father's will. If the incarnate Son's life is to be understood in terms of his free relation to the Father, it would seem to follow that there is in the divine eternity a freedom corresponding to it, so that to that freedom of God in creation and redemption, it can be argued – as Barth did argue at length – there corresponds what can only be called freedom in the relations of eternal Father, Son and Spirit.

The use of such an argument can be justified if it is held that freedom is a function of relations between persons and between persons and their world. Human freedom is what it is in a number of forms: in what takes place between God and man, man and man, and man and the world. What we thus have is an analogy of freedom, a freedom which takes a different shape in each case, appropriate to the character of the relation. What human freedom is can be understood only in the light of the freedom that is the gift of God through Son and Spirit. The question for this paper is whether the concept of the divine freedom from determination, revealed in God's freedom in creation, incarnation and redemption, is also of interest for the way we understand the structures of the non-personal created world.

That brings me to a third concept, one indicating the refusal of the early theologians to be content with a static doctrine of God. The concept of the divine energies appears to have developed as the result of thought about the divine activity in and towards the creation. Modern Orthodox theology, deriving from Palamas and what is probably excessive dependence on one letter of Basil, has tended to suggest an absolute distinction between the energies and the being of God. 'For Orthodox theology, the energies signify an exterior manifestation of the Trinity which cannot be interiorized, introduced, as it were, within the divine being, as its natural determination.'[7] But if 'Energies' "proceed" from God and manifest His own being',[8] it is difficult to deny that just as the divine freedom expressed in the world derives from the inner freedom of God, here it must be so also. Otherwise, the being of God is essentially unknowable in an epistemologically destructive sense, leading possibly also to an entirely static and motionless concept of eternity along Aristotelian lines. If we are entitled to move to concepts of God's being consisting in free relatedness, may we not also argue that there is also a dynamic to God's being, corresponding to the dynamic of freedom and relatedness? It must be repeated that we are not here engaging in a mapping of the inner being of God, but asking what concepts we may develop in order to characterise the kind of being that God is. The doctrine of the Trinity, accordingly, is that theologoumenon developed, in response to Christian experience, to show that God's being is not motionless, impassible eternity but a personal *taxis* of dynamic and free relations.

IV *Historical interlude*

If the very being of God is dynamic and energetic, it is strange that Christian doctrines of creation should so often have taken static form. Of course, it never was denied that the creation involved movement and change, even though that change was not always welcomed as an essential part of the process. But the fact that eschatologies have often conceived the creation as simply returning to its starting point is a symptom of a kind of

[7] Vladimir Lossky, *The Mystical Theology of the Eastern Church*, London: James Clarke, 1957, p. 80.

[8] Georges Florovsky, *Bible, Church and Tradition: An Eastern Orthodox View*, Belmont, Mass.: Nordland, 1972, p. 117.

static conception. The same has happened with doctrines of salvation as effecting the restoration of human beings to a lost innocence, rather than to an eschatological goal, and these have at the same time had the effect of conceiving redemption not as something that happens in and with the rest of the created order, but as salvation from it. These things are said often enough, and scarcely need repeating now, except insofar as we need reminding that there is a considerable difference between neoplatonic and trinitarian conceptions of creation, and that the former often appear to have overridden the latter.

Indeed, what I want to suggest is that some modern scientific theories look as though they are the result of a process almost of intellectual evolution, from static theories owing more to the Greek than to the Christian to a dynamism reflecting the more eschatological emphasis of a doctrine that pays attention to the role of the Holy Spirit. Here it is instructive to begin with a figure on the borderlands of modernity, who was also very much a theologian of the Holy Spirit, not least in his doctrine of creation, which to an extent shows the effect of its trinitarian dimension. 'For it is the Spirit who, everywhere diffused, sustains all things, causes them to grow, and quickens them in heaven and in earth.'[9]

Yet a recent study of Calvin as a sixteenth century figure shows that there is also a contradictory emphasis. William Bouwsma cites passages from the Reformer which indicate the influence on him of a pagan cosmology of a highly static kind. One quotation will make the point:

> Both Aristotle's unmoved mover and the spirituality of the heavenly bodies lurk behind Calvin's observation that 'God, when he revolves the world, remains consistent, so that what we call changes or turnings produce no variation in himself, but each revolution is coordinated with all the others.' He also slipped once into claiming that the heavens are 'eternal and exempt from alteration'.[10]

All this may be reason enough to see why Calvin opposed some of the claims of the new Copernican science. But even more

[9] John Calvin, *Institutes of the Christian Religion*, I.xiii.14.
[10] William J. Bouwsma, *John Calvin. A Sixteenth Century Portrait*, Oxford University Press, 1988, p. 73.

modern figures retained very much a static view of things. Again, one quotation, this time from Prigogine and Stengers, whom we shall meet again later:

> In the classical view [sc. of the physical world] the basic processes of nature were considered to be deterministic and reversible. Processes involving randomness or irreversibility were considered only exceptions.[11]

Determinism and reversibility both imply an essentially static universe, not in the sense that there is no movement, but that all that happens is decided in advance (determinism) and that any process can in theory be taken back the way it came. There is thus in principle no novelty. As in some forms of the ancient doctrine of creation, the end is not different from the beginning. The Newtonian cosmology thus shared some of the features of the essentially non-trinitarian doctrines of creation that tended to characterise the Western world before modern times.[12]

What has happened since Calvin's time is the development, partly under the impact of Christian theological impulses, of an increasingly dynamic conception of the universe. How far, or indeed whether at all, the development should be attributed to specifically theological impulses is at present the subject of much debate, initiated in large part by Michael Foster's famous paper which claimed about half a century ago that certain aspects of the Christian doctrine of creation were necessary conditions for the development of modern science.[13] (In much of this he was anticipated by Pierre Duhem many years before.) The claim is now sometimes dogmatically asserted, sometimes, though not so often, questioned, as in the recent study by Funkenstein. Probably there can be no certainty in historical judgements of this kind, though it must be significant that modern science happened in the Christian West and not

[11] Ilya Prigogine and Isabelle Stengers, *Order Out of Chaos. Man's New Dialogue with Nature*, London: Fontana, 1985, p. xxvii.

[12] It is remarkable how little Augustine's doctrine of creation is informed by trinitarian categories, in the sense that he does not articulate the doctrine christologically and pneumatologically.

[13] Michael B. Foster, 'The Christian Doctrine of Creation and the Rise of Modern Natural Science', *Mind* 43 (1934), pp. 446–468.

somewhere else. 'Things happened thus and therefore, thus they must have happened.'[14]

My project here is the more modest one of showing some correspondences between ancient trinitarian and modern scientific conceptuality. If that happens to support Foster's contention, so much the better. But it is not historical claims in themselves that are theologically important. The heart of the matter is ontological. What kind of world do we live in, and what are we to do in and towards it? They are the central systematic and, indeed, existential and moral questions.

V   *Contingency, relation and energy*

The three trinitarian concepts we have met are freedom, relation and energy. They are, as we have seen, interrelated in trinitarian theology, members of a cluster of linked concepts which attempt to characterise something of the being of God. I shall take them one at a time, inevitably involving overlap, and show how they, or something like them, appear in modern scientific conceptuality. Relation and energy are clearly concepts that appear in modern cosmology, and they will concern us eventually. But the joker in the pack is freedom. How does that fare when translated into the sphere of the physical world? The answer is that there can be no direct translation. Freedom is a word used of persons, divine and human, and can only in a highly questionable way be extended beyond that. Yet we have seen that the outcome of the free creation of the world by God is the otherness-in-relation of its being. It exists in its own way, but is none the less dependent for its existence on the activity of the creator. It is thus contingent upon God's creating, sustaining and redeeming action. Accordingly, it must be said that the concept of freedom is transmuted into contingence when we move from the personal to the non-personal sphere.

One meaning of contingence is of the world's dependence upon God for its being. But there is another meaning, and it is the one of which much has been made in recent writing. It means that the world does not *have* to be what or as it is. It is not

[14] R. Hooykaas, *Religion and the Rise of Modern Science*, Edinburgh, Scottish Academic Press, 1972, p. 162.

the same as freedom, but is rather the way of speaking of the distinctive form of being of the non-personal created world. Persons have – or should have – freedom; that is a mark of their distinctive character, and, in the case of finite persons, of their being in the image of God. The strength of Process thought is that it recognises the centrality of contingency; its weakness that it fails to distinguish between contingency and personality, so that everything has the same *kind* of freedom, albeit analogically. The claim here is that there is a qualitative – though not 'infinite qualitative' – distinction between freedom and contingency. Where persons have, or should have, freedom if they are to be themselves, the non-personal world is qualified by contingency.

As to that in which this contingency consists, there is, inevitably, disagreement. It is as difficult to define as freedom, although it is worth observing that, according to Funkenstein, the modern notion appears to have its basis in scholastic disputes about the absolute and ordained power of God.[15] We shall therefore outline the claims of some recent essays in the subject, all of whose writers are agreed that, although the Newtonian conceptuality may hold for some levels of reality, as a means of accounting for the behaviour of the universe as a whole it has had its day. Like the first evangelist, Arthur Peacocke states the difference between the old order and the new by means of a series of antitheses:

> *Then* ... the natural world was regarded as mechanically determined and predictable ...: *now* the world is regarded rather as the scene of the interplay of chance and of statistical, as well as causal, uniformity in which there is indeterminacy at the micro-level and unpredictability because of the complexity of causal chains at the macro-level, especially that of the biological.
>
> *Then* ... the natural world was still regarded as static in form ... essentially complete, unchanging and closed: *now* it is discovered to be dynamic – a nexus of evolving forms, essentially incomplete ...[16]

[15] Amos Funkenstein, *Theology and the Scientific Imagination from the Middle Ages to the Seventeenth Century*, Princeton University Press, 1986, pp. 121ff.

[16] Arthur Peacocke, *Creation and the World of Science*, Oxford: Clarendon Press, 1979, p. 62.

Like other similar theorists, Peacocke wishes to make it clear that indeterminacy does not imply the absence of causality. In fact it might be claimed that it is belief in the compossibility of the two that marks contemporary in contrast to classical science. According to Peacocke, the universe behaves in a law-like way, in which there operate networks of causally connected events. But the causality is not absolute – assimilated to some conception of logical necessity – for there is an ' "openness" in the texture of the nexus of natural events which was not generally appreciated before the revolution in physics . . . in the first decade of this century'.[17]

In his *Divine and Contingent Order,* T. F. Torrance, whose general theological position is rather different from that of Peacocke, nevertheless develops a similar concept of contingency. His contribution is to link it specifically with the notion of rationality. If once there was a tendency to identify the rational with the necessary, that is so no longer. The rationality of the world as discerned by modern science is located in patterns of things that are not bound to be what they are. It is a form of rationality, although it is essentially different from rationality as it is conceived by those philosophers who construe it on the model of logical necessity or euclidean geometry. 'Laws of nature . . . are not abstract generalizations, idealized laws prescinded from concrete, empirical reality, but objective contingent consistencies'.[18] That is to say, the rationality of scientific laws corresponds to the nature of the world, as non-contingent order: order that does not have to be as it is.

The notion of the contingence of the universe has been thrown into relief by recent accounts of the concept of chaos. This emphasises even more strongly the idea of the world as contingent but ordered, and at the same time reveals something of the sheer mystery of that order. In his study of recent developments, the journalist James Gleick gives an account of those developments which show, as he claims, that the failure of long-range weather forecasting derived not from human incapacity to gather sufficient data on which to base a prediction, but from the impossibility of being able to make that kind of

[17] Ibid., p. 59.
[18] T. F. Torrance, *Divine and Contingent Order*, Oxford University Press, 1981, p. 38.

prediction. The world is such that inherent contingencies within its structure mean that minor alterations of initial conditions rule out the possibility of certain prediction. There is chaos but stability, that is to say, contingence but reliability. 'Chaos is ubiquitous; it is stable; it is structured.' It is, in fact, part of the dynamics of the universe. 'Those studying chaotic dynamics discovered that the disorderly behavior of simple systems acted as a *creative* process. It generated complexity: richly organised patterns, sometimes stable and sometimes unstable, sometimes finite and sometimes infinite, but always with the fascination of living things.'[19] The universe is not only contingent – free in its own way; but the contingency operates so as to be creative.

Gleick's book opens with what has become perhaps the pictorial symbol of the notion of chaos, the 'Butterfly Effect – the notion that a butterfly stirring the air today in Peking can transform storm systems next month in New York'.[20] The fact that this concrete example illustrates even more remarkable and mysterious phenomena – for example, that minute sub-atomic changes in gases on the other side of the universe can affect the way things happen on this side – leads us into the next phase of our discussion, of the character of the universe as a *perichoresis* of interrelated dynamic systems. We have already come across the notion, in the quotations from Peacocke, and it seems that here the development of modern field theory in Faraday and Clerk Maxwell – two of the predecessors to whom Einstein repeatedly refers – has led inexorably to the conceptual echo of trinitarian theology in relativity theory and its developments.

To obtain a measure of what has happened, and, indeed, to show how the change in cosmology is similar to, even caused by, a theological change, we must pause to glance at the history of the concept of relation. In Aristotle, and certainly in logic until the time of Kant, relation is subordinate to substance. Relations are what take place or subsist between substances that are prior to them: something first exists, and then enters or finds itself in relation to other things, which may change its accidents, but not

[19] James Gleick, *Chaos. Making a New Science,* London: Sphere Books, 1987, pp. 76, 43.
[20] Ibid., p. 8.

what it really is (short of destroying it).[21] The notion is with us still, in the individualistic idea of a person as one who, in some measure already complete, enters into relations with other persons. Theologically speaking, as we have seen in chapter three, Augustine deprived the concept of theological power by treating relation as ontologically intermediate between substance and accident, thus (1) identifying – or initiating the process which eventually identified – the person and the relation: the person, in God at any rate, is an eternal relation; and (2) rendering person subordinate to being in the reality of God. By reifying relations in that way, he made the concept effectively redundant.[22] The tragic side of the matter is Augustine's failure to appropriate the Cappadocian conceptual advance according to which relations are between persons – as the Aristotelian concept suggests – yet are at the same time constitutive of what those persons are – here against Aristotle. The persons are not persons who then enter into relations, but are mutually constituted, made what they are, by virtue of their relations to one another.

What Augustine made effectively redundant in theology returns to transform science in the nineteenth and twentieth centuries. Relativity theory is the application to the universe of some such conception of relations as the trinitarian one just outlined. 'It [physics] now recognizes that, for an interaction to be real, the "nature" of the related things must derive from these relations, while at the same time the relations must derive from the "nature" of the things.'[23] Those words of Prigogine and Stengers lead us into the third of our concepts, that of energy, for it is evident that the physics of relativity also introduces a dynamism into the way things are conceived. There are no unchanging substances which enter into relations – as on the view of Aristotle and Newton alike – but the whole universe becomes conceivable as a dynamic structure of fields of force in mutually constitutive relations. To illustrate this dimension of the matter we turn to Prigogine and Stengers' central claim in their study of cosmology. This is that the notion of evolution cannot be restricted to the organic sphere alone but must be applied to the universe as a whole. Their thesis

---

[21] Aristotle, *Categories*, chapter 7.
[22] For a detailed defence of this claim, see ch. 3 above.
[23] Prigogine and Stengers, op. cit., p. 95.

illustrates something of the temporal irreversibility of the universe, its inherent directional dynamic.

Their repeated insistence is that science since Einstein has been forced to recognise what Einstein himself resisted, the inherent temporality of the cosmos. 'For us convinced physicists,' wrote Einstein, 'the distinction between past present and future is an illusion, though a persistent one.'[24] This means that Einstein's world, for all its relativity, remained finally static in the sense I have been using the word. Prigogine and Stengers are able to relate indeterminacy or contingence, relativity and a true dynamism. Theirs is a world whose reality is constituted by the arrow of time. It is a world congruent, though by no means identical, with that of Irenaeus, in the sense that it is consistent with his kind of eschatological dynamic.

There, of course, comes the difficulty. What is the relation between the kind of cosmological speculation in which these authors – or Capra[25] – engage, and a truly trinitarian eschatology? It is easy to generate, simply from the description of modern discoveries, a kind of secular or immanentist eschatology. But because trinitarian theology enables us to think of the world as at once absolutely other than God and completely dependent upon him, that step may be avoided. There is no absolute or necessary identity between the end of the universe as predicted by cosmologists and the eschatology that sees the end of the world as its perfection through the Holy Spirit. Nor, however, are we required to posit an absolute diastasis between the two. Trinitarian theology teaches that the world is destined for an absolute end, for perfection; it is directed to Christ, as it was created through him; but that through the action of the creator Spirit it is enabled to anticipate that end in the midst of time. We return to the concept of energies, and possibly to the Spirit as in some sense the energy of the Godhead. In such a way, we may understand the Holy Spirit as the divine energy releasing the energies of the world, enabling the world to realise its dynamic interrelatedness. Thus is God the Spirit conceived as the perfecting cause, the true source of the dynamic of the forward movement of the cosmos.

[24] Ibid., pp. 29f.
[25] Fritjof Capra, *The Tao of Physics. An Exploration of the Parallels between Modern Physics and Eastern Mysticism*, London: Fontana, 1983 (first ed. 1975).

Yet, of course – and here we take leave of all optimistic, immanentist, progressivist eschatologies: Peacocke, Process, Teilhard, and the rest – the dynamic of evolution is not coterminous with the dynamic of the Spirit, insofar as the latter is oriented to the one crucified in the midst of that very dynamic of energies of which we are speaking. That is to say, a theological account of creation must say that it has a destiny other than a continuing, if finite, progression to entropy and increasing complexity: the destiny of being enabled, through Jesus' offering of a perfect humanity to the Father, to praise its creator and return to him perfected. But there is overlap between the two, because the latter destiny is realised within the dynamics of the former. It is a far more complex matter than that revealed by scientific cosmology, because we shall have theologically to take account of such phenomena as evil and redemption. A merely natural theology of creation cannot take full account of the place of evil and its overcoming, because it has no criteria other than those provided by the discoveries of the natural sciences.

Trinitarian theology may have assisted in the development of the concepts with the help of which modern science has made its discoveries of the relationality, contingence and dynamic of the universe, but a return must be made to theology proper if further questions than those merely immanent in science are to be asked: different kinds of questions, but not entirely independent, as some schools of science and theology have sometimes urged, but different within relation. What I am suggesting is a different way of conducting the dialogue between theology and the sciences: by means of a comparison and contrast of overlapping concepts. Where the same, or similar, concepts are used in theology and science – analogically, metaphorically, or whatever – there exists the possibility of conversation.

VI   *Conclusion*

What is the point of all this? The playing of conceptual games? How much hangs on the dialogue of science and religion which we all take with such earnestness? We return to one of the points of trinitarian theology as having somewhere near its centre the question about the nature of the world in which we live. A non-determined world is a place where human beings are called to be free, and that means to enter into free and personal relations with each other and relations of dialogue with the created universe. (Prigogine and Stengers' work is subtitled: *Man's New Dialogue with Nature*.) Very near the end of the book, they quote a few lines in which that splendid old sceptic Lucretius argues that in a determined universe, a universe without *clinamen*, there would be no room for human freedom.[26] The agreement with an Epicurean shows among other things that concepts of an undetermined universe are not the prerogative of Christian theologians, and that is why we must beware of claiming along with some modern theologians too much of the credit for the development of modern science. And in any case, the chief foes of Lucretius – determinism, superstition and the anthropomorphic gods of the ancient world – are also ours. There we find the heart of the matter, that we are here engaged not merely in a dialogue between science and theology, but in an encounter between what makes for life and what for death. Ontology and ethics, creation and redemption, cannot be treated apart from one another.

The second question takes us to matters of similarly redemptive import. Suppose that we are able to transcend some of the weaknesses of Plato and Kant, and to find a way of suggesting, even in the light of modern historical understanding, a way in which words and the world in some way have a purchase on one another. What is the gain? We have already seen that we find concepts with the help of which we are enabled to come to terms with the being of God, ourselves and the created world. But, more important, we can also begin to find a way out of the cultural fragmentation that so bedevils the modern world. George Steiner has argued that in 'the break of the covenant between word and world' there has taken place 'one of the very few revolutions of spirit in Western history'.[27] Against that breach of covenant, the thrust of this paper is to suggest that the history of words, even words of metaphysical import, is not a field on which empty battles have been fought, nor is it one in which no progress is made in understanding the way things are.

[26] Prigogine and Stengers, op. cit., pp. 303–305.
[27] George Steiner, *Real Presences. Is there anything in what we say?* London: Faber & Faber, 1989, p. 93.

One of the things that the sciences have to teach – despite the relativistic scepticism of some modern philosophers of science – is that through the disciplined use of the imagination real insight in the meaning of things can be found and expressed in words.

The important lesson for the modern world to learn is that this is of far more than merely scientific import. If the fragment-ation and relativism that are the message of some writers in the humanities are to have the last word, the outlook for human community and human action in the world is bleak. With the loss of a common language there is lost also that communica-tion without which we are unable to live together and in the world. The renewal of language is thus the precondition for the renewal of social order. Such renewals will come when due attention is given to the doctrine of creation, not in abstraction from the doctrine of redemption, but as its counterpart. If the latter is neglected, the sin and evil that prevent the creation from becoming what it is called to be are ignored, and thus allowed to run their course unhindered. That is the danger of the sentimentalizing of creation to be found in much creation spirituality. But any treatment of redemption apart from its context, the creation, divorces human being from the world of which it is apart and to whose care it has been entrusted.

And so we return to the doctrine of the Trinity. As we have seen, the doctrine enables us to understand the world as truly itself, because created real and good by God, but also what it is only in continued dependence upon his conserving action. Creation through the Son and the Spirit ensures the affirma-tion both of the relatedness of the world to its maker and its dynamic teleology, its directedness to eschatological perfection. But it should never be forgotten that the doctrine is one forged under the impact of redemption, and specifically of that brought about by the incarnation, death, resurrection and ascension, achieved by the work of the eschatological Spirit, of the one through whom the world was made. Its function is thus to hold in relation the two central concerns of theologi-cal thought, creation and redemption, while distinguishing them.

A truly trinitarian doctrine of creation is a prime desider-atum for modern Christian theology because only by its means can the basis be laid for a proper alternative to the platonic Kantian options, with an account of whose strengths and weaknesses this paper began. Through it we shall learn to think, after both of those seminal thinkers, of the world as open to human language and the discovery of meaning, and yet, both because of its thralldom to evil and because of the mysterious depths given by its creator, also beyond the kind of final philosophical grasp that both of those thinkers in their different ways sought. World and word are thus to be understood as open to each other, but as so only through a process involving the redemption of human capacity and in a way that eludes any final conceptualization that would in effect cancel the openness. Our words can grasp only at anticipations of final truth, but they are through grace anticipations none the less. In such a case, the historicity of language is not a threat to the possibility of its expressing truth, but a positive gain, for history is the means by which the world is redeemed and brought to its proper perfection in Christ.

CHAPTER 9

THE INDISPENSABLE GOD?

The sovereignty of God and the problem of modern social order[1]

I *Religion today*

On the threshold of the modern age, John Calvin observed that there has been no social order which was not in some ways based upon belief in God.[2] While with greater knowledge of the world's civilisations we may ask whether there are non-theistic civilisations like the Confucian Chinese[3] or Buddhist, the fact remains that they have a religious basis in the broad sense that they understand their existence within the framework of a theological or quasi-theological scheme of things. The same is true of Plato's great if rather totalitarian attempt to base a political theory on the doctrine of the forms. At a time of supposed breakdown of an earlier religiously based order, one of which he was himself a strong critic, he believed, rightly or wrongly – for the need is not obvious – that some transcendent basis for social order was necessary. Some divinity is indispensable.

Similar points can be made about episodes in our own recent history, two of which are worth noting. 1. Early modernity was in no way an era dedicated to the expunging of the need to base social order in some (religious) conception of the unity of things. The typical theology of the Enlightenment was a form of

---

[1] First published in *Beyond Mere Health*, ed. Hilary D. Regan, Kew, Victoria: Australian Theological Forum, 1996, pp. 1–21. Reprinted by permission.

[2] 'Since from the beginning of the world there has been no region, no city, in short no household, that could do without religion, there lies in this a tacit confession of a sense of deity inscribed in the hearts of all.' *Institutes* I.iii.1 (McNeill and Battles, I, p. 44).

[3] Fung Yu-Lan, *A Short History of Chinese Philosophy*, New York: Macmillan, 1958.

philosophical theism developed as a response to a felt need for a more satisfactory religious basis for social order than the feuding creeds of a fragmented Christendom. What we call 'theism' has a historical location, as a seventeenth century attempt to find a common basis for the functioning of society. The plan was to ground social order in human nature, but a human nature understood in the light of a rationalistic version of the doctrine of creation.[4] This was driven by a metaphor of mechanism. The mechanism of social order was based in a natural order understood to have been created by a machine-maker deity. Speaking of Enlightenment America, Robert Jenson comments that 'Laws of political motion derived from analogy to the Newtonian laws of action and reaction pit interest against interest, faction against faction, power-center against power-center, to the good of all. The construction of such a polity was the great goal of those who established America's institutions.'[5] The God of the rational moral order thus provided a means of distinguishing between those things constitutive of society and those not necessary to its cohesion. Another way of putting the same matter would be to say that theism was an attempt to find a religious basis for a social order by the paring away of the elements of traditional Christian theology thought to be dispensable or actively harmful. Rational theism was to replace Christian dogma with a more universal basis for society. As we shall see, the effects of this are still with us.

2. It was one of the achievements of G. W. F. Hegel to have perceived the inadequacy of all the early modern programme. But there could be no simple return to the past. The Christian synthesis that had provided a basis for all forms of intellectual and social order during the period of Western Christendom was gone for ever. However, Hegel also believed that something at least as all-embracing was needed to replace the unifying vision of the Middle Ages, because some appropriately modern structure was needed for the stability of social order. But it had to be truly social, not simply mathematical and mechanical. His

[4] Christoph Schwöbel, 'After "Post-theism"', *Traditional Theism and its Modern Alternatives*, ed. Svend Anderson, Aarhus: Aarhus University Press, 1994, pp. 173–175.
[5] Robert W. Jenson, *Essays in Theology of Culture*, Grand Rapids: Eerdmans, 1995, p. 59.

proposal was to employ aspects of the Christian trinitarian vision in the service of a modernised Christendom. It is that programme whose death-throes we are experiencing today in the bankruptcy of theological liberalism, as well as in the inverted forms of Hegelianism that took shape in Marxism and other totalitarian systems. But even these anti-religious systems remind us again of the widely felt need for some kind of deity, if only a secularised one, as in the conception of history that takes the place of God in Marxism.

The point of this survey is to make us realise that it is our era that is out of step, and surely self-deceived, in claiming the viability of a purely secular basis for social institutions. This self-deception is still widespread, and found particularly in survivals of the doctrine of inevitable progress, for example in the continuing currency of the assumption that modernisation, however that is conceived, is both irreversible and will inevitably continue to take a secular direction. This is all we need, it is still naively supposed, for the success of technology will obviate the need for a religious underpinning of things. The absurd outbreak of faith in the capacities of The Net to provide a new world order is another symptom of this desperate modern desire to solve human problems merely technologically. Some serious theologians, as well as modernising secularists, still maintain faith in the irreversibility of secular modernism.

To this a range of responses is possible. We could draw upon the view that there is little sociological evidence for the irreversibility of secularism. It appears that some societies, in Latin America for example,[6] are going through forms of technological development without an accompanying secularism.[7]

---

[6] David Martin, *Tongues of Fire. The Explosion of Protestantism in Latin America*, London: Blackwell, 1990, pp. 274–275 for an argument for the contingency of at least one secularising tendency in modern culture.

[7] It may well be the case that the inevitable association of modernisation with the decline of religious belief is characteristic of the historical context of the West, where ecclesiastical institutions undermined their credibility by the way in which they appeared to respond purely negatively to the rise of the new science. Such considerations make it possible to claim that cultures with a less paranoid view of the interference of ecclesiastical institutions in the process of free thought and enquiry may well find that science and technology are one thing, secularism another. Modern science and irreligion are not necessarily associated, as some recent forms of cosmological speculation demonstrate only too well.

And in any case, there is some evidence that things are changing even in traditional Western societies. A recent report suggests an upturn in religious observance in Australia, particularly among young couples with children, and the reason given is in line with the general concern of this chapter. 'Much of the resurgence of interest in church can be attributed to young couples searching for ways to give their children a grounding in morality ...'[8] Rightly or wrongly, it is coming to be believed that some of the ills of the modern age are attributable to the loss of religious belief. We might put the matter still more strongly. It is a miracle that Christian belief has survived at all in an intellectual atmosphere poisoned against it by ideologies of all kinds. Now that the ideologies are changing, so may the prospects for renewal be greater.

A further piece of evidence that secularisation is not an irreversible feature of modern developments is shown by the emergence of New Age and other forms of religiosity. When Christian belief declines, it would appear that, to quote the famous saying, people do not believe in nothing; they rather believe in anything. And the surprising thing about the revival of pagan religion is that it is in its turn encouraging a revival of traditional religious forms, particularly those seeking a concept or experience of the spiritual or the Spirit. Nowhere is man's inherent religiosity demonstrated better than here, but also in the heart of the scientific world, where it becomes clear that science becomes a form of religion, and scientists indulge in all kinds of theological speculation. Religion is all around us, at least in the sense suggested by Tillich that we all have some ultimate concern, something that makes us tick more loudly than anything else, or as appears in Luther's more trenchant saying that whatever we hang our heart on serves as our God. It appears that, at least in some sense, God or a focus of worship is inescapable. In that respect Schleiermacher was right. There is a deep sense of religion in all of us. Or better, we should say with Calvin that we all have a *sensus deitatis*, an innate feel for divinity. In appealing to Calvin, who gets the balance better than both Schleiermacher and Tillich, we should remember that for him apart from the Christian gospel we all get our deity wrong, fabricating idols

[8] *Australian Outlook*, May 1995, p. 22.

which far from saving us in fact enslave us. That would seem to be a far more accurate way of looking at the modern condition. Rather than abandoning belief in some form of deity, the modern world has simply replaced the triune God with various false ones, money perhaps predominant among them.

II   *Society today*

But that leads us into further questions about the nature of the gods of the modern world, and particularly to the matter of pluralism. Pluralism is difficult to define, for it comes in many forms, but in general I mean by it the approach associated with some forms of postmodernism, according to which we are recommended simply to glory in particularity, variety and difference and allow the other to be the other, not a clone of ourselves. The mistake of all quests for *foundations*, of whatever kind, is that they are oppressive, forcing people into moulds.[9] It is fashionable to claim that we do not *need* such a unity nor do we in fact have one. We are, it is claimed, pluralistic and democratic societies, in which there is no one focus of unity, and that this is a good thing, heartily to be embraced.

But are we genuinely plural societies? The truth is rather that we are pluralist societies in certain respects, namely those fashionably thought not to have real impact upon the way our societies actually operate. As Lesslie Newbigin has repeatedly and convincingly argued, by relegating them to a merely 'private' sphere, modern societies effectively emasculate religious interests so that they cease to be truly constitutive of what a society really is.[10] Religion becomes what one does with one's solitude. The thesis must not be oversimplified. The point of the appeal to Newbigin is this. From the claim that we are pluralistic, according to the official doctrine, about overt religious beliefs, making religion a kind of option in the marketplace, it does not follow that we live in a genuinely plural society. The much vaunted pluralism conceals the fact that modern commercial and technological forces are exerting a homogenising and therefore unifying pressure on the way our

---

[9] Zygmunt Bauman, *Post-modern Ethics*, London: Blackwell, 1993.
[10] Lesslie Newbigin, *The Gospel in a Pluralist Society*, London: SPCK, 1989.

social order takes shape. Many of the intellectual influences that have shaped our modern world tend towards the abolition of differences, and in a number of ways. Both local communities and particular people are forced into modernising uniformities that deprive them of their distinctiveness. Zygmunt Bauman has seen in the modern quest for universality a move towards 'the progressive thinning down and eventually to the smothering, of present differences ...'.[11] He speaks of modernity as 'an arduous campaign to smother the differences and above all to eliminate all "wild" – autonomous, obstreperous and uncontrolled sources of moral judgement' (p. 12). Central to all this was the concept of the '*citizen* (the person with only such attributes as have been assigned by the laws of the single and uncontested authority acting on behalf of the unified and sovereign state) for the motley collection of parishioners, kinsmen and other locals' (p. 39).

A prominent aspect of this tendency is a move towards the elimination of the institutions and communities intermediate between the state and the individual person. It is these that are, in the view of acute observers of the modern scene like Michael Polanyi and Jonathan Sacks, crucial to the health of any open society.[12] But these focuses of local independence are inevitably suspect to authorities acting in the name of universal reason and modernity. In Britain, for example, it has been Conservative governments which have in recent years sought to reduce the autonomy of local government, the outcome being that their individualism has led to a centralising of government.

The historical irony of this is that a movement for human autonomy, often dedicated to freeing the human race from the tyranny of a homogenising God, has replaced that God with various rationalising forces which also work to produce homogeneity. But they are much worse, and for a number of reasons. I quote Robert Jenson again:

When communal vision of transcendent destiny fails,

[11] Bauman, *Post-modern Ethics*, p. 42, cf. p. 12.
[12] Michael Polanyi, *Personal Knowledge. Towards a Post-Critical Philosophy*, London: Routledge, 2nd ed. 1962; Jonathan Sacks, *The Persistence of Faith. Religion, Morality and Society in a Secular Age*, London: Weidenfeld and Nicolson, 1991.

temporal values become demonic; then, for example, the 'liberty' for which our state exists exhausts itself in the liberty of the state, and national security becomes the functioning political value. Since this turns rule over to police and army who are servants of the state, such a state has no actual rulers; it is but a self-perpetuating mindless process, a self-sustaining institutionalised public disorder, the usual word for which is 'fascism.'[13]

Why is this? The privatisation of ultimate questions like that concerning God means that they are displaced from the centre of thought, action and attention by penultimate interests; the creature is worshipped instead of the creator. Thus, we might say, idolatry is institutionalised, and we have, in Richard Neuhaus' expression, a naked public square.[14] The driving out of God from the public square can only have the effect of admitting seven devils far worse than those represented by the politicised Christianity which has been so roundly rejected by secular thinking. One does not need to dismiss the importance of economics to suggest that those who live only by such considerations are worshipping mammon in place of God.[15]

All of this raises the question of the sense in which the modern democratic world can be called 'totalitarian'. The danger of modern liberal democracy is that it will deceive us into believing that we are freer than we are. Here we must not forget the positive side of modern institutions. One cannot, without indulging in reactionary nostalgia, deny that we are freer in certain respects than in many alternative forms of organising society. But we live in a fool's paradise if we evade the pressures to homogenisation or the abolition of the personal differences that make each of us unique and lovable for ourselves. The context in which this chapter was first written, a conference on modern medical practice, suggests some examples, in that there is more than a suspicion that it is being used for 'quality control' – for example, in the practice of abortion as little more than a precaution against a small likelihood of

[13] Jenson, *Essays*, p. 64.
[14] Richard J. Neuhaus, *The Naked Public Square*, Grand Rapids: Eerdmans, 1984.
[15] It is often remarked that modern shopping malls are like cathedrals where the liturgy of shopping is enacted.

abnormality. Feminists like Germaine Greer are perhaps not altogether paranoid when they see moves towards totalitarian controls of women's bodies. She refers to 'the statement of a senior gynaecologist that in future all women will be hysterectomised when they have completed their family size and doped with oestrogen for the rest of their lives'.[16]

Here we reach one of the many paradoxes of modernity. In modern society regimentation goes hand in hand with a kind of anarchic individualism. The former we have already met in the tendency of modern regimes to attempt to impose dietary standards upon the public: for example, in the suggestion attributed to Mrs Bottomley that we should all eat three small potatoes each day. As Petr Scrabanek points out, people used to go to the doctor when they felt unwell. Now, the authorities attempt to impose upon us practices alleged to lengthen our lives or save the state money.[17] The individualism is the other side of the picture, when important decisions, like those about religious practice or sexual ethics, in which it was once rightly supposed that the community had some form of interest, are now left entirely to individual choice, choice, that is, however, subverted by propaganda and advertising.

Nor must it be forgotten that much theology is guilty of conniving with the modern drive to homogeneity. Michael J. Baxter has recently produced a sceptical appraisal of the fashionable tendency to what is called a 'public church' in the United States of America. Recent representatives of the approach are, he says:

> concerned only with those elements of Christianity that are translatable into values and principles that can then be applied to a U.S. public policy-making agenda. As a result, they put forth a domesticated version of Christianity and the church, one that conforms all too readily to the protocols of 'politics' as conventionally understood and practiced in the United States. In this way ... the public church does not

---

[16] Germaine Greer , 'We shall not be neutered', *The Spectator* 20 May 1995, p. 54. See also Caroline Richmond, 'A Womb of one's own', *The Spectator* 9 June 1995, giving evidence for the practice of giving women hysterectomies without their consent.

[17] Petr Skrabanek, *The Death of Humane Medicine and the Rise of Coercive Healthism*, London: Social Affairs Unit, 1994.

transform U.S. society; rather, U.S. society does not rest until the public church fits in with itself and with what it considers reasonable.[18]

Baxter also questions the assumption that the modern liberal democratic state is necessarily on the side of the angels, for the picture presented in the works he is considering

> fails to acknowledge the extent to which the role of the state in liberal democracy is in fact not limited but intrusive ... [I]t also fails to account for the role of corporations and other nonpublic organisations in the formation and exercise of political power. Then too, it shows virtually no appreciation of the role of advertising and the media in constructing the perceptions, desires, attitudes, and beliefs of the political subjects in this alleged 'arena of civil liberties'.[19]

And this brings us to another prominent feature of modern pluralism. It is its belief that we do not need any form of shared foundation for social order, which can simply be left to fend for itself. Against this, it must be asserted that it seems to be the case that even societies dedicated to pluralism, perhaps especially those, have a tendency to generate a myth or account of their basis. Perhaps 'pluralism' is such a myth, the last desperate gasp of the secular experiment. But pluralism is a chimera, because it unlikely that any social order could exist without some focus for or myth of unity that denies the very pluralism that is affirmed. This is because claims for truth will out, and they will be found to clash with one another. If we have no language and institutions in which to settle the inevitable disputes which accompany living in relation to others, those disputes will be likely to run out of control. We must therefore be sceptical of the claim that a society can be genuinely pluralistic, unless the plurality that it tolerates is underwritten by some form of shared basis in truth. The omens are not good for those who would claim a form of pluralism as itself some kind of unifying basis. Insofar as pluralism involves a suspension of judgement about the truth of the basis of life and a move to some form of relativism, there is in it probably the weakest focus of all. Susan Mendus has pointed out

---

[18] Michael J. Baxter, C.S.C. , 'Review Essay: the Non-Catholic Character of the "Public Church"', *Modern Theology* 11 (1995), pp. 243–258 (244).

[19] Baxter, 'Review Essay', pp. 253f.

that as a matter of historical fact, intellectual relativism generates social intolerance.[20] And Richard Neuhaus makes a similar point: 'Pluralism is a jealous god. When pluralism is established as dogma, there is not room for other dogmas.'[21] The reason is clear: if we have no agreed ways of facing and solving our moral differences, either conflict or repression is likely to be the outcome. We are irreducibly social beings, and cannot exist without some form of institutionalised relationships: law, education and medical care, quite apart from more basic necessities of food and shelter. Do the market or pluralistic individualism supply reasons for our continuing over and above this to behave in a civil manner towards one another? It seems more likely to be the case that, in the absence of an acknowledged basis of unity, social coercion, perhaps as an intolerant form of political correctness, but probably more institutionalised, will fill the vacuum. Whatever it is, it will provide the unifying framework traditionally supplied by God or religion. As Robert Jenson has commented, 'There never was, and in my opinion never will be, a polity without its religion.'[22]

III   *What kind of Deity?*

What theological response can there be to this depressing situation? If it is the case that the early church, in a situation similar to ours of supposed pluralism, both out-thought and out-lived the decadent classical civilisation in which it took shape, our challenge is to out-live and out-think decadent Western rationalism. It will be a more difficult task, from one point of view, because the church is already bound up with Western social history in a way that the ancient church was not. But it will be easier by virtue of the fact that we have at our disposal a fund of wisdom, of a great tradition of life and thought which is by no means at the end of its resources.[23] From that fund, I shall now try to bring to

[20] Susan Mendus, 'Introduction', *On Toleration*, edd. Susan Mendus and David Edwards, Oxford: Clarendon Press, 1987, p. 6.
[21] Neuhaus, *The Naked Public Square*, p. 148.
[22] Jenson, *Essays*, p. 98.
[23] This is the great strength of John Milbank, *Theology and Social Theory. Beyond Secular Reason*, Oxford: Blackwell, 1990.

bear some of the resources we have to contribute to lifting the dead hand of secular rationalism.

The conclusion of the argument so far is that, inescapably, something will perform the function of a deity. God, some god, is thus indeed indispensable, in the sense that all societies have one as a kind of ideal or focus of social unity. But the deity a society worships, whether that deity be avowed or unconscious, makes much difference to its life, so that much hangs on on which god it is that we hang our hearts. That is why there are a number of reasons why the God worshipped by Christians is indispensable for the good ordering of a free, just and tolerant society. In the remainder of the chapter, I want to advance a number of theses to develop such a claim.

1. First, and it is the only thing that finally justifies the claim, is that the God made known in Jesus Christ and the Spirit is the truth about our world and the shape that life must, if it is to be true life, take in it. If things are as Christians claim them to be, then the triune God is, as a matter of fact, the one without whom nothing is as it should be. The truth of this claim does not depend upon the power, 'success' or numbers of the church, though as a matter of fact I believe that societies are more satisfactorily ordered if this God is acknowledged at the centre of their lives; but this is secondary. Let me quote some words of P. T. Forsyth that make the point better than many:

> God is only God as absolute, eternal, holy love; His love conquers; it is the absolute power over us, and the final power over our world. All things work together for good to them that love God *in His universal, royal, holy, and final purpose* ... Such is the God of the Bible. He reveals Himself, but it is of His absolutely free and royal choice for His own holy end ... And God ceases to be God when he ceases to be such a God – the absolute, miraculous, personal, holy, and effective King and Lord of us and our world. To curtail his power is to infect Him with weakness; that is to say, it is to make Him a mixture of power and weakness – which again is to make Him a part of the world, and destroy Him altogether as God.[24]

[24] P. T. Forsyth, *The Principle of Authority*, London: Independent Press, 1952. 1st ed., 1913, pp. 371–372.

The Christian faith makes universal claims, because the God it worships and affirms – the triune God – is the universal creator and redeemer of all. That is thesis 1, and it determines all the others.

2. However, we should not express our claims to represent this God in too unqualified a manner. We cannot, for example, present too stark claims for the choice that has to be made. To present our audience with the alternatives of '*either* nihilism and chaos, *or* Christian social order and the "peaceful differ-ence" of the Trinity', according to Richard Roberts' character-isation of Milbank's thesis, may engender another attempt to impose some form of order upon society.[25] The reason why such stark alternatives cannot be accepted lies in what has already been said. If God is the creator of all things and the lord of history, then nihilism and chaos are not to be taken seriously as possibilities. Here we should recall an earlier experience of similar social decay. The world went on after the fall of Rome, and indeed that latter event gave Augustine the confidence to produce the work that formed the basis of the Christian civilisation to come. We may not enjoy the upheavals that may accompany the end of the Enlightenment attempt to become masters of the universe ourselves, but they will not necessarily prevent us from using them as the basis for a renewal of Christian thought and life.

Here a reference to Paul's eschatology is more than helpful. It is quite clear that for Paul the final judgement at the end of time was anticipated in the present by events which in some way prefigured it. He refers to a historical Roman who desecrated the temple at Jerusalem by placing in it the image of the emperor: 'the man of lawlessness ... who exalts himself against every so-called god and object of worship, so that he takes his seat in the temple of God, proclaiming himself to be God' (2 Thess. 2.3f). But, while time and history remain, it remains also the case that their lord prevents such demonic self-assertion from running out of control. Whether the meaning of v. 7: 'he who now restrains it will do so until he is out of the way' refers to God, Christ, the emperor or some angelic authority remains

---

[25] Richard Roberts 'Article Review: Transcendental Sociology? A Critique of John Milbank's *Theology and Social Theory. Beyond Secular Reason*', *Scottish Journal of Theology* 46 (1993), pp. 527–535 (p. 528).

irrelevant to the main point, which is that history is not out of the control of God and the mediators of his authority, who include duly constituted political authorities. This, then, is my first main claim: that a theology of divine sovereignty is the first foundation stone of the theology of social order. Thesis 2 is then that the sovereignty of God excludes any absolute pessimism. It is not we, but God, upon whom all things depend.

3. But it does not follow from this that a human moral response is irrelevant. The reverse is the case, for the shape that divine sovereignty takes in part depends upon the human response to grace. For that reason, we must ask a number of questions about how the universal claims of the Christian God are to be expressed. What kind of God do we worship, how does his reality express itself in history and what kind of demands, so far as society is concerned, does this impose upon the created order? How, in particular, should those who are called to represent the Christian gospel in the world seek to realise the claims of God over all the created order? That brings me to thesis 3: God is indispensable as providing a transcendent and eschatological framework for human social relationships. The experiment of the past few centuries according to which man is his own God or source of moral wisdom must be adjudged a pathetic failure, as it was bound to be. But it must also be confessed that the enterprise of seeking an immanent or this-worldly centre of meaning was undertaken for some good reasons. Not all was well with late Christian civilisation, as the Inquisition and wars of religion demonstrated only too well. But we know that story well enough for it to need no detailed rehearsal here. The reason for mentioning it is that it reminds us that nostalgia for the era of Christendom is misplaced, as is now very widely agreed, at least insofar as that involves the enforcement of Christianity by official means.[26] Both Christen-

---

[26] That does not deny that it may not be officially encouraged, though whether that would be a help I am not sure, and do not need to discuss here, nor that it is wrong to attempt to shape social order. The situation can be illustrated quite simply. A recent article suggested that it is wrong for the churches to attempt to impose their dislike of abortion on to the public. In reply, Michael Banner wondered what would have happened to the Christian campaign against slavery if such attitudes had prevailed. It would be sectarian to draw an absolute line between churchly ethics and those of the world around.

dom and its modern denial have lived by false eschatologies: premature attempts to impose the kingdom of God on earth. What is needed is a firm belief in the sovereignty of God, but less confidence in our ability to represent it in the world.

But what will fill their place? Given that both the (transcendent) past and the (immanent) present are in different ways profoundly unsatisfactory, where shall we look for salvation? Thesis 3A is that we require a *transcendent* source of truth, but one that needs to be carefully defined. Let us begin a construction with an appeal to the doctrine of the Trinity. In some recent writings, the value of a trinitarian model for social order has been claimed. The theology of God conceived to exist in the interrelationship of persons in which neither the one nor the many has priority over the other provides an alternative to the two poles of modern political thought, individualism, which elevates the many over the one, and collectivism, which does the reverse. Alongside this, and in development of it, we must set the theology of the person. If the divine persons are what they are in love and freedom, any social system which systematically deprives persons or groups of both love and freedom is to be questioned. Beyond any shadow of doubt, the doctrine of the Trinity has much to give us.

But it is not enough, because of the danger of an idealism in which the doctrine is used to justify an unthinking appeal to that which happens to be the fashionable political or social theory. We are all in favour of relational conceptions of humanity and the world, all in favour of love and freedom – well, most of us anyway. What makes a difference is how we construe them. No trinitarian theology is adequate without attention first to the particular shape taken by the life, death and resurrection of the second person of the Trinity incarnate, Jesus of Nazareth, and second to the characteristic form taken by the work of the Spirit who, by relating people and things to Jesus, brings about their proper perfection. To transcendence must be added eschatology.

How this is to be understood can be developed with a glance at the topic of the two cities, famously presented by Augustine as the heavenly and earthly cities. They were Augustine's concrete way of speaking of the relation of eternity and time with specific reference to social and political order. Until the end of time, the two cities are intermingled, so that throughout our fallen time divine eternity continues to impinge by virtue of the presence of the eternal to time. However, there are difficulties with Augustine's way of construing the relation, which was characteristically platonic. The city of God was for him a timeless reality, transcending the earthly city and imping-ing upon it in various ways. Furthermore, the eternal city is represented by angels, as is made clear by the large amount of space dedicated to their place in the created order by Augus-tine in the *City of God*.[27] What is wrong with this? First, its platonism tended to produce an other-worldly emphasis which undervalued the life of this world. Second is the fact that, whether true to Augustine's vision or not, it did come about that the vision operated oppressively, in coming to justify the imposition upon a social order of a faith whose basis must remain in free response to the gospel. Both considerations require a re-examination of the place of eschatology in our understanding of the relation of the two cities. Augustine has a transcendent framework for social order, but one whose escha-tology was questionable because contaminated by the platonic opposition of time and eternity. This brings me to thesis 3B. What is needed is an eschatological reading of the two cities: not contrasting eternity with time, so much as seeing this life in the light of the world to come.

The inadequacies of the Augustinian eschatology derive from weak christology and pneumatology. As so often in Augustine's theology, there is a tendency for the distinctive forms of action attributed to Son and Spirit to be redistributed to intermediate agencies, in the context of a strongly unitary conception of divine action. Because Jesus Christ and the Holy Spirit tend to be displaced by the angels, the character of divine action in history is understood too unitarily, so that two biblical notes tend to be lost or at least underplayed. One is the dynamism of the biblical God's eternity, for example that expressed in the vision of the latter chapters of the book of Revelation, with its clear incarnational note. The writer sees a vision of the holy city coming down from heaven to earth, in such a way that the

---

[27] Augustine, *City of God*, books xi and xii in particular. See, for example, xi.9: 'Angels form the greater part of the heavenly city . . .'

historical incarnation bears down upon history and *within* history from eternity. Revelation 21.3 uses the christology of John 1.14 – that the Word became flesh – eschatologically: 'Behold, the dwelling of God is with men. He will dwell with them, and they shall be his people, and God himself will be with them.' The coming of Christ to the world is the coming of final salvation in the here and now.Where he is, the world to come begins already.

We shall, then, begin an elucidation of the bearing of eschatology on social order with christology. The life, death and resurrection of Jesus show the way by which God's recapitulation of the human story engages with the powers of darkness and brings fallen human life to its promised perfection. Here is not a political programme, but action, teaching and a death. Insofar as there is a political programme in the divine economy it is realised by the gathering of a community around the crucified and risen Lord. Insofar as it depicts a mode of human action, it is manifestly non-coercive. That is not to be taken sentimentally. The records of the teaching of Jesus suggest that what he says is to be understood in terms of both giving and the requirement of obedience, of promise and threat alike; of grace and judgement, we might say in summary. As man, Jesus exercises the action of divine sovereignty in both grace and judgement, but he does it in a way that takes him to the cross. Albert Schweitzer famously saw that eschatology is the key to the meaning of Jesus' death, but he understood it wrongly. He believed that Jesus went to the cross in the hope of forcing God's hand, compelling him to bring in the end of the world:

> Jesus ... lays hold of the wheel of the world to set it moving on that last revolution which is to bring all ordinary history to a close. It refuses to turn, and He throws Himself upon it. Then it does turn, and crushes Him.[28]

Rather, the action of Jesus in going to the cross means the opposite: he leaves the outcome to God the Father, trusting in his sovereignty. That is the model for human action in the

---

[28] Albert Schweitzer, *The Quest of the Historical Jesus. A Critical Study of its Progress from Reimarus to Wrede*, E.T. by W. Montgomery, London: A. and C. Black, 3rd edn., 1954, pp. 368–369.

world. The failure of both Christendom and modernity is precisely to attempt to move the wheel of history for ourselves.

What part, then, does our theology of the Spirit play in all this? This was the aspect Schweitzer missed. It is the Spirit who brings in the eschatological age, and his action is paradigmatically realised in the resurrection of Jesus from the dead. The point about the action of God the Spirit is that it gives substance to anticipations of the recapitulation (Eph. 1) of all things to be achieved in Christ. There are two focuses to the Spirit's action in this respect, judgement and redemption. The Spirit acts to convict the world of sin – see, for example, John 16.8–11 – exposing its disobedience and unbelief. In a similar context to this one – a paper entitled, 'Is there an Ordering Principle?' – Robert Jenson has observed that, 'Eschatological vision always starts with the perception of damnation.'[29] But, certainly so far as the judgement of the end is anticipated in the present, that judgement serves the greater end of redemption, of the reconciliation of all things in Christ the mediator of creation. That, too is the Spirit's function in reordering the fallen world by redirecting it to its true end in Jesus Christ. The Spirit is thus the agent and mediator of the rule of Christ in both judgement and salvation until he hands over the rule to God the Father at the end of the age. That is the only principle of social order that we need, and it is more concerned with ordering than with order, with an action taking place rather than the rigid structure envisaged in some conservative theories of social order. To summarise thesis 3: the transcendent basis we need for social order is the sovereign action of God made real in Christ and the Spirit, because only there do we learn how God actually works in the world.

4. The outcome of all this is that in place of the traditional theology of the two cities, we require a conception of the action of the sovereign God taking place through both church and world. The world and the church are, alike but in different ways, the subjects and objects of divine eschatological action. The way in which the sovereignty of God operates through what we call the world is through both grace and judgement. There is wholesome and saving action in the sphere of the world. One

[29] Jenson, *Essays*, p. 75.

of the many points of the parable of the Good Samaritan, as Barth long ago pointed out, is that gracious and godly action is found precisely in those places we tend to call world rather than church. That holds for large areas of modern medical practice. But there is also judgement. If our modern world has systematically organised its life so as to worship the creature rather than the creator, then either its repentance or its doom cannot be far away.

But that is not to deny the primary place that the church is called to have in the purposes of God. To understand how it can be that the church must be understood as a, perhaps the, major focus of the working of divine sovereignty in the world, we must turn to the doctrine of election. In its traditional Western form, election tended to be of individuals and was oriented on the future kingdom. Election was primarily to do with the future fate of individual believers. But the biblical focus is much more centrally on election to a historical task. The historical task of the church is not to attempt to order society, not to attempt to grasp the reins of worldly power, but to accept a call to be a community of life centred on worship. Worship has all the features that our modern world most desperately needs, because it orients human life to one who reminds us that we are creatures, and do not make our world. It places us before the absolute sovereignty of the sovereign God. Moreover, relation to that authority is realised through Christ and the Spirit, so that we emphasise not only God's otherness, but his nearness in reconciliation and redemption. It is as a community of worship that the church implicitly acts as a vehicle of divine judgement upon and salvation from all those idolatrous forms of life that, in both church and world, would worship anything other than the creator. Thesis 4 holds then that because the church is a community whose orientation is transcendent and eschatological, she provides, precisely as a worshipping community and as a result of her orientation, the strongest possible counterweight to a world dedicated to merely this-worldly goals.

5. The focus on worship is also important because it avoids a merely moralistic definition of the church. Activism is the modern church's characteristic sin. But there are ethical dimensions, and they centre on the church as an intermediate community, one of those communities of concrete human relationship

where we learn to become truly ourselves. As I have already suggested, the health of society is bound up with the health of those communities, which, because they are intermediate between the state and the individual, maintain a balance between the one and the many. They are bulwarks against both collectivism and individualism, both of which deprive human being of its space to be. Because of her orientation to the sovereign triune God, the church's moral and social calling, as *the* intermediate community, is to be an echo in time of the communion of Father, Son and Spirit in eternity.

Of course, here too we must not idealise. The theology of divine sovereignty and the eschatological dimension I have stressed together entail that the relation between church and world is a complex one, because there is no absolute distinction between them. Both spheres of sovereignty are peopled by human beings made in the image of God and only more or less partly realising the form of life that entails. The walls dividing church from world are permeable. On the one hand, the church is not immune from patterns of being characteristic of worldly – fallen – existence, as the sociology of modern sexual behaviour illustrates all too well. On the other hand, even in a supposedly secular society the fact of the existence of a worshipping community inevitably shapes the way in which life in the 'world' takes form. Religion, including traditional Christian faith, does have an impact on society in all kinds of ways. That the leader of the British Labour Party is a practising Christian and that 20 per cent – or whatever – of Australians attend church will have all kinds of effect upon the way things go from day to day.

Thus, without being idealistic, it is possible to claim that the church has an indispensable role to play even, perhaps especially, in the societies that appear to have written her off. Here her public character is important, not public in the sense attacked earlier, as in some way assimilated to contemporary patterns of thought and behaviour, but as being publicly different. It is only so that she may be a vehicle of divine judgement and grace, for example, in reminding all society that unless it serves a truth that is beyond it, the naked public square will soon be filled by demons. More important, such a community plays the positive role of representing promise: that hope does not depend upon playing god, upon economic development, upon technological progress, but upon response to grace and truth. It is there to witness to the God who is indispensable because he is the sovereign lord who calls all into reconciled relationship with him through Jesus Christ and in the Spirit. Thesis 5 is then that the church is indispensable to society as a minority community calling upon the wider world also to worship, and prepared to pay the price for that witness.

Let me then draw two conclusions. 1. There are, in the theology of the triune God, resources for a non-coercive conception of social unity, and therefore of a social order that is open and plural rather than pluralistic. But not any Trinity will do, only one formed by attention to the way in which God acts in the incarnation and atoning death and resurrection of Jesus and in the eschatological action of the Holy Spirit in both church and world. There is certainly order in the heavenly city, and it is one derived from the worship of God. *Disorder* derives from the worship of the creature instead of the creator. Order is not an end in itself, but exists for the end of human love and freedom. We may therefore accept neither a postmodern vision of sheer disorder, nor a modern vision of an order imposed by reason or force. That is why our God who is a God of order through freedom – freedom to be with, from and for the other – is indispensable for a social order in which both individuality and sociality have due place.

2. The church is indispensable to modern social order because, and in as much as, the God she worships is indispensable to the good ordering of all societies, whether that be recognised or not. But, as our christology and eschatology suggest, she may not take that as a licence to act coercively. Her indispensability is a relative indispensability, relative that is to the overall workings of divine sovereignty. The calling of the church is to embody, but not compel, this vision. This means that the most effective way to operate in the modern world is as a church, perhaps generally a minority church, which does not trim its teaching to the fashions of the present but actively orients its life to the cross and resurrection of the incarnate Lord. This means that the church as an institution has to learn the lesson that the best way to gain its political life and influence is to lose it. Her God is indispensable for the life of the world, but exercises his sovereignty in his own way and own time.

Chapter 10

ATONEMENT AND THE PROJECT OF CREATION

An interpretation of Colossians 1.15–23[1]

I *To broaden the focus*

According to John Thompson in a recent study of the doctrine of the Trinity, it is the conviction of Eberhard Jüngel, along with Moltmann, von Balthasar and Barth, that the cross is the key to the trinitarian nature of God.[2] But is it? Can it not equally be argued that it is a weakness of Western theology that it has tended to treat the significance of the cross in relative abstraction from the incarnation, resurrection, or, for that matter, creation, so that it has appeared to teach strange doctrines in which the cross is a kind of punitive exercise rather than the centre of the whole justifying action of God? We shall therefore ask in this chapter what is the *contribution* the atonement makes to trinitarian theology; and, conversely, what does the Trinity contribute to an understanding of the atonement? One benefit of the project is that it may enable us to understand the relation of economic and ontological Trinity more systematically than seems to be the case in much recent theology. That is to say: might the atonement be of more assistance in maintaining a due sense of the relation between what we may say of God in relation to the world and God in himself than either Barth's stress on the freedom of God or the more recent fashion for speaking of a suffering God?

---

[1] A slightly revised version of a paper published in *Dialog* 35 (Winter 1996), pp. 35–41. Reprinted by permission.

[2] John Thompson, *Modern Trinitarian Perspectives*, Oxford and New York: Oxford University Press, 1994, p. 58.

The heart of the matter is this. It is indeed necessary to understand the atonement as a divine act, something achieved by God in order to save the human race from a plight of its own making which would negate God's purposes for good for both it and the world. But to concentrate on the suffering of God raises problems. On the one hand, it tends to reduce atonement to theodicy: as if the problem is not human offence and sin, but the evil for which God is in some sense responsible. There is a problem of theodicy in a world of suffering, but it is not the same as that of atonement, and if it supplants the latter, it undermines the gospel of the grace of God in face of human enmity towards him. On the other hand, it calls attention away from the fact that atonement is also a human act, an act, that is, of the incarnate Son whose life, death and resurrection realise, in the Spirit, a human conquest of evil which those who come to God through him may subsequently share. To place the weight on a suffering God deprives the incarnate Son of his proper work, as Andrew Walker has argued.[3]

Already, as soon as these points are made, the necessity for a discussion of the trinitarian dimensions of the topic becomes manifest. In what sense is atonement the work of the Father, and how is that work mediated by the Son and the Spirit? Clearly, it has always been seen as the work of God the Father, but sometimes the impression has been given that in some sense the Father punishes the Son as man in place of the sinner. The objections to this have been so well rehearsed that there is no need for repetition. But why does the accusation continue to be made if it is not because something, somewhere, continues to be lacking? This chapter is designed to demonstrate that attention to the pneumatological dimensions enables the development of a more truly trinitarian construction of the matter, and in two respects in particular. First, it places the atonement in the broader context of God's plan for the whole created order. And second it enables the character of the atonement as a truly human act to come more into the centre of the picture. We shall begin with the former consideration, in order to place the atonement in the whole economy of God.

[3] Andrew Walker, in an unpublished paper.

II   *Creation as project*

The fashion for 'creation spirituality' and the disrepute into which the doctrine of original sin has fallen both testify to the Achilles' heel of the Western tradition of atonement theology, Catholic and Evangelical alike. While critics of the mainstream tradition tend to parody it, there are elements of truth in what they say, and as follows. First, much difficulty has been generated by a tendency to conceive of the original creation as absolutely, rather than relatively, perfect, so that salvation, however it is understood, comes to be understood in terms of restitution to an original state. If everything is absolutely perfect in the beginning, salvation can only mean a going back to something already achieved. I do not here want to join the now fashionable band of those who hold that in some way the creation was not complete in the 'beginning', and that it is still in some way still in process. Oliver O'Donovan has argued recently that this is to misconstrue the relation between creation and providence:

> That which most distinguishes the concept of creation is that it is complete. Creation is the given totality of order which forms the presupposition of historical existence. ... Because created order is given, because it is secure, we dare to be certain that God will vindicate it in history.[4]

As will become clear, however, it is also necessary, without undermining that statement – which in its own way repeats Barth's distinction between creation and providence[5] – to speak of the relative perfection of creation in the beginning to make the point that creation is not a timeless whole, as it was made in Augustine, but has a temporality and a directedness to an end

[4] Oliver O'Donovan, *Resurrection and Moral Order. An Outline for Evangelical Ethics*, Leicester: Inter-Varsity Press and Grand Rapids: Eerdmans, 1986, pp. 60f.

[5] Karl Barth, *Church Dogmatics* III/3, Edinburgh: T. & T. Clark, 1960, p. 13. The differences between the concepts of creation and providence are, then, first that providence presupposes creation, presupposes that there is something to provide for; and second that creation presupposes providence, for although it is a finished act, it is not the finished act of the deist machine maker, but of one who has in view the care for and governing of the creation.

which is greater than its beginnings, and that they belong to its nature as creation.

Second, there has been a tendency to conceive human salvation as being in some way apart from the rest of the created order, as, for example, the salvation of the soul apart from the body or of the believer in some way out of the created order and apart from it. To be sure, the situation has never been quite so simple as its detractors sometimes suggest, and certainly not where the doctrine of the resurrection of the body has been taught. But behind the distortions lie two formative influences which have always thrown the theology of the resurrection into the shade. First is Origen's doctrine of a first creation of disembodied, rational spirits, whose pre-mundane fall became the occasion for the creation of the material world, which is as a result treated as the place where the fall of the spirits is corrected. This inevitably suggests both that the material world is chiefly instrumental to the purpose of salvation rather than in some way being involved in it; and that salvation consists in a return to an original and absolute perfection. The second influence is Augustine's equally problematic doctrine of the limited number of those who will eventually be saved, perhaps best exemplified in Anselm's long discussion of whether the number of the saved will equal the number of the fallen angels.[6] It is the introduction of what can only be called semi-gnostic features into the doctrine of creation that has opened the doors to the current excesses of creation spirituality, which themselves run the risk of denying the reality of sin and the need of the whole created order for redemption.

In face of all such tendencies, we need to recover the notion of creation as project. That is to say, we need to understand it as something God creates not as a timelessly perfect whole, but as an order of things that is planned to go somewhere; to be completed or perfected, and so *projected* into time. It may be that it is right to see an anticipation of this in the divine rest on the seventh day, along with the Fourth Gospel's taking up of this theme in its characterisation of Jesus' activity as the continuation of the work of God the Father, which has clearly not yet finished (John 5.17). But the notion of project certainly

[6] Anselm, *Cur Deus Homo*, I. 16–18.

comes to the surface in the great christology of Colossians 1, which will form the basis for this chapter: 'through him (Christ) to reconcile to himself all things, whether on earth or in heaven' (Col. 1.20).

On the basis of this affirmation, and in so far as atonement can be taken literally to mean 'at-one-ment' – that is, as bringing God and the creation into reconciled relation – it would follow that full and universal atonement happens only at the end. Only when all things are reconciled to him will the world be finally in its projected relation to God. Our question then is: what is the place of the historical atonement achieved by Jesus Christ in realising the project? More generally we may ask, what is the relation of Jesus of Nazareth to the final reconciliation? We shall approach that question through a number of preliminary points.

There are a variety of ways in which an eschatological resolution of the project of creation can be conceived to take form, although they fall into two classes which are in the end absolutely opposed to one another. First, and still among us despite the battering they have taken, are processive notions that in some way derive from the modern idea of progress and suppose that in some way history itself is a process of evolution (and surely that metaphor is significant) or development which is moving immanently towards its promised end. Christology is the key to the form this – and, as we shall see, the rival eschatology – takes. While there is a place for Christ in the progressive conception, it tends to be a cosmic Christ shorn of his historical particularity and especially of the centrality of his substitutionary death. The Christ of exponents of the processive eschatology I have sketched is, like the Christ of Colossians, a universal figure, conceived to work immanently to bring history to its fulfilment, but he tends to be conceived in abstraction from Jesus of Nazareth. Important is not the historical Jesus so much as the one who is agent of human and cosmic development and renewal wherever that is found. The reason is plain: if history has some kind of inbuilt 'Christic' direction, the historic cross, which represents a rupture of the seamless web of history, becomes an embarrassment or irrelevance. The significance of Jesus on this account tends to be restricted to his instantiation as a crucial mover in a general process.

Conceptions such as these find favour with some exponents of creation spirituality, for they appeal to a universality that is not restricted to one particular religion, and with some feminists, particularly those who can be described as 'ecofeminists'.

However, the processive eschatology is no longer credible, for reasons 'secular' and theological alike. Despite the outbreak of optimism in early modernity, actual history has always been against it. In the first place, history itself, as it takes place, provides no suggestion that it is in itself any more than a combination of benefit and disaster, with neither taking, or likely to take, the upper hand. There is no manifest and unambiguous *progress*. (One could easily be far more pessimistic.) Alongside the fact that modern science is enabling us – that is, those benefiting from it – to live longer is also the fact that those same techniques enable us to consign millions to death by improved methods of oppression and killing. Second, the current projections of the future of the universe as a whole are of a progressive (*sic!*) running down into a death by extreme heat or cold, so that, because the predictable end, both human and cosmic, can only be death, there is no resolution apart from some kind of transformative eschatology. Apart, that is to say, from a conception of God's action in the world which takes far more seriously sin, death and evil as forces which threaten the project, and threaten it radically, there is either no project, or it is destined for failure.

This means that a second possible form of eschatology is necessary, one which accepts the necessity of a transformation of history if it is to move towards its goal. It is a form that must go through the narrow gate of the historic cross and resurrection of Jesus of Nazareth. Our passage makes clear that the redirection of creation to its end finally takes shape only in so far as Jesus Christ makes 'peace by the blood of his cross', and thus only as the particular historical figure who can die upon a cross. While there is clearly a 'cosmic' christology in Colossians and other books of the New Testament, it always has two aspects. There is no cosmic christology apart from the narratives of ministry and death; that is to say, there is no eschatology without first passing through death, cosmic and personal alike. Here the accounts of the ministry in the Synoptic Gospels and the Pauline – and not only Pauline – cosmic Christ agree precisely. The gospels show that it is in the human acts of this man restoring the created order to its true destiny that the promised reconciliation of all things is realised and anticipated.[7] But it does not happen as part of a continuity. 'Rather, the continuity of the world is broken in such an elemental way that the previous life-time comes to appear hopelessly aged, something to which the future of the kingdom of God cannot connect in any way – except, that is, through an elemental crisis in reality that once was.'[8] Apart from divine action in Jesus, the project will not be realised.

III   *The crisis in context*

The elemental crisis comes to a centre in the death of Jesus. But what is its significance in our context? Jesus' recorded activities imply a particular diagnosis of the condition of the creation in both its personal and non-personal dimensions. This is particularly evident in the exorcisms, which show the human condition enslaved to forces beyond its control, but the same can apply to all forms of sickness as well as to moral and social disorder. The reason is that in the ministry of Jesus we see the beginning of a titanic struggle against those powers which impede what I have called the project of creation. They are the things which prevent the created order and its various components from achieving their destined perfection. But they are not to be understood merely as temporary impediments to the onward march of evolution or history. They are actively evil in such a way as to represent a crisis, for they led to the execution of the one who by his activity in all its forms restored the projected direction of the created order, both human and non-human, and realised by anticipation the promised perfection of the end time.

It is the resurrection of the crucified which both realises and guarantees that this man is the mediator of the reconciliation

---

[7] Surely that is the point of his activities of healing and exorcism, and even the so-called 'nature miracles' here fit into the same pattern. Here is the agent of creation restoring his Father's world to its true allegiance and so true being.

[8] Eberhard Jüngel, *Theological Essays II*, ed. J. B. Webster, Edinburgh: T. & T. Clark, 1995, p. 91.

of all things. But, again, it restores the creation only as project. One of the few links between the eschatologies of the synoptic gospels and Paul brings out this very point. 'For he must reign until he has put all his enemies under his feet' (1 Cor. 15.25). The reign of Christ, his kingship, consists in continuing warfare against those things that hold creation in thrall, and so continue to thwart the project. And, it must not be forgotten, there is an ethic of the kingdom also, and it continues the note of crisis, of a final battle against the enemy. 'For we are not contending against flesh and blood, but against principalities, against the powers, against the world rulers of this present darkness ...' (Eph. 6.11). Only eschatologically is the completion of the project guaranteed.

But why should the activities and fate of this man be granted universal significance in this context? The answer is to be found in the answers to two further questions: who is this, and what does he do? Colossians is clear about the first, even though an articulation of its meaning is by no means straightforward. Jesus of Nazareth is *also* the 'cosmic Christ', the one from whom all things come and to whom they move ('all things were created through him and for him', v. 16). What is achieved in Jesus' ministry is accordingly the work of the one through whom the creation was made returning to his realm in human actuality, in such a way that by means of his action and passion, and what God achieves through them, the project of creation is redirected to its proper end – the at-one-ment of all things with God.

The shape this redemptive and redirecting action takes is best articulated with an elaboration of another central affirmation of our text, that Jesus Christ 'is the image of the invisible God' (v. 15). The notion of the image of God brings together all of our themes so far. Its use in Genesis, along with Genesis' account of the fall, suggests that in some way or other the project of creation is bound up with its being entrusted by God to the human race, so that its outcome is bound up with human being-in-relation to God. Failure in the latter involves the whole created order in fallenness. Thus the doctrine of the image of God points to a way of human being in relation to God on which the future of the whole in some way depends. The future of the whole depends upon this particular part. In that sense, we must affirm the traditional slogan, 'man is a microcosm', the one in whom the whole finds its meaning. A failure of at-one-ness here entails a failure of the whole project, which can therefore be achieved only by the reconciliation of those whose breach frustrates the destined outcome. It is the human frustration of the divine purposes in and for creation which accounts for the 'elemental crisis in reality' to which reference has already been made.

The change that is brought about by Jesus is indicated by the fact that according to our passage not the human race as a whole but Jesus Christ 'is the image of the invisible God ...'. Indeed the prominence of that confession at the head of the passage suggests that much of what it has to say is an elaboration of what it means to claim this for the risen Christ. That Jesus Christ is the true image of God involves a number of consequences for our thesis. As Pannenberg has pointed out, when it is used of Jesus, it implies that he is not only the one of whom we are copies – the prototype – but also the one who actualises the true human destiny by what he achieves.[9] The reconciliation of all things to God can be achieved only by him who is at once Christ the creator *and* a human being who restores the project of creation to its proper destiny by what he does. Because he is Christ the mediator of creation, he is of universal significance. But because he is Jesus of Nazareth, who lived, taught, acted as the agent of the eschatological kingdom, suffered, died and was raised, his universal significance is realised in a particular way – a way corresponding to the form of his action and fate.

IV   Inaugurated universality

In speaking of Jesus in this way we meet a universality which comes about only in and through time: an inaugurated universality. The beginning, the creation, was, as we have seen, a relative perfection: a perfection understood only in the light of a completion that is to come. This is a project whose fulfilment will be only at the end, when there will be universal at-one-ment,

---

[9] Wolfhart Pannenberg, *Systematic Theology Volume II*, E.T. by G. W. Bromiley, Edinburgh: T. & T. Clark, 1994, pp. 215–217.

however that is conceived to take place. The question for us concerns how this eschatological destiny shapes life in the present; and the answer, as we have seen, is only by atonement, which means not perfection *simpliciter*, but perfection through redemption, reconciliation.

In a book some of the ramifications of which this chapter is designed to explore, I suggested that the metaphors through which the divine-human action of the incarnate Son is realistically conceived are mainly three.[10] They enable us to conceive the kind of action which is taking place, and also in its light, by a kind of negative reflection, the evil which is being overcome or healed. Metaphors of victory show that the atonement is a battle against evil, fought by God as man, and with the weapons only of defenceless human action. Metaphors of legality show the atonement as making possible the forgiveness of sin conceived as breach of divine law, by God the Son himself enduring as man the consequences of that breach. Metaphors of sacrifice show the atonement as a cleansing of the pollution incurred by the creation as the result of human sin. From the point of view of each of them in different ways the atonement is seen to be that historical action in which, by overcoming in the human activity and suffering of Jesus the enemies of creation's true flourishing, God enables the creation to achieve that which was purposed for it, the reconciliation of all things in Christ.

The third of the metaphors is in many ways the crucial one, because of the central significance of sacrifice for our theme. What is the project of creation? At this stage we need to specify it in more detail. God created the world so that the created order should be offered back to its creator, perfected, and perfected as the result of the true dominion exercised by God's vice-gerent, the human creature. Corresponding to the creator's gift of the creation, is the creature's glad and willing praise of the creator's goodness in a sacrifice of praise and thanksgiving. At the centre of this response is the gift of the whole human person, body and soul, what Paul called in a metaphorical reversal whose implications are of immense signifi-

---

[10] Colin E. Gunton, *The Actuality of Atonement. A Study of Metaphor, Rationality and the Christian Tradition*, Edinburgh: T. & T. Clark and Grand Rapids: Eerdmans, 1989, chapters 3–5.

cance, a *living* sacrifice, achieved through the renewal of the mind. This perfect sacrifice is achievable only *eschatologically.* 'You ... he now has reconciled in his body of flesh by his death, in order to present you holy and blameless and irreproachable before him ...' (Col 1.22). The human project is to be completed in the presentation before God of a form of life made possible by Christ's atoning death. But what form of life? We cannot understand it without reference to the cross.

To return to our characterisation of the ministry of Jesus, we can now see that his death, on this account, represents *on one level* the response to the ministry by the forces opposed to the creation's perfection. It is thus a microcosm of human resistance to the project of creation, concentrated at the point where its reign is threatened. On another level, however, it is the offering up to God the Father by Jesus Christ the incarnate Son of a certain form of human living and dying, as a 'sacrifice'. How does it overcome the enemies of the creation? Here we reach an important implication of the notion of creation as project. Projects take time, and if it is indeed true that the project is completed only through time, it follows that reconciliation it is not achieved universally, in the sense of timelessly, but by the action of temporal *particulars.* Yet there is also a sense in which, if not the completion, yet its inauguration is achieved by one particular: the whole career of Jesus from conception and birth through to ascension. It is in this way that he becomes the microcosm, the part which represents the whole. How, then, can this particular be the means of the perfection of the whole? We return to the significance of this sacrifice as the one that makes other – *living* sacrifices – possible and actual.

Here three themes are intertwined. First is the substitutionary sacrifice, the sacrifice of exchange. One cannot explain how this can be, though there are ways of giving what it means conceptual shape. Among other things, a sacrifice is something or someone which or who is taken from the whole – the whole community, or indeed the whole world – and is offered to God in place of the others: *in place of* because apart from what the sacrificed is and does they cannot, by virtue of their bondage to evil, be made perfect. But a sacrifice, to be acceptable, must be perfect. It follows that nothing that belongs to the fallen creation can become a *sacrifice,* a gift of the creation offered in praise to God, apart from cleansing. This is because, as things stand, the whole of created reality participates in the pollution disseminated by sin, and the microcosm, the one made in the image of God, is no longer able to represent the whole. As made in the image of God, we involve the whole of that world in pollution. This means that nothing created can, apart from redemption, any more be offered as a sacrifice of praise to the creator.

This in turn implies that, on one level, only God can provide the sacrifice (Genesis 22!) by taking on himself the consequences and weight of the accumulated evil. Therefore he *gives up*, sacrifices, his only Son (Rom. 8.32). The one who entrusted the world, as project, to those made in his image, himself provides the means of its redirection. On another level, as Anselm rightly noted, only the one responsible for the sin could appropriately make restoration. Redemption must also be an authentically human action – a true and unpolluted sacrifice of praise to God. Here it is that Jesus, taking flesh from the polluted whole, must – through the Spirit – *become* perfect, because it is only as such that his gift is acceptable to God and so in turn is able to *become* the means of the perfecting of others ('being made perfect he became the source of eternal salvation to all who obey . . .', Heb. 5.9). The cleansing of one, particular, person becomes the means of the cleansing of the whole, though only at the end will this be complete. In the meantime, particular transformations and so *projectings* toward eschatological perfection take place as by the Spirit other created beings are brought through Christ to God the Father. In a slightly different context – though perhaps not so different – Paul uses the analogy of the part being the means for the sanctification of the whole. 'If the dough offered as the first-fruits be holy, so is the whole lump . . .' (Rom. 11.16).

The second theme is given by the resurrection and ascension, which continue our pneumatological direction. They are the means by which the one perfect sacrifice, consisting in a death, is made the way for *living* sacrifices by others, though they too involve a kind of – and sometimes an actual – death, as baptism and the ethic of taking up the cross make clear. The risen and ascended Christ is the one who, by virtue of his acceptance by God the Father, becomes the source of the perfecting gifts of the Spirit to those who put their faith in him. For our purposes, the point of the resurrection is that it is at once personal, cosmic and eschatological. It is personal in being the resurrection of a person, but it is cosmic in being the resurrection of the body. It is, as the transformation of the whole person into the conditions of the age to come – and not a resuscitation[11] – thus universal as the archetype of the destiny of the believer – 'the first-born from the dead' (v. 18) – and accordingly of the promised perfection of the whole creation. Just as those made in the image of God are, by virtue of sin, the heart of the problem, so in Christ they are in the beginning of the solution, or, better, the first fruits (1 Cor. 15.20, 23).

Third is the church. It is of significance here that there is a place for the church in Colossians' cosmic christology, again showing that this Christ cannot be reduced to a general cosmic force. For many interpreters, this introduction into the text is a puzzle, and attempts have been made to explain it as an interpolation, because it supposedly does not belong in the logic of the passage. But that is precisely to miss the point. The reason for such incomprehension is to be found in the very history of the Christian theology of salvation with which this chapter began. The church is an irrelevance in this passage only if salvation is salvation out of or in some way in distinction from the rest of the created order, of souls rather than bodies, and if her business is not directly with the reconciliation of *all things* in Christ. But if it is those created in the image of God whose sin is the chief impediment to the completion of the project, their reconciliation is at the centre. Thus we may say that the church is elected as the *particular* means by which *particular* anticipations of the promised reconciliation of all things in Christ are achieved.

Reconciliation, as the work of the perfecting Spirit, is achieved by relating people and things to God through Christ. The worship of the community is therefore to be seen as God's chosen means by which the communion of the last days is realised. Worship is an end in itself: the self-offering – living sacrifice – of the people to God in praise and thanks. But it is

---

[11] Thus, as Pannenberg sees, it is a metaphorical yet still a real, raising. Pannenberg, *Systematic Theology Volume II*, pp. 346–348.

also the way by which a reconciled relation to God is constituted. The Word makes known the way to God and calls the
world to believe. The inauguration of the new relation is
baptism, as a sharing in the atoning death of Jesus and an
appropriation of the way to God that is achieved. The Lord's
Supper, as the anticipation of the eschatological banquet,
provides orientation and food for the period 'between the
times'. And life in the community of the faithful in all its
dimensions is also part of the project, as a schooling in the ways
of the eschatological kingdom, again, an end in itself but also
the way by which the church calls the whole world to 'be
reconciled to God' (2 Cor. 5.20).[12]

As the use of water, bread and wine suggest, the rites of
relation to the risen Christ take up into their action the created
order as a whole. Sacraments represent and inaugurate the
perfecting of the creation by offering it through Christ to God.
The church, by offering up human life in this way also offers
up, in anticipation, the whole creation in praise to its maker. As
Bryan Spinks has written, 'the eucharist, pinpointed in the
worshippers receiving the bread and the wine, represents the
eschatological firstfruits of the redemption and sanctification
of the whole cosmos'.[13] But because the church, as the elect
community, is the chosen place for these particular gifts and
graces, it does not follow that the creator Spirit is unable to use
other means for the purposes of reconciliation. Wherever there
is between human beings the kind of love instantiated in Jesus
and wherever there is good use of the created world for science
and art; wherever, that is to say, the world in all its aspects is
enabled to praise its creator, there is the work of the perfecting
Spirit.

To complete the chapter we do, therefore, require after all a
form of creation spirituality: an understanding of the created
order not as the subject of some kind of 'spiritual' or spiritualising interpretation, not as an object of some kind of idolatrous

[12] In a full treatment, more would need to be said of the church's relation to
Israel. 'Paul can say that according to the counsel of God the (temporary)
rejection of the Jewish people of God has become the means to the reconciling of the cosmos (Rom. 11.15).' Pannenberg, *Systematic Theology Volume II*, p.
413.

[13] Bryan Spinks, 'Trinitarian Theology and the Eucharistic Prayer', *Studia
Liturgica* 26 (1996), pp. 209–224.

service in which the creation is re-divinised, but as an ethic of sacrifice. The human calling is to enable the whole creation to praise its creator by particular instances of faithful action towards both other people and the world: by proper relationality and by loving dominion. The eschatological completion of the project, inaugurated at the creation and re-established by Jesus, is thus anticipated in all forms of human action and worldly event that are enabled by the Holy Spirit as he relates the world to the Father through Jesus Christ, crucified, risen and ascended.

CHAPTER 11

BEING AND CONCEPT
Concluding theological postscript

I *On speaking of the Unknowable God*

In the foregoing chapters much has been spoken or implied about the being of the triune God. Speaking about God is the most perilous of all theological enterprises, and should not be entered upon lightly. The chief reason for caution, however, is not the modern claim that we cannot penetrate the veil of phenomena or of 'experience' to the realities which may or may not underlie, but the *theological* peril that we may violate the unknowableness of God by essaying a speculative construction of what we suppose God to be. To use a modern idiom, we run the risk of 'objectifying' God: of turning him into a static and impersonal object to be subjected to our unfettered intellectual control, or into an abstraction, the object of pure speculation and the projection on to eternity of conceptual patterns from the merely finite world.

The positive function of the doctrine of the unknowability of God is to preserve the freedom and, so to speak, personal privacy of God's being. To be personal is to exist in relation, indeed, but also to be defined by one's otherness to all other beings. There are therefore strict limits to what we may claim to know of any other person, let alone of God. Yet it must be borne in mind that corresponding to the Scylla of thinking that we know too much, there is a corresponding Charybdis, with its own arrogance, of claiming that we know too little to be able to speak at all. There lies the weakness of so much modern theology, in reducing the knowledge of God to a speaking *about* ourselves or our supposed experience rather than *from* the God made known in Christ. It is important here to stress that we know other human persons in their otherness – indeed, that it is there that we most truly know them, as in large measure unknown. So it is with the knowledge of God, whose unknowability is therefore to be understood relationally – in terms of the relation with us into which he has freely entered in Christ and the Spirit – and not absolutely.

It is not therefore entirely paradoxical to say that we know God in his unknowability: according to the limits of, on the one hand, his revelation, however that be supposed to take shape, and, on the other, of our personal and conceptual possibilities. (We may speak similarly of our knowledge of those finite persons with whom we have dealings.) The nature of those conceptual possibilities has been a matter of intense debate in Western thought, which in recent centuries has tended to claim too much for human scientific and rational achievement, too little for the possibilities of genuine theological knowledge. In chapter three it was argued that the theological dimension of the problem has much to do with something lying further back than merely the modern age in our intellectual history. Augustine's legacy to his descendants was to locate the unknowability of God in the wrong place: not in the otherness of the personal, but in the platonically conceived otherness – 'transcendence' – of the material or sensible and 'spiritual' or intelligible worlds. Whether that be the reason, the fact is that trinitarian theology has come into disrepute as being concerned chiefly with the defence and articulation of given and apparently paradoxical statements of dogma. It has rarely seemed to be the living heart of worship and life.

One of the fruits of the Augustinian legacy, as it comes to us through the fire of the Enlightenment's criticism of dogma, is a tendency to misunderstand the point of trinitarian theology. What has happened in recent discussion is that the intellectual situation has been understood in an over simple fashion, in two respects in particular, both of them presupposing a more static conception of dogmatic development than that with which I have tried to work. The first is that according to which it is held that the classical doctrine of the Trinity is to be understood as a 'model', developed in its entirety in the past, which may now be obsolete *because the precise form of words in which it was formulated no longer satisfies modern rational criteria or theological developments.*

The second is that there are two trinitarian 'analogies', the 'psychological' and the 'social', which are (more or less) fixed in form and present clearly demarcated alternative options for those who wish to continue to be trinitarian theologians. It should be clear by now that, although there is developed in this book what can be called a social rather than a psychological approach, those ways of speaking are highly inadequate. There is not a 'model' known as trinitarian doctrine, a fixed set of formularies, but rather a process of intellectual development – a tradition – during the course of which a number of conceptual possibilities have been shaped. It is the possibilities of these concepts for our knowledge of God, ourselves and our world that I wish to develop, not the defence of formulae or the elaboration of theories about the social life of the inner Trinity. What do the concepts do or allow us to say?

II *Some theological decisions*

One, perhaps *the*, point of trinitarian theology is that it enables us to develop an ontology of the personal, or, better, an understanding of God as the personal creator and redeemer of the world, and so the basis of the priority of the personal elsewhere, too. In what sense is God personal? The answer from all that has gone before is clear: he is personal as being three persons in relation, of having his being in what Father, Son and Holy Spirit give to and receive from each other in the freedom of their unknowable eternity. This means that we must reject the claim of Barth and other modern theologians that personality is a function of the one God, made known, in Barth's terminology, in three modes of being. The objection to Barth's development is not that it is modalist, for it is not, even though it does not finally guard against suspicions of that tendency. It is rather that it fails to reclaim the relational view of the person from the ravages of modern individualism. To be personal, as we have seen, is not to be an individual centre of consciousness or something like that – although that may be part of the matter – but to be one whose being consists in relations of mutual constitution with other persons. That is one of the glories of trinitarian thinking, for it enables unique and fruitful insight into the nature of being – all being – in relation.

As we have seen, to have his being in relation means that God is personal as a communion of Father, Son and Holy Spirit. Whence does this communion derive? According to Zizioulas, it derives from the Father, who is to be conceived as the cause of communion in the Trinity.[1] While such a claim preserves the due priority of the Father in the Godhead, I do not believe that it allows for an adequate theology of the mutual constitution of Father, Son and Spirit. Should it not rather be said that communion is a function of – a way of characterising – the relations of all three, just as freedom is to be conceived as a relation between beings, rather than as some contentless absolute? Whatever the priority of the Father, it must not be conceived in such a way as to detract from the fact that all three persons are together the cause of the communion in which they exist in relations of mutual and reciprocal constitution. Thus the Father is what he is not only because he begets the Son, but also because the Son responds in the way made known in his obedience as incarnate, and so can be understood to be the one who shares in the constitution of the being of God by means of his eternal response of obedience and love. Similarly, the movement of the Spirit can be argued also to be constitutive of the being of God the Father, in that it is the Spirit who ensures that the love of Father and Son is not simply mutual love, but moves outward, so that creation and redemption are indeed free acts of God, but acts grounded in his being as love.[2] Beyond this, it would be better to preserve an element of reserve, and to say that God's unknowableness prevents us from further enquiry into the *cause* of his being who and what he is.

That this is not simply a matter of pointless speculation is shown by two considerations. The first is the implication of such a theology of communion for our understanding of the being of the church and of human being in the world, drawn out as they have been in previous chapters. The way we think of

---

[1] John D. Zizioulas, *Being as Communion*, London: Darton Longman and Todd, 1985, pp. 40f.

[2] That, surely, is the point of the much cited passage from Richard of St Victor, for example pp. 89f above.

God affects the way we think of that which he creates and redeems. It will be evident, for example, that the theology of the church essayed here will be more congregational in its structure than Zizioulas' strongly episcopal ecclesiology that tends to see the bishop as representing the Father. There are similar implications for our view of human society in general. The second consideration concerns the other side of the matter of the known and the unknown, and it is that a refusal to speculate about inner causality prevents encroachment beyond the limits of what is made known of God in the economy of creation and salvation as it is recorded in Scripture. Certain conceptual developments are licensed by trinitarian theology, but they must also be controlled by due consideration of the infinity of God and the finitude of the human knower.

It is at this point that we come up against an important matter of interpretation. There is, in the biblical representation of the way in which the acts of God take shape in time, some support for Zizioulas' giving of priority to the Father. It is often said that when the New Testament writers use the word 'God' *simpliciter*, they are referring to God the Father, so that Irenaeus is true to Scripture in speaking of Son and Spirit as the two hands of God, the two agencies by which the work of God the Father is done in the world. Indeed, Paul's account of the progress of the risen and conquering Christ in 1 Corinthians 15 ends with the confession that when he hands the Kingdom over to the Father, God will be all in all (v. 28). Here, however, the priority of the Father is not ontological but economic. Such talk of the divine economy has indeed implications for what we may say about the being of God eternally, and would seem to suggest a subordination of *taxis* – of ordering within the divine life – but not one of deity or regard. It is as truly divine to be the obedient self-giving Son as it is to be the Father who sends and the Spirit who renews and perfects. Only by virtue of the particularity and relatedness of all three is God God.

Therefore, while it is right to affirm both Western and Eastern emphases on the Father as the 'fount' of the Trinity – though noting and disapproving its possibly impersonal connotations – this should not be at the expense of being able to speak of a kind of equality. Here I am indebted to Professor T. F. Torrance for some words of Gregory of Nazianzus which achieve the right kind of balance: 'I should like to call the Father the greater, because from him flows both the equality and being of the equals, but I am afraid to use the word origin (*arche*) lest I should make him the origin of inferiors....'[3] Despite the danger that it might suggest a subordination of the personal to the impersonal, the use of the concept of the *homoousion* – probably best translated today as 'one in being' rather than 'of one substance' – is of great value in this context. It should not be understood as in any way implying that God is in some sense 'substance', or that there is impersonal being under- or over-lying the three persons in relation. Its function rather is to ensure that we do not suppose there to be degrees of deity in the Godhead. The Son and the Spirit are as truly and fully God as is the Father, in and through their economically subordinate functions of doing the will of the Father in the world.

Another important function of the *homoousion* is that it enables a theology of the Trinity to express the oneness of the being and act of God. One danger of the concept of communion – and especially of a 'social' analogy of the Trinity – is of a form of tritheism which appears to relate the three persons in such a way as to suggest that they have distinct wills. Here lies the importance of the doctrine of the *perichoresis*, the interanimation in relation, of Father, Son and Spirit that is such that all that is done is indeed the act of all three. Thus far, we may accept the principle, so influential in the West in particular, that the acts of the triune God in the world are undivided. But this principle, like so many others – including the *homoousion* – can be the source of confusion unless it is carefully qualified. If it is so stressed, as it tends to be stressed in Augustine, that the distinctiveness and particularity of the actions of Son and Spirit in the economy are overridden, the doctrine of the Trinity is divorced from its basis in history and made an irrelevance. The principle, and its associated concepts of *homoousios* and *perichoresis*, are vital devices to ensure that trinitarian language does not lapse into tritheism. But it is equally important to maintain a way of speaking of the distinct modes of divine action that are made known in biblical revelation.

[3] Gregory of Nazianzus, *Or* 40.43.

The real difficulties come when we try to conceptualise the relations of Son and Spirit to each other and to the Father. Here it has to be said that the doctrine of the *Filioque*, that the Spirit proceeds from the Father *and the Son*, has been the source of a number of weaknesses, and particularly of a tendency in the West so to subordinate the Spirit to the Son that he appears to be given little more of a function than the application of the work of Christ to believer, church and the rest. On the other hand, however, there is, in the East, as is often pointed out, the parallel danger of a direct ascent through the Spirit to the Father in a way that can sometimes appear to bypass the work of Christ. Can a way be found that avoids the twin pitfalls?

To begin a clarification, a little must be said about the relation of the persons in the economy of salvation. As the 'self-effacing' person of the Trinity, the Spirit's primary function is to lead to Christ, the way to the Father. That encapsulates the essential asymmetry of the relationships in the economy of salvation. The Spirit is the giver of faith, not in himself nor even, strictly speaking, in Christ, but in the Father through Christ. In that respect, we return to the theme that God *simpliciter* is God the Father, the fount and goal of our being. But we neither receive our being in the first place apart from Christ, the mediator of creation and salvation, nor are directed to our goal apart from the Spirit, the perfecting cause.

In order to do a measure of justice to the concerns of both East and West, Thomas Smail has suggested the following ways of putting the matter. He argues that is it not enough to amend the creed to read '. . . who proceeds from the Father *through the Son*', because 'it suggests that there is a one-way dependence of the Spirit and his work upon the Son and his work'. It can be argued that the kind of theology which led to the adoption of the *Filioque* clause has prevented Western theology from being able to give the Holy Spirit due place in its developments, for example, in showing how the Christ who is later to pour out the Spirit is during his ministry very much the gift of and dependent upon the guidance of the Spirit, and, indeed, is raised from the dead by the Spirit's power. Therefore Smail suggests that, in order to give in the creed the weight to the Son and Spirit that would do justice to their place in the economy of salvation, we would need to say about the Spirit that 'he proceeds from the Father *through the Son*'; but we would also need to say about the Son that he is 'eternally begotten of the Father *through the Spirit*'. In that way what we say about the relationships of Father, Son and Spirit in God would more faithfully reflect what the New Testament obliges us to say about the relationships revealed in the life and in the resurrection of Jesus.[4]

That, in the end, is the point of the struggle for an adequate trinitarian conceptuality: not as some abstract test of orthodoxy, but as a way of expressing coherently and as well as possible what it is that we are granted to know of the God to whom we are related by the Spirit through Jesus Christ.

How, then, shall we define the persons as a result of whose relatedness we may speak of the being of the one God in communion? Most attempts to define the concept in the history of theology have proved disastrous, as a number of instances in the previous chapters have shown. Particularly to be avoided is the definition of person as *relation*, for the reasons that it tends to define the personal in terms of the impersonal, and that it therefore muddies the waters, making it difficult to speak of the relations *between* the persons that are so important if we are to hold the unity and threeness of God in appropriate tension and balance. If it is true – and the main thesis of this book has been designed to argue that it is – that the ground of being of the world and all in it is a personal God, then the person is not only a logically primitive notion, as Strawson importantly argued,[5] but, as Zizioulas has contended, an *ontologically* primitive reality also. Therefore we cannot do justice to its reality by attempting to define it in other terms, especially terms drawn from impersonal realities.

One way to attempt a definition is to use a tautology in which the terms mutually define each other, as in Calvin's nearly successful definition:

'Person,' therefore, I call a 'subsistence' in God's essence,

[4] Thomas A. Smail, 'The Holy Trinity and the Resurrection of Jesus', *Different Gospels*, ed. Andrew Walker, London: Hodder and Stoughton, 1988, pp. 63–96 (pp. 76–78).
[5] P. F. Strawson, *Individuals. An Essay in Descriptive Metaphysics*, London: Methuen, 1959, pp. 101ff.

which, while being related to the others, is distinguished by an incommunicable quality. By the term 'subsistence' we would understand something different from 'essence.'[6]

It does seem that Calvin here commits the characteristic sin of Western trinitarianism, of seeing the persons not as constituting the being of God by their mutual relations but as in some way inhering in being that is in some sense prior to them. That is certainly the interpretation of Claude Welch.[7] Yet Calvin's attempt is without doubt an indication of what must conceptually be done in order to secure all the dimensions of a doctrine of the one God who exists only in the communion of the three: the interrelatedness of the persons and the unique individuality-in-relation of each.

In general, however, the best way to define the person is ostensively, by indicating where persons are to be found and the way that they are conceived to be and act. That is what has been attempted in different ways in this book. In the next section we shall move to a discussion of two concepts which place the person, and indeed, the person in relation to the world, in such a way that the core meaning of the concept, as it emerges in trinitarian thinking, can at least be indicated.

III   *Otherness and relation*

One of the lessons to be learned from the foregoing excursions into trinitarian ontology is the importance of the concepts of otherness and relation as ways of characterising the personal being of God without encroaching on his unknowableness. In that respect, they would serve either to replace or to interpret the overused and confusing terms 'transcendence' and 'immanence'. To speak of the transcendence of God is indeed one way of speaking of his otherness, but it has two drawbacks. The first is that it can so easily be construed quantitatively, as in the sometimes discussed topic of how much transcendence modern theology can tolerate; and the second, related to it, is the danger that it will be conceived as the opposite or contrary

---

[6] John Calvin, *Institutes of the Christian Religion*, I.xiii.6.
[7] Claude Welch, *The Trinity in Contemporary Theology*, London: SCM Press, 1953, pp. 190f.

quality to immanence, so that the two appear to be alternatives, and the more transcendent God is conceived to be, the less immanent. Over against such a separation, it can be argued that otherness and relation are superior terms for performing the function that transcendence and immanence are usually given. The reason is that they are not alternatives or contraries, as the latter tend to be, but correlatives which require and interpret each other. Only that which is other than something else can be related to it. Otherness and relation can therefore be conceived as correlatives rather than rivals.

The point can be illustrated with reference to many of the themes of this book, and first the most basic relation of all, that between God and the world. The claim has been made in a number of chapters that all forms of monism which rule out the otherness of God to humankind or the world violate, by incorporating it into the being of God, the freedom of the world to be itself. This is undoubtedly true of pantheisms of all kinds, for if God is ontologically too close to the world, the world becomes simply a function of his being and so unable to be itself. Otherness – the ontological distinction or infinite qualitative difference between God and that which is not God – is important both for the contingency of the created order and for the freedom of the human person. In a trinitarian understanding, because God has otherness – personal freedom and 'space' – within the dynamics of his being, he is able to grant to the world space to be itself.

But otherness is a concept important for finite relationships also. Of our relation to the non-human world, it must be said that we make a mistake if we do not take due account of our otherness from it. To personalise the world or to make it the object of worship, as may be the case in some forms of 'creation-centred spirituality', is to misconstrue its nature, and so our responsibility for its being truly itself. Similar considerations are equally important, although in a different way, in our conceptions of inter-personal relations. Here there are two central dimensions to be considered. One is the uniqueness and particularity of each person: what we might call the finite qualitative distinction between one person and any other: the unique distinctness of every person. All monistic or totalitarian societies which violate this violate the being of the person. The second is the essential privacy of the person. Even within the closeness of a marriage, it is important not to speak of a union of a couple if this suggests some kind of merging into the other. To relate rightly to other people is to intend them in their otherness and particularity, to allow them room to be themselves.

On the other hand, otherness without relation is as destructive as relation without otherness. It is instructive to note that, according to Coleridge's brilliant analysis, a theology which absolutely separates the world from relation to God – the otherness without relation which is deism – by reflex replicates the same problems as those of pantheism. Because of a lack of true personal relation of God to the world, a relation logically conceived comes into play, with the result that the world becomes as much rolled up into the being of God as it is in pantheism. Here, the notion of otherness in relation is of crucial importance. The doctrine of creation, trinitarianly conceived, enables us to understand the world as other than God, but as the product of a free act of creation and of a continuing free relatedness. Only if the universe is based in the act of one whose being is personal freedom can it be conceived both as real in itself and as related to the creator who holds it in being, whose free act through the Spirit delimits and so establishes its own proper freedom to be itself.

The same kind of logic applies when we speak of the being of realities which comprise the created world. If there is no otherness, the world is just a blank homogeneity, and the richness and variety which we appear to see around us merely the play of underlying simplicity. (That appears to be the position of some Indian religious systems.) If, on the other hand, there is not the perichoretic and dynamic interplay which was part of the burden of chapter eight, the final truth about our world is an irrational pluralism, in which no sense can be made of the concept of a universe. Here, too, otherness and relation are essential concepts if we are to understand the variety within unity of the world made by the God who is himself neither blank unity nor dissipated plurality. The claim made in chapter eight is that some of the concepts used in recent cosmology appear to echo the trinitarian conceptuality of the Fathers. Without claiming dependence of the former on the latter, it is at least justifiable to suggest that the conceptuality gives rise to a conception of the world not inconsistent with a Christian doctrine of creation.

Similar considerations apply to the relations of human beings, as we have seen in a number of the chapters. The point has been made often enough in the foregoing pages that neither a collectivist nor an individualist conception of human being in the world is adequate to the way we are. In this respect, the trinitarian conceptuality at the very least gives food for thought about what it is to be human in society. Here, too, there is need for both otherness and relation. Indeed, in our fragmented and perplexed society, it may be that theology has here insights with redemptive possibilities. And that leads to the chief reason for including a chapter on the church in a volume chiefly dedicated to ontology. We live in a fallen world, and need to be reminded that to speak of otherness and relation, even to institute programmes for realising them, is not enough. The world, and not only the human world, is re-established in the cross of him through whom it came to be and and through whom it is re-constituted by the free act of the eschatological Spirit. The church, however lamentably it has failed in its calling, continues to be a reminder, through its orientation to the triune God, of the shape a true human society must take. But the being of the church, too, if it is not to fall ever and again into ideological distortions, must be shaped, formed, by its relation to the triune God, and so *thought* by analogy with his being.

IV   *An ontology of sacrifice*

It is hoped that in what has gone before the twin aims of this work have been at least advanced: to show the doctrine of the Trinity not as a closed dogma, to be swallowed or not as the case may be, but as a continuing enterprise of conceptual refinement and development. At one of the stages of the organisation of this work, I was tempted, in echo of Orwell's title, to call it *Homage to Cappadocia*. Wiser counsels have since prevailed, because it is not my concern to canonise any theologian or school, and particularly not to play the East against the West.

Despite all that has been learned, and must continue to be learned, from those theologians we call Cappadocian, from one point of view mine is a very Western concern. It seems to me that the interest in recent Western theology in humanisation rather than divinisation is the key to the trinitarian outworking of the Christian gospel. What is needed is a theology which enables humankind and the world to be themselves, in the image of God and destined for the praise of God in their own ways, but as contingent and finite beings.

Within the broad framework of a trinitarian theology, it becomes possible, as we have seen, to understand God and the world as related in otherness. It is one thing to be God, another to be the world. And yet the world can fulfil its created destiny only in relation to God. The theology of the Trinity provides, in this context, a way of embracing those relations to God we call creation and redemption within a conceptual framework which links the two without confusion, so that redemption is seen as the restoring and completing of that which was 'in the beginning'. That which was begun through the Son and in the Spirit, has its destiny in being returned, perfected, to the Father through their redeeming agency.

Perhaps one central notion which can create links between all aspects of what is being said here is sacrifice, construed chiefly in terms of gift. According to this conception, to be is to exist in a dynamic of mutual giving and receiving.[8] That is a 'sacrificial' ontology of God, for, as we have seen, the Trinity is a conception of God as three persons constituted by their relations of reciprocal giving and receiving. Sacrifice is also a way of understanding the end for which the world is made: to echo the mutual giving and receiving of Father, Son and Spirit within the dynamics of space and time, as a sacrifice of praise. Thus creation can be understood as the sheer gift of God, the free giving of shape in otherness to that which echoes eternal giving and receiving of Father, Son and Spirit.

Similarly, the fallenness of the creation can be understood to derive from the disabling of creation's ability to praise its

---

[8] Colin Gunton, 'The Sacrifice and the Sacrifices: From Metaphor to Transcendental?', *Trinity, Incarnation and Atonement. Philosophical and Theological Essays*, edd. Ronald J. Feenstra and Cornelius Plantinga, Jr., University of Notre Dame Press, 1990, pp. 210–229.

creator, and to consist in the fact that the dynamic of sacrifice fails to take place. The interrelatedness of the human race manifests an otherness of alienation, rather than of salutary relation, or love, while the non-human creation shares in the disorder. It is for the redemption of this world, to restore and perfect its capacity to praise its maker – in other words, to bring it into true otherness and relation in its various dimensions – that the Father 'gives up' the Son into that relation with the world which involves his bearing its disorder and stain; and the incarnate Son reciprocates, in the Spirit, the Father's sacrifice by giving up his life as a perfect offering of human praise and obedience.

It is by the agency of that same Spirit that the human creation is, from time to time, enabled through the sacrifice of Christ to offer back the creation, human and non-human, perfected, as its sacrifice of praise. It is thus our sacrifice – the living sacrifice – which is the human analogy of the Trinity in time. All true human giving and receiving of love, all the arts and crafts and industry that effect a liberating human dominion over the creation, in a word all truly human action in relation to other people and the world, are finite echoes, achieved through the Father's gift of himself in the Son and the Spirit, of the giving and receiving that Father, Son and Spirit are in eternity. This book is offered in the hope that it will in its own way share, and enable a sharing, in the sacrifice of praise to which all life is called in Christ.

BIBLIOGRAPHY OF MODERN WRITERS

Anderson, Ray S., *Historical Transcendence and the Reality of God*, London: Geoffrey Chapman, 1975

Ayer, A. J., 'The Concept of a Person', *The Concept of a Person and Other Essays*, London: Macmillan, 1963

Bailey, Derrick Sherwin, *The Man-Woman Relation in Christian Thought*, London: Longmans, 1959

Barfield, Owen, *What Coleridge Thought*, Middletown, Connecticut: Wesleyan University Press, 1971

Barth, Karl, *Church Dogmatics*, E.T. and ed. by G. W. Bromiley and T. F. Torrance, Edinburgh: T. & T. Clark, 1956–1975, Vols I/1, II/1, II/2, III/1, III/2, III/4

Bouwsma, William J., *John Calvin. A Sixteenth Century Portrait*, Oxford University Press, 1988

British Council of Churches, *The Forgotten Trinity. 1. Report of the BCC Study Commission on Trinitarian Doctrine Today*, London: British Council of Churches, 1989

Brown, David, *The Divine Trinity*, London: Duckworth, 1985

Brunner, Emil, *Man in Revolt. A Christian Anthropology*, E.T. by Olive Wyon, London: Lutterworth, 1939

Buckley, Michael, *At the Origins of Modern Atheism*, New Haven and London: Yale University Press, 1987

Calvin, John, *Institutes of the Christian Religion*, E.T. and ed. by J. T. McNeill and F. L. Battles, 2 vols., London: SCM Press, 1960

Campenhausen, Hans von, *Ecclesiastical Authority and Spiritual Power in the Church of the First Three Centuries*, E.T. by J. A. Baker, California: University of Stanford Press, 1963

Capra, Fritjof, *The Tao of Physics. An Exploration of the Parallels between Modern Physics and Eastern Mysticism*, London: Fontana, 1983 (first ed. 1975)

Cohn, Norman, *The Pursuit of the Millennium*, London: Secker and Warburg, 1957

Coleridge, Samuel Taylor, 'On the Prometheus of Aeschylus', *The Complete Works of Samuel Taylor Coleridge*, ed. W. G. T. Shedd, New York: Harper and Brothers, 1853, Vol. 4, pp. 344–365.
    'Notes on Waterland's Vindication of Christ's Divinity', *Complete Works*, op. cit., Vol. 5, pp. 404–416
    'Essay on Faith', in *Complete Works*, op. cit., Vol. 5, pp. 557–565
    On the Constitution of the Church and State, *The Collected Works of Samuel Taylor Coleridge*, ed. John Colmer, London: Routledge, 1976, Vol. 10

Cupitt, Don, *Taking Leave of God*, London: SCM Press, 1980

Descartes, René, *Meditations on the First Philosophy*, in *The Philosophical Works of Descartes*, E.T. by Elizabeth Haldane and G. R. T. Ross, Cambridge University Press, second ed., 1931, Vol. I

Dodds, E. R., *The Greeks and the Irrational*, University of California Press, 1951

Elrod, John W., *Kierkegaard and Christendom*, Princeton University Press, 1981

Faraday, Michael, 'A Speculation touching Electric Conduction and the Nature of Matter', *On the Primary Forces of Electricity*, ed. Richard Laming, 1938

Farley, Edward, *Ecclesial Man. A Social Phenomenology of Faith and Reality*, Philadelphia: Fortress Press, 1975

Feuerbach, Ludwig, *The Essence of Christianity*, E.T. by George Eliot, New York: Harper and Bros., 1957 ed.

Flew, R. Newton, *Jesus and his Church*, London: Epworth Press, 1960

Florovsky, Georges, *Bible, Church and Tradition: An Eastern Orthodox View*, Belmont, Mass.: Nordland, 1972

Foster, Michael B., 'The Christian Doctrine of Creation and the Rise of Modern Natural Science', *Mind* 43 (1934), pp. 446–468

Funkenstein, Amos, *Theology and the Scientific Imagination from the Middle Ages to the Seventeenth Century*, Princeton University Press, 1986

Gibbs, J. G., *Creation and Redemption: A Study in Pauline Theology*, Supplement to *Novum Testamentum* xxvi, Leiden, 1971

Gleick, James, *Chaos. Making a New Science,* London: Sphere Books, 1987

Gunton, Colin E., *Becoming and Being. The Doctrine of God in Charles Hartshorne and Karl Barth,* Oxford and New York: Oxford University Press, 1978

Yesterday and Today. A Study of Continuities in Christology, London: Darton, Longman and Todd, 1983

Enlightenment and Alienation. An Essay Towards a Trinitarian Theology, Basingstoke: Marshall, Morgan and Scott, 1985

'Creation and Recreation. An Exploration of Some Themes in Aesthetics and Theology', *Modern Theology* 2 (1985), pp. 1–19

'Barth on the Western Intellectual Tradition. Towards a Theology After Christendom', *Theology Beyond Christendom. Essays on the Centenary of the Birth of Karl Barth May 10, 1886,* ed. John Thompson, Pennsylvania: Pickwick Press, 1986, pp. 285–301

The Actuality of Atonement. A Study of Metaphor, Rationality and the Christian Tradition, Edinburgh: T. & T. Clark, 1988

'Two Dogmas Revisited. Edward Irving's Christology', *Scottish Journal of Theology* 41 (1988), pp. 359–376

'The Sacrifice and the Sacrifices: From Metaphor to Transcendental?', *Trinity, Incarnation and Atonement. Philosophical and Theological Essays,* edd. Ronald J. Feenstra and Cornelius Plantinga, Jr., University of Notre Dame Press, 1990, pp. 210–229

The One, the Three and the Many. God, Creation and the Culture of Modernity. The 1992 Bampton Lectures, Cambridge University Press, 1993

Hall, Douglas John, *Imaging God. Dominion as Stewardship,* Grand Rapids: Eerdmans, 1986

Hardy, Daniel W., 'Coleridge on the Trinity', *Anglican Theological Review* LXIX (1988), pp. 145–155

God's Ways with the World. Thinking and Practising Christian Faith, Edinburgh: T. & T. Clark, 1996

Harnack, Adolph, *History of Dogma,* E.T. by Neil Buchanan and others of third ed., London: Williams and Norgate, 1897, Vol. III

History of Dogma, E.T. by E. B. Speirs and James Millar, London: Williams and Norgate, 1898, Vol. IV

Hartshorne, Charles and Reese, W. L., editors, *Philosophers Speak of God*, University of Chicago Press, 1953

Hill, W. J., *The Three-Personed God. The Trinity as the Mystery of Salvation*, Washington: Catholic University of America Press, 1982

Hodgson, Peter C., *Winds of the Spirit. A Constructive Christian Theology*, London: SCM Press, 1994

Hooykaas, R., *Religion and the Rise of Modern Science*, Edinburgh: Scottish Academic Press, 1972

Höpfl, Harro, *The Christian Polity of John Calvin*, Cambridge University Press, 1982

Irving, Edward, *The Collected Writings of Edward Irving*, Vol. V, ed. G. Carlyle, London: Alexander Strahan, 1865.

Jenson, Robert W., *Alpha and Omega. A Study in the Theology of Karl Barth*, New York: Thomas Nelson & Sons, 1963
God After God. The God of the Past and the God of the Future, Seen in the Work of Karl Barth, Indianapolis and New York: Bobbs-Merrill, 1969
The Knowledge of Things Hoped For. The Sense of Theological Discourse, New York: Oxford University Press, 1969
Story and Promise. A Brief Theology of the Gospel about Jesus, Philadelphia: Fortress Press, 1973
Visible Words. The Interpretation and Practice of Christian Sacraments, Philadelphia: Fortress Press, 1978
The Triune Identity, Philadelphia: Fortress Press, 1982
'The Triune God', *Christian Dogmatics*, edd. C. E. Braaten and R. W. Jenson, Philadelphia: Fortress Press, 1984, Vol. I, pp. 83–191
'The Holy Spirit', *Christian Dogmatics*, op. cit., Vol. II, pp. 101–178
America's Theologian. A Recommendation of Jonathan Edwards, New York and Oxford: Oxford University Press, 1988
'The Community of the Resurrection'. Paper read to the Society for the Study of Theology, Leeds, England, 1988

Jüngel, Eberhard, *The Doctrine of the Trinity*, E.T. by Horton Harris, Edinburgh: Scottish Academic Press, 1976
God as the Mystery of the World. On the Foundation of the Theology of the Crucified One in the Dispute between Theism and Atheism, E.T. by D. L. Guder, Edinburgh: T. & T. Clark, 1983

Zur Freiheit eines Christenmenschen. Eine Erinnerung an Luthers Schrift, München: Christian Kaiser, 1987

Kaiser, Christopher B., *The Doctrine of God. An Historical Survey,* London: Marshall, Morgan and Scott, 1982

Kasper, Walter, *The God of Jesus Christ,* E.T. by M. J. O'Donnell, London: SCM Press, 1984

Kierkegaard, Soren, *Concluding Unscientific Postscript,* E.T. by D. F. Swenson and W. Lowrie, Princeton University Press, 1941

Two Ages. The Age of Revolution and the Present Age, E.T. and ed. by H. V. and E. Hong, Princeton University Press, 1978

The Sickness unto Death, E.T. by Walter Lowrie, in *Fear and Trembling and the Sickness unto Death,* Princeton University Press, 1954

Kimel, Alvin, editor, *Speaking the Christian God. The Holy Trinity and the Challenge of Feminism,* Leominster: Gracewing, 1992

LaCugna, Catherine Mowry, *God For Us. The Trinity and Christian Life,* New York: HarperCollins, and Edinburgh: T. & T. Clark, 1991

Lewis, H. D., *The Elusive Self,* London: Macmillan, 1982

Linzey, Andrew, 'The Neglected Creature. The Doctrine of the Non-human Creation and its Relation with the Human in the Thought of Karl Barth', PhD, University of London, 1986

Lossky, Vladimir, *The Mystical Theology of the Eastern Church,* London: James Clarke, 1957

Lovibond, Sabina, *Realism and Imagination in Ethics,* University of Minnesota Press, 1983

Lubac, Henri de, *The Splendour of the Church,* London: Sheed and Ward, 1956

Luther, Martin, *The Freedom of a Christian.* In *Three Treatises,* Philadelphia: Fortress Press, 1960

McFarland, Thomas, *Coleridge and the Pantheist Tradition,* Oxford: Clarendon Press, 1969

MacFarlane, Graham, 'Strange News from Another Star. An Anthropological Insight from Edward Irving', *Persons, Divine and Human. King's College Essays in Theological Anthropology,* edd. Colin E. Gunton and Christoph Schwöbel, Edinburgh: T. & T. Clark, 1991, pp. 98–119

McKenna, Stephen, 'Introduction' to *Saint Augustine. The Trinity*, Washington, D.C.: Catholic University of America Press, 1963

Mackey, James P., *The Christian Experience of God as Trinity*, London: SCM Press, 1983

Macmurray, John, *Persons in Relation*, London: Faber and Faber, 1961

Marx, Karl, *Works, March 1843 to August 1844*, in Karl Marx, Frederick Engels, *Collected Works*, Vol. 3, London: Lawrence and Wishart, 1975

Moltmann, Jürgen, *The Crucified God*, London: SCM Press, 1974
   The Trinity and the Kingdom of God, London: SCM Press, 1981
   The Coming of God, London: SCM Press, 1996

Owen, John, *Of Toleration*, in *Works*, ed. W. H. Goold, Edinburgh: T. & T. Clark, 1862, Vol. VIII, pp. 163–206
   The True Nature of a Gospel Church, *Works*, op. cit., Vol. XVI

Pannenberg, Wolfhart, 'The Question of God', *Basic Questions in Theology*, Vol. 2, E.T. by G. H. Kehm, London: SCM Press, 1971, pp. 201–233
   Systematic Theology Volume 1, E.T. by Geoffrey W. Bromiley, Edinburgh: T. & T. Clark, 1991
   Systematic Theology Volume 2, E.T. by Geoffrey W. Bromiley, Edinburgh: T. & T. Clark, 1994

Parfit, Derek, *Reasons and Persons*, Oxford University Press, 1984

Peacocke, Arthur, *Creation and the World of Science*, Oxford: Clarendon Press, 1979

Peters, Ted, *God as Trinity. Relationality and Temporality in Divine Life*, Louisville, Kentucky: Westminster/John Knox Press, 1993

Prickett, Stephen, *Words and the Word. Language, Poetics and Biblical Interpretation*, Cambridge University Press, 1986

Prigogine, Ilya, and Isabelle Stengers, *Order Out of Chaos. Man's New Dialogue with Nature*, London: Fontana, 1985

Rade, Martin, 'Der Sprung in Luthers Kirchenbegriff und die Entstehung der Landeskirche', *Ausgewählte Schriften*, Band 3, ed. Christoph Schwöbel, Gütersloh: Gerd Mohn, 1988, pp. 151–166

Rahner, Karl, *The Trinity*, E.T. by Joseph Donceel, London: Burns and Oates, 1970

Roberts, Richard, 'Der Stellenwert des kirchlichen Amtes', *Zeitschrift für Theologie und Kirche* 83 (1986), pp. 382f

Schleiermacher, F. D. E., *The Christian Faith*, E.T. by H. R. Mackintosh and J. S. Stewart, Edinburgh: T. & T. Clark, 1928

Schlink, Edmund, *The Coming Christ and the Coming Church*, Edinburgh: Oliver and Boyd, 1967

Schwöbel, Christoph, 'Introduction. The Renaissance of Trinitarian Theology: Reasons, Problems and Tasks', *Trinitarian Theology Today. Essays in Divine Being and Act*, Edinburgh: T. & T. Clark, 1995, pp. 1–30

'Particularity, Universality and the Religions. Towards a Christian Theology of Religions' in ed. Gavin D'Costa, *Christian Uniqueness Reconsidered. The Myth of a Pluralistic Theology of Religions*, New York: Orbis Books, 1990, pp. 30–46

'God, Creation and the Christian Community. The Dogmatic Basis of a Christian Ethic of Createdness', *The Doctrine of Creation*, ed. Colin E. Gunton, Edinburgh: T. & T. Clark, forthcoming

Sell, Alan, 'Ecclesiastical Integrity and Failure', Society for the Study of Theology, 1987

Smail, Thomas A., 'The Holy Trinity and the Resurrection of Jesus', *Different Gospels*, ed. Andrew Walker, London: Hodder and Stoughton, 1988, pp. 63–96

Strawson, P. F., *Individuals. An Essay in Descriptive Metaphysics*, London: Macmillan, 1982

Sutherland, Stewart R., 'A Theological Fable', *King's Theological Review* 6 (1983), pp. 17–19

TeSelle, Eugene, *Augustine the Theologian*, London: Burns and Oates, 1970

Thompson, John, *Modern Trinitarian Perspectives*, Oxford and New York: Oxford University Press, 1994.

Torrance, Alan J. *Persons in Communion. Trinitarian Description and Human Participation*, Edinburgh: T. & T. Clark, 1996

Torrance, Thomas F., *Divine and Contingent Order*, Oxford University Press, 1981

Theology in Reconciliation, London: Geoffrey Chapman, 1975

Transformation and Convergence in the Frame of Knowledge. Explorations in the Interrelations of Scientific and Theological Enterprise, Belfast: Christian Journals, 1984

The Trinitarian Faith, Edinburgh, T. & T. Clark, 1988

Vatican II, *The Conciliar and Post Conciliar Documents*, ed. A. Flannery, Leominster: Fowler Wright, 1975

Wainwright, Arthur W., *The Trinity in the New Testament*, London: SPCK, 1969

Walker, Andrew, 'The Concept of the Person in Social Science', paper prepared, 1985, for the British Council of Churches' Study Commission on Trinitarian Doctrine Today

Ward, Keith, *Holding Fast to God*, London: SPCK, 1982

Welch, Claude, *The Trinity in Contemporary Theology*, London: SCM Press, 1953

Wendebourg, Dorothea, 'From the Cappadocian Fathers to Gregory Palamas. The Defeat of Trinitarian Theology', *Studia Patristica* 17.1 (1982), pp. 194–198

Whyte, James, 'The Problem of Authority', *King's Theological Review* 7 (1984), pp. 37–43

Wiles, M. F. 'Eternal Generation', *Journal of Theological Studies* 12 (1961), pp. 284–291

Wolff, Hans Walter, *Anthropology of the Old Testament*, E.T. by Margaret Kohl, London: SCM Press, 1974

Wolfson, H. A., *The Philosophy of the Church Fathers*, Cambridge, Mass.: Harvard University Press, 1956

Yerkes, James, *The Christology of Hegel*, Albany: State University of New York Press, 1983

Yoder, John Howard, *The Politics of Jesus*, Grand Rapids: Eerdmans, 1972

The Priestly Kingdom. Social Ethics as Gospel, Notre Dame University Press, 1984

Yu, Carver T., *Being and Relation. A Theological Critique of Western Dualism and Individualism*, Edinburgh: Scottish Academic Press, 1987

Zizioulas, John D., *Being as Communion. Studies in Personhood and the Church*, London: Darton, Longman and Todd, 1985

'On Being a Person. The Ontology of Personhood', *Persons, Divine and Human. King's College Essays in Theological Anthropology*, edd. Colin E. Gunton and Christoph Schwöbel, Edinburgh: T. & T. Clark, 1991

Index of Subjects

Index of Authors